I hope this book will inspire you to walk the path of the Hearth Witch. While you may begin to learn how to work with natural resources from books like this one, the true teaching only comes when you start listening to the land and its plants and animals.

When the sacred within you recognises the sacred that surrounds you everywhere, a deeper spiritual reality opens up in which all space becomes sacred space, all time becomes sacred time, and all acts become sacred acts.

This is the true path of the Hearth Witch. Walk it in beauty.

Anna Franklin

THE
HEARTH

Witch's
YEAR

Anna Franklin is a third-degree witch and high priestess of the Hearth of Arianrhod, and she has been a practicing Pagan for more than forty years. She is the author of over thirty books. Her books have been translated into nine languages.

Anna has contributed hundreds of articles to Pagan magazines and has appeared on radio and TV. She lives and works in a village in the English Midlands, where she grows her own herbs, fruit, and vegetables and generally lives the Pagan life. Visit her online at www.AnnaFranklin.co.uk.

THE
HEARTH
Witch's
YEAR

RITUALS, RECIPES & REMEDIES
THROUGH THE SEASONS

ANNA FRANKLIN

Llewellyn Publications
WOODBURY, MINNESOTA

FIRST EDITION
Second Printing, 2021

Book design by Rebecca Zins
Cover design by Shira Atakpu
Interior floral woodcut © 1167 Decorative Cuts (New York: Dover Publications, 2007)
Llewellyn is a registered trademark of Llewellyn Worldwide Ltd.

NOTE: The information in this book is provided for educational
and entertainment purposes only. It does not constitute
a recommendation for use.

Library of Congress Cataloging-in-Publication Data
Names: Franklin, Anna, author.
Title: The hearth witch's year : rituals, recipes & remedies through the seasons / Anna Franklin.
Description: First edition. | Woodbury, Minnesota : Llewellyn Publications, [2020] | Includes bibliographical references and index. | Summary: "*The Hearth Witch's Year* examines how the natural tides of the year shape the hearth witch's spiritual life, looking at how nature influenced spiritual practice in the ancient Pagan world and how it should influence us today, because when we are separated from nature, we are separated from our spiritual source. It includes seasonal rituals, practices, and recipes for every month of the year"—Provided by publisher.
Identifiers: LCCN 2020038124 (print) | LCCN 2020038125 (ebook) | ISBN 9780738764979 (paperback) | ISBN 9780738765174 (ebook)
Subjects: LCSH: Witchcraft. | Year—Religious aspects—Paganism.
Classification: LCC BF1566 .F6955 2020 (print) | LCC BF1566 (ebook) | DDC 203/.3—dc23
LC record available at https://lccn.loc.gov/2020038124
LC ebook record available at https://lccn.loc.gov/2020038125

Llewellyn Worldwide Ltd. does not participate in, endorse, or have any authority or responsibility concerning private business transactions between our authors and the public.

All mail addressed to the author is forwarded but the publisher cannot, unless specifically instructed by the author, give out an address or phone number.

Any internet references contained in this work are current at publication time, but the publisher cannot guarantee that a specific location will continue to be maintained. Please refer to the publisher's website for links to authors' websites and other sources.

Llewellyn Publications
A Division of Llewellyn Worldwide Ltd.
2143 Wooddale Drive
Woodbury MN 55125-2989

www.llewellyn.com
Printed in the United States of America

Contents

February 23

THE PURIFICATION MONTH

March 47

THE GREEN SHOOTS MONTH

April 67

THE MONTH OF OPENING

May 83

THE MERRY MONTH

June 99

THE MONTH OF GLORY

July 115

THE GOLDEN MONTH

August   125

THE HARVEST MONTH

September   139

THE MONTH OF COMPLETION

October 153

THE EMBER MONTH

November 171

THE DEAD MONTH

December 191

THE MONTH OF REBIRTH

CONCLUSION   217

APPENDIX: WEIGHTS AND MEASURES   219

BIBLIOGRAPHY   225

INDEX   229

RECIPE INDEX   239

Introduction

My year as a Hearth Witch is a cycle—the balmy days of spring, when life returns
and I begin work on the garden and go out to collect nature's first wild gifts. The
full days of summer, when I am busy weeding and hoeing, collecting and preparing
herbs and remedies to see me through the year. Then comes the abundant bounty of
autumn, when the hedgerows are full of wild fruit and nuts, when all the work on
the vegetable plot pays off and I get busy preserving it, freezing and canning, making
jams and wines. Finally come the frozen days of winter, when I cleave to my hearth
fire and turn my attention to indoor activities. Then the year begins anew and the
whole cycle starts again, never the same twice but a continuing cycle nonetheless.
The magical and spiritual rituals I celebrate throughout the year reflect this cycle.

The natural cycle of the year is the basis of the eight sabbats observed in modern Paganism—the first stirrings of spring at Imbolc, the gaining of the light after
Ostara, the flowering of the earth at Beltane, the zenith of the sun at Midsummer,
the first fruits at Lughnasa, the completion of the harvest at autumn equinox as the

light begins to decline, the death tide of Samhain with the coming of winter, and the rekindling of the year at Yule, as the Sun is reborn.

However, for our ancestors, the cycle of the year was much more personal since most of them worked on the land and depended on it for survival. They were acutely aware of the tides of energy flowing into, then out of the world—energy both spiritual and physical—and instead of trying to dominate these tides, worked with them, marking them with a myriad of feasts and festivals, myths and folklore. All these together give us half-blind modern Pagans with all our distractions, cushioned by central heating and a constant supply of food from the shops, places to start to make our own profound connections. I look to the clues that nature gives me to tell me when to plant my garden or harvest my crops and, moreover, when to celebrate a spiritual feast.

The Greeks and Romans left us a wealth of written material documenting their beliefs and religious practices, but the Pagan Celts left us nothing—all we know of them comes from much later Christian chroniclers, who failed to record any earlier Pagan ritual practices. However, when the Christian church stamped out Paganism throughout northern Europe, the old festivals proved difficult or even impossible to get rid of, and the church was forced to incorporate them into the liturgical calendar, but appropriated to various saints' days. Some of the old Pagan gods were even turned into Christian saints to make the transition easier. We can also look at the folklore customs of the year, which may stem from earlier Pagan practices in some instances (though this is debatable) but which were certainly practiced by people intimately concerned with the cycles of nature. These things taken together give us an insight into the year that goes beyond the eight sabbats.

But while we can look to the past, we must also recognise that we work here and now and that cycles change. When the dinosaurs walked the earth, the planet was on the other side of the galaxy.[1] In the Bronze Age, because of precession, the solstices and equinoxes fell in different constellations to where they fall now. The hawthorn no longer blossoms at Beltane here in Britain because eleven days were dropped from the calendar in 1752, when the Gregorian calendar replaced the old Julian calendar, meaning that the cycle shifted on. Some people celebrated their festivals on the new-style dates, while others stubbornly stuck to the old-style dates. And let's not forget that climate change brings still larger swings in the natural world.

---

[1]   Jessie Christiansen, https://www.sciencealert.com/dinosaurs-roamed-the-earth-on-the-other -side-of-the-milky-way, November 2019.

The spiritual lessons of the gods are always there, if only we have the ability to look and see. Though we long for this knowledge, we can die of thirst beside its fountain without being aware of its presence. The pattern of the year tells us that there are times when such knowledge is easier to access—when there is a confluence of the season, the pattern of the stars, the time, the place, the preparation of ourselves and myriad other cycles that overlap. Sometimes only a few of those things converge and we get a partial connection, or at another time different things converge and we get something else again. And then there are the times when everything aligns and we experience a profound and life-changing gnosis. So we watch for the signs and signals—the pattern of the year, the currents and moods of Mother Nature, the places we work, the synchronicities that give us clues as to our direction: the clews that take us through the labyrinth. These opportunities are always flowing, always changing. The cycles that unite at one Samhain will never be repeated again—ever. Every year will be different. We can only try to discern the patterns, the myriad cycles, large and small, and find the intersecting points where we can stand and drink from the fountain of spiritual wisdom.

I've written in this book about how the year and the patterns of nature influence me here in England and how I sometimes take inspiration from ancient practices, but putting them in the context of my own time and place, I've had to leave a lot out or the book would extend to several volumes! Where you work is different, even if you live only a few miles away from me, but if you are on a different continent or in the Southern Hemisphere, it will be very, very different. The message of this book is to go out and understand the natural cycles where you live, and respond to them rather than impose something that doesn't fit.

According to our coven bard, Dave the Flute, witchcraft is like making good tea. If you follow the way of the Abrahamic religions of the book—referential, scripture based—you are told what to believe and the actions you must take to be successful. Take mug, put in teabag, pour on boiling water, take teabag out, add milk, and serve. It may be quite a foul cup of tea and you might have preferred some sugar, but you have done as you were told. But a witch would also prod the bag to see what it was doing, note the colour of the tea as it got stronger and compare with past experience of tea making, giving it a taste to see how it was doing, and end up with an ace cup of tea. The witchcraft method is experiential, personal, and unscripted. It is the path untrodden—revelation through your own effort.

THE WOLF MONTH

January

• • • • •

As the days lengthen the cold strengthens, as the old saying goes. January is a time of ice and snow, sleet and hail, bitter winds and biting rain. It is such a wild and threatening month that in the *Anglo Saxon Chronicle* January was called the *Wul-manoth* ("wolf month") and in Scots Gaelic it was *faoilteach* or *faoilleach*, which means both "wild" and "wolf." For the Lakota Sioux of the Eastern USA, the month of January was the period of the hardship moon, and the Germans once called it the hard month.[2] It was a cruel month for our ancestors, with short hours of daylight, frozen and unyielding ground, no fresh food, and the weather preventing both work and travel. It is still a hard month for wildlife, and for many creatures, especially small birds, finding enough food to survive takes up almost every hour of daylight.

---

2 Nilsson, *Primitive Time-Reckoning.*

In January we are deep in the winter season of the Crone Goddess, who comes into her full power during the twelve days of Yule, accompanied by various spiteful winter spirits. In some German-speaking regions, in the spirit of Yuletide misrule, guisers dress up as the host of Perchta, the winter hag, in horned wooden masks with snouts and beaks and black sheepskins or hoods of badger or bear fur. They take part in processions and ecstatic dances, blowing horns, clashing symbols and bells, threatening bad children and rewarding good ones. The Perchten run through the streets with glowing embers in their mouths, as if breathing fire. They rush into houses to "clean" them and chase the shrieking children. The guisers claim the offerings that have been set out for Perchta.[3] They appear alone or in groups, especially on three specific winter nights, called the "rough nights": the Eve of St. Nicholas, the Eve of the Winter Solstice, and before Epiphany. They carry bells and other loud instruments to dispel winter. It is believed that the quality and abundance of the next harvest, as well as the wellbeing of the people, are dependent on the performances of the Perchten.

Our modern calendar is based on the old Roman one, which ordered the months from January to December from about 700 BCE. The Romans called the first month Januarius after the god Janus ("door"), the two-faced god who simultaneously looked back to the past and forward to the future and presided over all beginnings and endings, movement and change.[4] He was considered the initiator of all things and was worshipped not just at the New Year but at the beginning of any enterprise, such as the harvest and planting times, marriages, deaths, and other commencements. In Rome any rite or religious act began with an invocation of Janus and finished with an invocation to Vesta, the hearth goddess.

Though the days are cold and dark, we passed the shortest day in December, with the rebirth of the Sun at Yule, and though we know that January and February will be the coldest, wettest, and windiest of the year, we can comfort ourselves that, inch by inch, minute by precious minute, the days are gradually getting longer. This is not really very noticeable until Imbolc, but it is happening. The Sun Child, born at Yule, is growing and gaining strength.

---

3 Max Dashu, *The Tregenda of the Old Goddess, Witches, and Spirits*, http://www.suppressedhistories
.net/secrethistory/witchtregenda.html.
4 Franz Altheim, A *History of Roman Religion* (London: Methuen, 1938).

January is the time for the comfort of the hearth fire's warmth, hearty food, and curtains shut tight against the cold and dark. It's a time to withdraw from the hustle and bustle of the busy warmer months and let the direction of the coming year emerge. January brings a whole new year yet to unfold, full of possibilities for the next twelve months. The rituals of January are concerned with setting the tone for the coming year with acts of sympathetic magic, banishing the baneful spirits of the darkest days, and waking up the land in preparation for the return to work on it.

Early January

January 1: NEW YEAR'S DAY

We still celebrate New Year's Day as an important holiday and a day of firsts. Its ancient customs have persisted into the modern age—a firm break with the past and the previous year must be made, and all tasks must be finished before the New Year begins. In the past, everything done or seen on New Year's Day was considered to have a magical or symbolic significance, and it was important to begin the year as you meant to go on. This included feasting well to ensure food for the coming year, not starting the year as a debtor, and not giving anything away, which would mean giving your luck away. No substance of any kind was allowed to be removed from the house on New Year's Day—not even dirty water, sweepings from the floor, or ashes from the hearth. One of the unluckiest things to do was give a neighbour fire from your hearth, which would ensure a death within that family during the coming year.

In ancient Rome, in celebrations that might still seem entirely familiar to us today, the Kalends (first day) of January were celebrated with singing and dancing all night long in the streets, with men wearing women's clothes and people wearing masks and disguises. Libanius, the famous Greek sophist of the fourth century CE, wrote:

> The festival of the Kalends is celebrated everywhere as far as the limits of the Roman Empire extend....Everywhere may be seen carousals and well-laden tables; luxurious abundance is found in the houses of the rich, but also in the houses of the poor better food than usual is put upon the table. The impulse to spend seizes everyone. He who the whole year through has taken pleasure in saving and piling up his pence, becomes suddenly extravagant.[5]

---

5   Quoted in Miles, *Christmas in Ritual and Tradition*.

The Christians took a dim view of this continuation of Pagan customs. Caesarius of Arles (sixth century CE) castigated that

> the heathen put on counterfeit forms and monstrous faces....Some are clothes in the hides of cattle, others put on the heads of beasts...furthermore those who have been born men are clothed in women's dress... blushing not to clothe their warlike arms in women's garments...[6]

Even priests were accused of wearing masks, dressing as women, and singing lewd songs.

Because it was the start of a whole new year, it was a day for taking omens. In the eleventh century, Buchard of Worms wrote:

> Have you celebrated the calends of January according to pagan customs?...to wit: arranging stones on your table or giving a feast, leading dancers or singers through the streets and squares, taking a seat upon your roof while wearing your sword in order to see and know what will happen in the new year, sitting atop of a bull's hide where the roads cross to read the future, on the night of January 1 cooking bread for yourself to know whether the new year will be prosperous according to whether the dough rises? If yes, because you have abandoned God your creator, and have turned to vain idols and become apostate, you will fast on all the official days for two years.[7]

Divinations continued to be widely practiced into very recent times. In Lithuania on New Year's Eve, nine separate bread rolls, each with a different item (tokens representing money, a cradle, bread, a ring, a death's head, an old man, an old woman, a ladder, a key), were baked into dough and laid beneath nine plates, and everyone had three grabs at them. Whatever he or she got would be their lot during the year. Germans put a leaf of periwinkle on a plate filled with water, and if it remained green until the following night, good health was assured for the coming year. If it stained, though, it meant illness; if it turned black, death would follow. In Macedonia St. Basil's cake was baked with a silver coin in it. The person who found the coin in his or her piece would prosper during the year. On the Isle of Man, it was a custom to fill a thimble with salt and upset it on a plate, one thimbleful for each person in the house.

---

6   Quoted in Matthews, *The Winter Solstice*.
7   Quoted in Walter, *Christianity*.

This was put aside for the night and examined the next morning. If any of the heaps of salt had fallen over, that person would die in the coming year.

In Britain, in the spirit of ensuring prosperity for the coming year with sympathetic magic, gifts were once given at New Year's rather than Christmas.[8] Children in West Glamorgan went from house to house with good wishes for the New Year, carrying apples stuck full of corn, variously coloured and decorated with a sprig of evergreen.[9] For the same reason, on the Scottish borders, care was taken that no one entered a house empty-handed on New Year's Day; in England a visitor had to bring something to eat or drink. Romanians threw handfuls of corn at one another with some appropriate greeting, such as:

> *May you live*
> *May you flourish*
> *Like apple trees*
> *Like pear trees*
> *In springtime*
> *Like wealthy autumn*
> *Of all things plentiful.*[10]

In Russia corn sheaves were piled upon a table and in the midst of them was set a large pie. The father of the family took his seat behind the sheaves and asked his children if they could see him. When they replied in the negative, he would declare that he hoped the corn would grow as high in his fields so that he would be just as invisible when he walked there at harvest time.

On the first day of the New Year, the first drawn water from a well or spring gained magical properties. A Highland practice was to send someone on the last night of the year to draw a pitcher of water in silence and without the vessel touching the ground. The water was drunk on New Year's morning as a charm against witchcraft and the evil eye. At Bromyard in Herefordshire it was the custom at midnight on New Year's Eve to rush to the nearest spring to snatch the "cream of the well" (the first pitcher of water) and with it the prospect of the best luck. In Pembrokeshire early on New Year's morning, crowds of boys went round the neighbourhood with a vessel of cold

---

8   Kightly, *The Customs and Ceremonies of Britain*.

9   *Gentleman's Magazine*, March 1819.

10   Miles, *Christmas in Ritual and Tradition*.

spring water, and using a twig of box, rosemary, or myrtle, they would sprinkle the hands and faces of anyone they met in return for a copper or two.[11]

Rite of New Beginnings

The infant Sun God, reborn at winter solstice, has spent twelve days growing and gaining strength. Until this day all has been uncertain, but now he is strong enough to battle the cold and darkness and start to bring back light and warmth. We are ready to start the New Year, and it is time to let go of the past—the old year and all its problems—and look forward.

Spend some time meditating on what you need to leave behind with the old year and what your goals are for the new year. What do you want to learn and achieve? What could you do to make your life better? Write these New Year's goals down in a short list.

Prepare an apple stuck with wheat, barley, or some other grain and sprigs of bay and rosemary. Tie it with a red ribbon. This is a symbol of love, wholeness, and prosperity.

Have ready an incense composed of frankincense grains and juniper berries or needles (or a few drops of juniper essential oil) and a charcoal block to burn it on, in a dish on a heatproof mat. Place a feather beside it. Put two white candles on your altar.

Light the candles and the charcoal. Say:

> Lord and Lady, on this day of endings and beginnings,
>
> On this the first day of the first month of the year, I honour you.
>
> At this time of change and transition, I call upon you.
>
> As I stand on the threshold of the year, I invoke you.

Sprinkle the incense onto the charcoal. Using the feather, waft the smoke over yourself as an act of purification, saying:

> Let me be cleansed of the past
>
> Open the west door and let the old year go!

Think about what you want to release—bad habits, negativity, toxic relationships, and so on, and let them drift away. Visualise the past flowing away behind you, taking all its ills with it.

---

11 Owen, *Welsh Folk Customs.*

Take up the apple. Say:

> *Let me make a prosperous new beginning*
> *Open the east door and let the New Year in!*

Visualise your future streaming towards you, full of possibilities, prosperity, and joy. Take up your list of goals and read them out loud in the presence of the Lord and Lady. If you wish, you can perform divinations after reading out your goals and make this part of the ritual, seeking guidance through the tarot, runes, or whichever method you prefer.

When you are ready to close, say:

> *Lord and Lady, witness that I begin anew.*
> *Be with me, lighting my path and guiding my feet.*
> *This rite is ended. Blessed be.*

Put out the candles.

January 3: HONOURING THE HOUSEHOLD DEITIES

In the depths of winter, we spend more time in our houses, relying on their shelter to keep us safe and cosy. It is important to honour the spirit of your home at all times of year, but especially now. When you think of your home as having an indwelling spirit, it can make a huge difference to the quality of life within it. Every house has its own spirit—what we detect as an atmosphere when we enter it. This was really brought home to me recently when the coven rented a holiday cottage for a spiritual retreat. The place had been unsympathetically renovated to accommodate as many people as possible and seemed atmospherically and spiritually dead when we arrived. We started to make offerings to the house spirit with food from each meal (which was later emptied outside for the birds) and we lit candles and spoke to the household spirits. Within two days, the house woke up and started to take notice, and we were warmly welcomed; the withdrawn house began to enjoy having us there and became positively cheerful.

A belief in house spirits is very ancient. In Persia and China it was always the custom to make offerings to the house spirit before entering a dwelling, while a similar custom in northern Europe involved taking bread and salt when visiting a home.[12] The Romans honoured protective spirits called Lares. The *Lar Familiaris* ("household

---

12   Eric Maple, "The House," *Man, Myth and Magic* (Leeds: BPC Publishing, 1970).

lar") was given monthly offerings of garlands placed on the hearth as well as daily offerings at mealtimes. They also had an annual feast called the Compitalia that was celebrated at this time of year, which gave rise to some of our Christmas customs, such as the use of lights.

Honouring the House Spirits

For the ancients, the hearth was also the altar of the household gods, where offerings could be made. You can use your mantelpiece as an altar—many people do—or you can make a small shrine or niche with a representation of your house spirit. Offer a small portion of each meal with the simple words "House spirit, I honour you." Put this food out for the birds later. Light a candle at your chosen place with the same words. On special occasions, honour your house spirit with a garland on the hearth or shrine.

January 5: TWELFTH NIGHT

Twelfth Night (January 5) and Twelfth Day (January 6) are generally considered to be the ending of the Christmas season. Today most people just think of it as the time to take down the Christmas decorations, but in the past it was a major festival surrounded by its own myths and customs. It was a time for one last fling with games, dressing up, and plays, all managed by the Lord of Misrule, who held sway during the season of Yule and the twelve days that followed it. The Tudor court held huge feasts, while in Victorian England the shops were open late, selling cakes decorated with stars, castles, lions, dragons, kings, knights, and serpents painted onto white icing. The king and queen of the feast were chosen by a concealed ring or a pea and bean hidden in the cake.[13]

It was both a propitious and a dangerous time, standing between the holiday period and the return to work, between winter and the coming of spring, between the old and new year. Any such liminal time is surrounded by taboos and propitiations. In many places bonfires were lit, sometimes thirteen fires, one for each of the twelve days of Christmas and a thirteenth, called the Judas Fire, which was put out during the proceedings to extinguish any negativity that might attach to the coming year.[14]

---

13   *Brewers Dictionary of Phrase and Fable*, Blitz Editions (Leicester, 1990) and
      http://www.pepysdiary.com.
14   Roud, *The English Year*.

Many of the customs of Twelfth Night concern the Crone or Hag Goddess, who rules the winter quarter of the year, like the German Perchta, to whom this night is sacred and who was placated with houses decorated with evergreens and food left out for her on Twelfth Night.[15] If she was pleased, she would leave small presents and treats for the children.

Twelfth Night and Twelfth Day was the time to expel the winter spirits of chaos and bane and send them back to the underworld in a ritual battle between the forces of growth and summer and the forces of death and winter. The malicious Greek *Kallikantzaroi* appear during the twelve days, and the signal for their final departure comes on Twelfth Night with the Kalanda festival, when the Blessing of the Waters ceremony takes place. Some holy water is put into vessels, and with these and incense the priests make a round of the village, sprinkling the people and their houses, which makes the winter spirits flee.

. . . .

TWELFTH NIGHT CAKE

2¼ POUNDS MIXED DRIED SULTANAS, RAISINS, AND CURRANTS

2 OUNCES MIXED PEEL

¼ PINT WHISKEY

¼ PINT MILK

12 OUNCES BUTTER

12 OUNCES MUSCAVADO SUGAR

4 EGGS, BEATEN

1 POUND, 4 OUNCES PLAIN FLOUR

1 LEVEL TABLESPOON BAKING POWDER

2 LEVEL TEASPOONS MIXED SPICE

2 OUNCES GLACÉ CHERRIES

2 OUNCES CHOPPED WALNUTS

Place the dried fruit and peel in a bowl. Stir in the whiskey and milk, cover, and leave overnight. Heat the oven to 140°C/275°F/gas mark 1. Oil a large tin (approximately 12 inches × 10 inches) and line the base and

---

15   Miles, *Christmas in Ritual and Tradition.*

sides with greaseproof paper. Brush the paper with oil. Cream the butter and sugar, add the beaten eggs a little at a time. If the mixture curdles, add a little flour. Sift the flour, baking powder, and spice, and fold into the creamed mixture. Add the fruit, nuts, and whiskey/milk mixture. Stir well. Turn into the tin. Bake in the centre of the oven for 2¼ to 2½ hours. Leave to cool in the tin. Turn out and remove the paper. If you really must, you can sprinkle more whiskey on top. The cake can be iced and decorated with stars, ribbons, wheat ears, nuts, and glacé fruit.

January 6: EPIPHANY

In the Christian calendar this is the Feast of the Epiphany, latterly said to mark the visit of the wise men to the infant Jesus, though in some sections of the early church it was considered Christ's birthday. St. Epiphanius of Salamis (c. 315–403 CE) wrote that January 6 was Christ's epiphany ("appearance"):

> Christ was born on the sixth day of January after thirteen days of the winter solstice and of the increase of the light and day…For on the twenty-fifth day of December the division takes place which is the solstice, and the day begins to lengthen its light, receiving an increase, and there are thirteen days of it up to the sixth day of January, until the day of the birth of Christ…for it needs must have been that this should be a figure of our Lord Jesus Christ Himself and of His twelve disciples, who made up the number of the thirteen days of the increase of the light.[16]

However, this day was previously celebrated as the birth—or epiphany—of the vegetation and vine god Dionysus. Indeed, Epiphanius complained that

> the leaders of the idol-cults…in many places keep highest festival on this same night of Epiphany…at Alexandria, in the Koreion as it is called—an immense temple—that is to say, the Precinct of the Virgin; after they have kept all-night vigil with songs and music, chanting to their idol, when the vigil is over, at cockcrow, they descend with lights into an underground crypt, and carry up a wooden image lying naked

16 *The Panarion of Epiphanius of Salamis* (trans. Frank Williams), online at https://archive.org /stream/EpiphaniusPanarionBksIIIIII1/Epiphanius%20-%20_Panarion_%20-%20Bks%20II%20 %26%20III%20-%201_djvu.txt, accessed 9.1.20.

on a litter…And they carry round the image itself, circumambulating seven times the innermost temple, to the accompaniment of pipes, tabors and hymns, and with merry-making they carry it down again underground. And if they are asked the meaning of this mystery, they answer and say: "To-day at this hour the Maiden, that is, the Virgin, gave birth to the Aion."[17]

Aion or Aeon was a syncretic god, usually identified as Dionysus but also containing elements of Cronos, Osiris, and Apollo, worshipped in multicultural Alexandria. Aion was a god of time, the revolutions of the stars and the zodiac, eternity, and the afterlife.[18] He was generally depicted as a young man but also as an old man who sloughs off age to become young again—an image of a god (or year) reborn annually and one we still use in depictions of the old year as an ancient man and the new year as a babe.

Like other feast days around this period, Epiphany was widely associated with the winter crone. In Carinthia it was called Berchtentag[19] after the hag Bechta, and in Italy the hag goddess of the twelve nights is Befana, her name a corruption of Epiphania ("epiphany"). Though her role has largely been taken over by Santa Claus in modern Italy, she was once the yuletide gift-bringer. Sicilians especially honoured Befana, also called *la Strega* ("the witch") or *la Vecchia* ("the old woman"). Befana descended from the mountains, riding on her broom, and entered houses through the chimneys, leaving presents for children. Children left notes for her in the chimney. For those children who had been naughty, she left only coal (shops sold *carbone*, a sweet that looks like coal) or a birch rod (to be spanked with). Witch-like images of Befana were placed in the windows of houses and there were processions through the streets. Singers serenaded houses where cloth images of Befana were placed in the windows or carried her image from house to house while carolling. The Befana dolls were afterwards burned, probably in token of the passing of the old year. Omens were taken from the fire; if the smoke blew towards the east, it was an indication that the harvest would be good. If the smoke blew towards the west, it would be poor.

The rites of the Epiphany signal that the darkest time has ended.

---

17 Ibid. and Hugo Rahner, *Greek Myths and Christian Mystery* (Biblo-Moser, 1963).
18 http://hermeticmagick.com/content/deities/aion.html.
19 Ibid.

Hag Goddess Ritual

I shall be honouring the winter witch Goddess tonight, decorating my altar with evergreens and my witchy dolls and lighting a candle to her, saying:

> Hag Goddess, who comes at twilight
>
> With your wind-shredded clothes and witch's hat
>
> All hail to you! This is your season,
>
> And I give you due honour.

January 7: THE RETURN TO WORK

In the past, women returned to their spinning duties on the first day after the twelve days of Christmas, or St. Distaff's Day. It was a sign that the festive period was over and things were back to normal. It is also called "Rock Day," with rock being an alternative name for the spindle or distaff. St. Distaff is not a real saint, and the term is something of a joke.

The men did not return to work until after Plough Monday, the traditional start of the agricultural year falling on the first Monday after Twelfth Night. References to Plough Monday date back to the late fifteenth century. In some areas, particularly in northern England and East Anglia, the plough might be blessed at the church, then dragged from house to house throughout the village in a procession with the ploughmen collecting money, a necessary seasonal supplement to income when there was no work on the land. If anyone refused to contribute, they might find their front gardens ploughed up. The ploughmen were often accompanied by musicians and winter characters like the Hag, a boy dressed as an old woman called the Bessy, and a man in the role of the fool, who wore animal skins, a hairy cap, and had an animal tail hanging from his back.

Ritual for Returning the Corn Dolly to the Earth

This is the time to return the corn dolly—the spirit of vegetation that the coven made at the autumn equinox—to the earth. I go out into the garden, dig a small hole, lay the corn dolly in it, and say:

> The light is returning and spring will come
>
> Let life return to the earth.

I cover up the corn dolly with soil, then say:

> Blessed be.

Mid-January

January 17: OLD TWELFTH NIGHT WASSAILING

This is one of the traditional days (along with Twelfth Night, Twelfth Day, and Old Twelfth Day) for wassailing the orchards, waking up the spirit of vegetation and the land itself, and energising the move towards spring.

Today, most people think of wassailing only in connection with toasting the apple orchards. However, in the past wassailing was a widespread custom associated with wishing health to people, crops, and animals; apple trees were wassailed to make them bear fruit, and even bees were wassailed to make them produce more honey. Cattle were toasted to keep them healthy; the prize cow was given a special cake with a hole in the middle (a symbol of the sun) and regaled with the words:

Fill your cups, my merry men all!

For here's the best ox in the stall!

Oh, he is the best ox; of that there's no mistake,

And so let us crown him with the Twelfth cake!

The cake was hooked over one of its horns. In parts of Scotland, the sea was similarly honoured, with ale poured into the waves in the hope that this would encourage good fishing in the coming year.[20]

Wassailing the orchards usually involved either the landowner or specially selected bands of wassailers visiting the orchard at night, selecting the oldest or most fruitful tree (known in Somerset as the Apple Tree Man) to represent the whole orchard. The tree might be beaten with sticks in order to wake it up after its winter sleep. Bread or cakes soaked in cider would be placed in the tree's branches and the wassail song sung, then loud noises made to frighten winter spirits away from the orchard.

The word *wassail* comes from the Anglo-Saxon phrase *Wæs hal*, which was used as a greeting. *Wæs* means "to be" and *hal* means "hale" or "whole." The greeting often accompanied the welcoming of a guest with a cup of ale or mead, and so became a toast (the correct response to which is *drinc hale*, meaning "I drink to your good

---

20   Carmichael, *Carmina Gadelica*.

health") and eventually wassailing, the act of toasting someone or something on special occasions with spiced ale, cider, or wine.

In the coven we see it as the last of our three rituals of the Yuletide season that finally closes the barren winter cycle and brings back the energy of growth into the land. We tap the apple tree three times to wake it up, pour cider onto its roots, and put apple cake or toast into its branches to honour it. It's a very joyful occasion when we wear garlands of ivy and bang drums to banish all the spirits of winter bane before passing around the wassail cup full of spiced cider or apple wine—at which point it gets even merrier. We take it in turns to host the event; some of us only have one apple or pear tree, others several. If you don't have fruit trees of your own, perhaps you can get together with friends who do or even perform the ritual in a local orchard or park where fruit trees grow. Wassailing ceremonies are becoming more and more popular, even among non-Pagans.

Wassailing Ritual

The ritual is carried out in the fruit orchard. Wear a garland of ivy. Choose the largest and most productive tree on the plot to stand for all the rest. Tap the trunk of the tree three times to wake it up with your wand, and say:

> Apples and pears with right good corn
> Come in plenty to everyone.
> Eat good cake and drink hot ale
> Give to the earth and she'll not fail!

Place the cake in the main fork of the tree. The wassail drink is thrown three times at the roots of the tree with the chant:

> Here's to thee, old apple tree!
> Whence thou may'st bud
> And whence thou may'st blow
> Hats full! Caps full! Bushel-bags full!
> And pockets full too!

The wassail bowl is recharged, and all drink to the health of the orchard as you say "Wassail!" Drums and musical instruments are played to wake up the spirits of vegetation and drive away the spirits of winter.

You can then take a burning brand and carry it around the property to infuse the spirit of warmth and fire into the earth, purifying it and bringing luck for the coming year. Everyone gathers around the fire and refills the wassail bowl for a final toast of "wassail."

. . . . . .
Wassail

2¼ PINTS HARD CIDER

3 APPLES, PEELED, CORED, AND GRATED

2 OUNCES BROWN SUGAR

½ TEASPOON GROUND GINGER

GRATED NUTMEG

Put a ¼ pint of cider in a pan and add the grated apples. Cook until the apples are soft and add the brown sugar, ginger, and the other 2 pints of cider. Heat through but do not allow to boil. To serve, add some grated nutmeg and pour into a large cup or bowl.

. . . .
Dorset Apple Cake

100 GRAMS BUTTER

225 GRAMS SELF-RAISING FLOUR

PINCH OF SALT

225 GRAMS APPLES, PEELED, CORED, AND FINELY CHOPPED

100 GRAMS SUGAR

1 EGG, BEATEN

MILK

Using your fingertips, rub the butter into the flour and salt until it resembles breadcrumbs. Add the apples and sugar, then mix in the egg and enough milk to make a stiff dough. Pour into an 8-inch tin and bake at 190°C/375°F/gas mark 5 for 45 minutes.

ffffff

Late January

Now we enter the sign of Aquarius, the water bearer, who pours out a trickle of stars into the mouth of Piscis Austrinus, the southern fish.[21] The constellation is found in a region of the sky often called "the sea" as many watery constellations are found there, including Eridanus the river, Cetus the whale, and Pisces the fishes.

The Greeks saw the constellation as Ganymede, the cup bearer to the god Zeus, who stole the youth away after becoming captivated by his beauty, or they associated it with Deucalion, the son of Prometheus who built a ship to survive a great flood.[22] The constellation was certainly associated with floods and water in general; in Babylonian lore it was connected with Ea, god of water and wisdom, commonly depicted holding an overflowing vase, who ruled the southernmost quarter of the sun's path through the zodiac called the Way of Ea, corresponding to the period of 45 days on either side of winter solstice. (Pisces contained the winter solstice in the Early Bronze Age.)[23]

The ancient Egyptians thought that it represented Hapi, the god of the Nile, whose annual flooding brought fertility when Aquarius put his jar into the river, which marked the beginning of spring.

The Winter Blues

While I long for spring, the long, dark hours and the wintry weather of January is taking its toll in my house, with seasonal coughs and colds and dry, chapped skin, as well as a touch of the January blues now that the festive period is over, so I am making up a batch of seasonal remedies.

. . . .

HONEY LIP SALVE

7 TABLESPOONS OLIVE OIL

2 TEASPOONS RUNNY HONEY

6 TABLESPOONS BEESWAX, GRATED

---

21 Krupp, *Beyond the Blue Horizon.*

22 Robert Bruce Thompson & Barbara Fritchman Thompson, *Illustrated Guide to Astronomical Wonders* (O'Reilly Media, 2007).

23 Hugh Thurston, *Early Astronomy* (Springer Series in Statistics, 1993).

In a double boiler, warm the oil and honey together; do not boil. Remove from the heat and stir in the beeswax until it has melted. Pour into small pots and seal.

. . . .
LEMON COUGH AND COLD TEA

Put the juice from one lemon (rich in vitamin C) into a cup and top up with boiling water. Add a couple teaspoons of honey, which has antiviral properties, before drinking.

. . . .
WINTER BLUES TEA

Winter can be slightly depressing, and a cup of this can help lift your mood.

    1 TEASPOON LEMON BALM

    1 TEASPOON CAMOMILE

    PINCH OF SAFFRON

    1 CUP BOILING WATER

Combine the herbs and put into a teapot. Cover with the boiling water and leave to infuse for 10 minutes. Strain into a cup and sweeten with honey.

January 31: IMBOLC EVE

Winter certainly makes me appreciate my hearth fire all the more, but it had an even greater importance for our ancestors. Imagine frozen, blustery winter days, when there was little work that could be done on the land, when the hours of daylight were short and the nights long. Fire meant the difference between survival and death, between comfort and cold pain. It was the centre of activity, where everyone gathered to eat and cook, sit and warm themselves, and talk and listen to the stories of the bards.

Nowadays, most people do not have a big open fire where they cook and sit in the evenings. This doesn't matter; remember that the hearth is a symbol for the hospitality and living spirit of the home. By connecting with the energies of the hearth, you can invite ancient magic into your life and learn to make your home a happier, more

. . . . .

attractive place, whether you are living in a bedsit in the middle of the city or a pretty cottage in the countryside. The principle is the same. It is a refuge, a place of worship, the shrine of the sacred flame, and a celebration of life. You can use candles and oil lamps instead of a fire to symbolise the living flame that embodies the presence of the Hearth Goddess.

The Goddess of hearth and fire dwells within every hearth, whether large or small, and she is known in every culture and always served by women. In many places the Hearth Goddess has a special feast day at this time. In Greek myth the Hearth Goddess was called Hestia; she refused a throne on Olympus to look after the hearth and never took part in the wars and arguments of the gods. Instead she is the calm centre, the safe haven of the home, where people can seek refuge and shelter. She is the gentlest and most principled of all the gods, representing security and the solemn duty of hospitality presiding over all hearth and altar fires. In Rome she was called Vesta, the virgin fire goddess worshipped in a state cult and in private households every day. In Celtic lore she is Brighid, a pan-Celtic goddess, appearing as Brighid or Brigit in Ireland, Brigantia in Northern England, Bride in Scotland, and Brigandu in Brittany. She was converted into a Christian saint, and within living memory in Ireland, the fire was kindled with invocations to Brighid by the woman of every house. In Lithuania the Hearth Goddess was Gabija, whose name means "to cover up" and refers to the practice of the mistress of the house banking the fire at night so that it will neither go out nor spread from the hearth. She was invoked at all family rituals and occasions since without her they would not be possible. Like Brighid, she had special festivals at the beginning of February dedicated to the renewal of the hearth fire and the household gods.

Tomorrow we will celebrate the festival of Imbolc as the festival of the Goddess of the hearth fire, but I honour her each day when I light my fire:

> *Hearth Goddess, I honour you.*
> *Bring your presence in the living flame into my home*
> *And bless me with your gifts of light and warmth.*

If you have no fire, light a candle on your mantelpiece or altar to bring the Hearth Goddess, in the form of a living flame, into your home and into your heart.

THE PURIFICATION MONTH

· · · · ·

February, though the shortest month of the year, is said to have the worst weather. Native American tribes called the full moon of February[24] the Snow Moon, the Hunger Moon, or the Storm Moon.[25] In the mornings, my garden pond is frozen and the plants are rimmed with frost. A blanket of powdery white snow covers the earth, showing the angular marks of bird feet, printed like runes on the ground, as the hungry birds try to find a fallen seed or a scrap of bread. Winter seems to be dragging on, and if we didn't see signs that spring is around the corner, it might be considered the dreariest month of all. Yet the rain, the cold, and the snow are cleansing the face of the earth, destroying harmful bacteria, soaking the soil with life-giving moisture, and filling the rivers and reservoirs, all of which will ensure good crops later in the year.

---

24   Every nineteen years there is no full moon in February at all!

25   *The Old Farmer's Almanac*, https://www.farmersalmanac.com/full-moon-names, accessed 19.10.18.

Just as the earth is being washed clean, many ancient festivals of February reflect the theme of purification. The name of the month itself is derived from the Latin *februarius*, which means "purification." According to the Roman writer Ovid, in ancient times purgation was called *Februa*: "Of this our month of February came…For our religious fathers did maintain, purgations expiated every stain of guilt and sin."[26] He explained that the custom had come from Greece, where it was held that pure lustrations could cleanse any sin or impious deed. In the oldest calendars, February was the last month of the Roman year, and the idea seems to have been to propitiate the spirits of the gods and ancestors, atone for any offence given to them, and so prepare for spring and the coming year with a clean slate.

The ancient Greeks celebrated the Lesser Eleusinian Mysteries this month, during which those who were planning to participate in the Greater Eleusinian Mysteries in September went to Athens to be purified of any ritual impurity or sin (*miasma*).[27] As Clement of Alexandria wrote: "The mysteries of the Greeks begin with purification,"[28] and in most mystery traditions, ritual purification is necessary before the would-be initiate can approach the gods. At the centre of the Eleusinian Mysteries were the agricultural goddess Demeter and her daughter Persephone, the goddess of spring who was associated with purity. Representations show Demeter seated on the *kiste* (the basket that held the ritual implements of the Greater Mysteries, which would not be revealed until the autumn equinox), with the initiate holding out his hand to touch the snake that coils from the kiste to Demeter's lap.[29] The snake symbolised mystery and rebirth, and the fact that the initiate was ready to receive the mysteries at the autumn equinox.

Just as people purified themselves, their homes, and the tombs of their ancestors at this time of year, there are many stories of goddesses cleansing themselves in sacred waters in order to renew themselves and restore their virginity. The Greek goddess of love, Aphrodite, renewed her virginity every year by bathing in the sea at her birthplace of Paphos in Crete. Artemis, the moon and hunt goddess, refreshed her virginity by bathing every year in a sacred fountain, while Hera, the Queen of Heaven, bathed in the spring at Kanathos near Argos in order to become a maiden

---

26   Ovid, *Fasti* (trans. J. Frazer), https://www.theoi.com/Text/OvidFasti1.html, accessed 13.5.19.
27   Stephanie Goodart, *The Lesser Mysteries of Eleusis*, https://cac45ab95b3277b3fdfd-31778daf558bd d39a1732c0a6dfa8bd4.ssl.cf5.rackcdn.com/05_goodart.pdf, accessed 13.5.19
28   Ibid.
29   Ibid.

once more.[30] Even in Christian lore, Candlemas (February 2) is the feast of the purification of the Virgin Mary. The maiden goddess is associated with purity, new beginnings, and regeneration, so these seem to be metaphors for the old year being washed away and turned into spring.

Similarly, there was a Scottish tradition that at the beginning of spring the Cailleach ("hag" or "veiled one") drank from the Well of Youth and transformed into the youthful maiden Bride.[31] The Cailleach ruled the winter months, while Bride (Brighid/Brigit) ruled the summer months. The Cailleach is the female personification of winter. Her staff freezes the ground, and she brings storms and bad weather, though she protects deer and wolves and is the mother of all the gods.[32] *Là Fhèill Brìghde* (St. Bride's Day, February 1) was said to be the day that the Cailleach gathered her firewood for the rest of the winter. If she intended the winter to last a good deal longer, she made sure that the weather was bright and sunny so she could go out and collect plenty of fuel. If the weather was terrible, it meant that the Cailleach was asleep and would soon run out of wood, so winter was nearly over.

In Scotland, St. Bride's Day was considered the beginning of spring, with Bride melting the river ice. According to Scottish folklorist Alexander Carmichael,

> Bride with her white wand is said to breathe life into the mouth of the dead Winter and to bring him to open his eyes to the tears and the smiles, the sighs and the laughter of Spring. The venom of the cold is said to tremble for its safety on Bride's Day and to flee for its life on Patrick's Day.[33]

As Nigel Pennick puts it,

> At this time of year, Brighid symbolises the opening out of enclosed, invisible nature concealed in the darkness of wintertide into the visible world of light.[34]

---

30 Pausanias, ii.38.2, online at http://www.perseus.tufts.edu/hopper /text?doc=Perseus:text:1999.01.0160, accessed 13.5.19.

31 Carmichael, *Carmina Gadelica*.

32 Mackenzie, *Wonder Tales from Scottish Myth and Legend*.

33 Carmichael, *Carmina Gadelica*.

34 Pennick, *The Goddess Year*.

In Scotland the serpent, sometimes called the noble queen, is supposed to emerge from its hollow among the hills on St. Bride's Day:

> On the day of Bride of the white hills
>
> The noble queen will come from the knoll.
>
> I will not molest the noble queen
>
> Nor will the noble queen molest me.[35]

The serpent sloughs off its skin annually and is thereby renewed, making it an ancient symbol of regeneration. Snakes and maidens also featured in the February celebrations of the Roman goddess Juno Sospita (Juno the Saviour). At the beginning of February, the consuls made a sacrifice to her, while young girls offered barley cakes to the sacred snake in her grove. If their offerings were accepted, their virginity was confirmed and the year's fertility assured.

During this month animals begin to shake off their winter sleep and emerge from hibernation. Some are said to come out to check the weather on Bride's Day or Candlemas, testing whether it is safe to emerge or if they need to go back to sleep. Badgers were reputed to emerge at noon and if they saw their shadows, they went back to their setts. If they didn't see their shadows, they stayed out, and the worst of winter was over. In Huntingdonshire the day was even called Badger's Day.[36] A similar folk belief persists in America as Groundhog Day.

The year is awakening, new and pure, waiting for life to mark it. The lengthening days that follow Imbolc hold the promise of spring and the rebirth of plant life, and the yearly cycle of work on the land begins once more as the earth is prepared for the seed.[37] I think of February as a time of purification during which we can banish negativity in all its forms. It is a time to cleanse, physically and spiritually, and prepare for the busy season to come as, day by day, the light increases, and we embark on the many personal and spiritual lessons the year will bring.

35   Carmichael, *Carmina Gadelica.*

36   Pennick, *Folklore of East Anglia.*

37   Owen, *Welsh Folk Customs.*

Early February

February 1: IMBOLC

February opens with Imbolc, one of the quarterly festivals of the old Irish and one of the eight sabbats of the modern Pagan year. The term Imbolc (alt. Imbolg/Oimelc) only occurs in the literature of Ireland and probably means "parturition" or "lactation."[38] A fifteenth-century quatrain said this of Imbolc:

> To taste of every food in order,
>
> This is proper at Imbolc,
>
> Washing of hand and foot and head;
>
> It is to you thus I relate.[39]

This suggests it might have been a time of feasting and purification. Little else is recorded of its customs except that it was accounted the first day of spring and the time ewes came into milk. In Christian times it seems to have been completely subsumed in the feast day of St. Brighid (alt. Brigid/Bride/Brigit),[40] and indeed, modern Pagans often celebrate Imbolc as the festival of the goddess Brighid. From the tenth-century *Cormac's Glossary*:

> Brigit i.e. a poetess, daughter of the Dagda. This is Brigit the female sage, or woman of wisdom, i.e. Brigit the goddess whom poets adored, because very great and very famous was her protecting care. It is therefore they call her goddess of poets by this name. Whose sisters were Brigit the female physician [woman of leechcraft], Brigit the female smith [woman of smithwork]; from whose names with all Irishmen a goddess was called Brigit. Brigit, then, breo-aigit, breo-shaigit, "a fiery arrow."[41]

This single source gives us most of the ideas we have today about the goddess Brighid: three sisters or a triple deity with the Brighid of poetry, prophecy, and

---

38   Ó hÓgáin, *Myth, Legend and Romance*.

39   Kuno Meyer's translation as found in Kenneth Hurlstone Jackson's *Studies in Early Celtic Nature Poetry* (Cambridge: University Press, 1935).

40   Blackburn and Holford-Strevens, *The Oxford Companion to the Year*.

41   Cormac's Glossary, https://archive.org/stream/sanaschormaiccooostokgoog /sanaschormaiccooostokgoog_djvu.txt, accessed 10.4.19.

inspiration, the Brighid of healing, and the Brighid of fire, who oversees the hearth and forge and who is the patroness of craftsmen and women.

Most of the tales we have that expand these concepts come from the later legends of the saint the Christian church turned her into.[42] However, since many of the practices around the saint's feast day concern fire, fertility, and the birth of young animals, it seems entirely probable that these originally related to the goddess Brighid at Imbolc.[43]

While Cormac's interpretation of her name as "fiery arrow" may be fanciful, she was certainly connected with fire. In one tale, St. Brighid was born at sunrise on the threshold of the house as her mother was on her way out to milk the cow, and immediately a tower of flame emerged from her forehead that stretched from earth to heaven, fulfilling a druid's prophecy that she would neither be born inside nor out, nor during the day or night. Later, a house she was in flamed up to heaven and a fiery pillar rose from her head. She also hung her cloak on sunbeams, cow dung blazed before her, and flames engulfed her body without burning her. In another tale, she carried a burning coal in her apron.

Furthermore, the saint is said to have founded an abbey at Kildare (*Cull Dara* = "temple of the oak"), where a perpetual fire, held to burn without ash or waste, was kept burning by a college of nineteen women called *Inghean an Dagha* ("daughters of the flame"), who fed the fire each night and kept it from dying; on the twentieth day it was believed that Brighid herself tended the flame. Men were forbidden to enter this sanctuary. This sounds very much like the rites of a Pagan temple, a sacred hearth tended by virgin priestesses akin to the fire of the Vestal Virgins of Rome, given a thin Christian veneer. Nevertheless, the abbey kept the flame burning until 1220 CE, when Henry de Loundres, the Archbishop of Dublin, shocked at this evidence of fire worship, issued an edict ordering the flame to be extinguished, condemning it as "pagan superstition."[44]

In 1969 the Catholic Church officially removed Brighid from the list of accepted saints, finding no evidence that she ever existed. The goddess Brighid, however, was certainly a pan-Celtic deity. Her association with the hearth fire, by way of the erst-

---

42   Gilbride & Aster Breo, *Finding Brighid in the Ancient Lore,* https://clannbhride.wordpress.com /articles-and-essays/finding-brighid-in-the-ancient-lore, accessed 26.9.18.

43   Ó hÓgáin, *Myth, Legend and Romance.*

44   Jones and Pennick, A *History of Pagan Europe.*

while saint, persists in Ireland to this day. Within living memory, the domestic fire was kindled with invocations to Brighid, and I often use this traditional prayer[45] to kindle my hearth fire:

> I will build the hearth as Brighid would build it.
> Guarding the hearth, guarding the floor,
> Guarding the household all.

Imbolc Ritual

I celebrate Imbolc as the festival of the flame—the domestic hearth fire, so crucial at this cold time of year, as well as the fire of the sun as the days increase in length. Both of these fall under the auspices of the goddess Brighid. She is called "daughter of the bear" as she comes after the first rising of the star Arcturus, the Bear Keeper, over the horizon at Imbolc. She is born at sunrise and is the herald of new beginnings. When she comes, she kindles the first stirrings of spring in the belly of the earth. I honour the Hearth Goddess, thank her for her gifts of warmth and prosperity, and ask for her blessing, as well as consider how I will use her creative and healing fire in the coming year.

Decorate your hearth or altar with any wild greenery you can find and the first flowers of spring (such as snowdrops), white crystals, and glass vessels of spring water. You will need one white candle and three red candles. Prepare a Brighid doll, a figure in the shape of a woman made from a sheaf of wheat or oats (this is distinct from the corn dolly, representing the grain god, which we returned to the earth in January). This can be done as simply or intricately as you wish. Alternatively, you can use a doll or Goddess statue. Decorate it with shells, stones, and ribbons. Place a bright white crystal over its heart—this is called the Guiding Star of Brighid. Also prepare a white wand by stripping a twig of birch or willow, and an oblong basket for Brighid's bed dressed with pretty fabric and other decorations you think suitable.

Light the white candle and say:

> Goddess Brighid, lady of the sudden flame,
> Bring me your fiery inspiration.
> Come to my hearth; your bed is prepared.
> Goddess Brighid, come in!

---

45 Danaher, *The Year in Ireland.*

Repeat until you feel the presence of the Goddess:

Brighid, come in!

Brighid, come in!

Brighid, come in!

When you are ready, lay the Brighid doll in the bed and say:

Brighid with her white wand breathes life into the mouth of dead winter.

Lay the white wand alongside the icon and say:

The earth warms in the feeble embrace of the Imbolc sun,

and winter moves to spring. Brighid, I honour you tonight.

Light the first red candle. Say:

The fire of the hearth is the dwelling place of the Goddess. The hearth is the sacred
centre of the home. It warms, it comforts, it nourishes. It draws home the weary
traveller. It is the place where the gods and humankind may meet. Lady of the
Triple Flame, warm my hearth and home with your living presence.

Meditate on the inspiration of your own hearth fire and home, what it means to you, what you wish for in the future, and how you might use it in the service of others and the Goddess.

Light the second red candle and say:

Lady of the Triple Flame, beloved Goddess of poets and craftspeople, you are the
fire of inspiration, the fire in the head, the touch of the gods that stokes the forge of
creativity. I ask you to inspire me and kindle my inner spark.

Think about the inspiration of Brighid's "fire in the head," what it means to you, and what you wish for in the future in connection with creativity and craftsmanship, and how you might use these in the service of others and the Goddess.

Light the third red candle and say:

Lady of the Triple Flame, you are the fire of healing that flows from the heart of
the Goddess. Gentle Goddess of healing, light the fire of healing within me.

Meditate on the inspiration of healing, what it means to you, and what you wish for in the future in connection with the healing fire, and how you might use it in the service of others and the Goddess. Then say:

Brighid, I honour you tonight. You bring the return of spring and the renewal of the earth. I will honour them. You bring the gifts of the Triple Flame; I will honour them and use them in your service.

Let this ritual end with love and blessings, and allow the candles to burn themselves out.

February 2: CANDLEMAS

Whereas February 1 is Imbolc and Brighid's Day, February 2 is Candlemas Day, the Christian feast of the purification of the Blessed Virgin Mary. According to Mosaic law, a woman is unclean for forty days after giving birth to a male child and needs to be purified before she can re-enter society, so when the church decided to fix Christ's birthday on December 25 (after celebrating it all around the calendar at various times), this dated the purification of Mary to the beginning of February. It is said that as Mary entered the temple, an old man called Simeon recognised the baby as the promised Messiah and hailed him as a "light to lighten the Gentiles."[46] The Roman Catholic Church uses Candlemas as the time to bless the candles for the coming ritual year and embraces the old Pagan symbolism of light redeeming the darkness in spring.

The Celtic Church in Ireland, finding that the worship of the Pagan goddess Brighid was too deeply ingrained to be eradicated, turned her into a saint and gave her the role of nursemaid to the infant Jesus, even though St. Brighid was supposed to have lived in Ireland hundreds of years later, in the fifth or sixth century CE. She is alleged to have distracted King Herod's soldiers when they were pursuing the holy family by dancing with two candles, allowing the holy family to escape.

Like many church feasts and customs, Candlemas was a direct takeover of pre-existing Pagan festivals. Pope Innocent asked,

> Why do we in this feast carry candles?...Because the gentiles dedicated the month of February to the infernal gods, and as...Pluto stole Proserpine, and her mother, Ceres, sought her in the night with lighted candles, so they, at the beginning of this month, walked about the city with lighted candles; because the holy fathers could not utterly extirpate this custom, they ordained that Christians should carry about candles

---

46   Luke 2.22–40.

in honour of the blessed virgin Mary: and thus what was done before to the honour of Ceres is now done to the honour of the Virgin.[47]

The purifications of the ancient Greek Lesser Eleusinian Mysteries were celebrated around the beginning of this month with candlelight processions in honour of the agricultural goddess Demeter and her daughter, the spring goddess Persephone (Ceres and Proserpine respectively in Roman mythology) and marked Persephone's release from the underworld and her return to the land in spring. In Rome the Feriae Sementivae was held in honour of the agricultural goddess Ceres and Tellus (Mother Earth), with the protection of the goddesses invoked to defend the newly sown seed from bad weather and frost. They were given sacrifices and offerings such as spelt bread, and small decorated clay discs were hung on the trees to ward off evil spirits and negativity. Also in Rome, candles were burned to the goddess Juno Februa, or Juno the Purifier (mother of the god Mars, who protected the crops) to scare away evil spirits.[48] The light of the candles echoes the increase of the sun's light and is perhaps an act of sympathetic magic, while fire, of course, is the ultimate agent of purification.

Though we now consider Twelfth Night to be the end of the Christmas season, in the past many considered it to be Candlemas; even now in Rome, the manger scenes are left up until Candlemas. In England the Yule log was often burned up until Candlemas Eve. Like Twelfth Night, it was marked by games, dancing, and feasting, presided over by the Lord of Misrule or Abbot of Unreason. The coming of Candlemas was inextricably linked to the ending of the winter season of rest and withdrawal. Very little work was done on the land from Halloween till Candlemas, and many Candlemas carols talk of the return to work. This was also the day that servants had to hand back the candles they had been given in the autumn to light their quarters since it was considered that artificial light was no longer required after this point,[49] which gave rise to the saying "Candlemas, candleless."[50]

47   Quoted by William Hone, *The Every-Day Book: or, The Guide to the Year: Relating the Popular Amusements, Sports, Ceremonies, Manners, Customs, and Events, Incident to the Three Hundred and Sixty-Five Days in Past and Present Times; Being a Series of Five Thousand Anecdotes and Facts* (London: W. Tegg and Co., 1878).
48   *Brewer's Dictionary of Phrase and Fable*, Blitz Editions (Leicester: Bookmart Ltd., 1990).
49   Owen, *Welsh Folk Customs*.
50   Bogle, *A Book of Feasts and Seasons*.

Candlemas Ceremony

At Candlemas, take the besom and sweep through the house, saying: "Let winter's grip be swept away." Start at the top of the house and work your way down, eventually sweeping through the back door. Light a white candle in each window of the house, saying "The light grows" with each one.

If you can, make a fire in the hearth or garden to burn the last of the Yuletide greenery. I always keep a piece of holly from Yule for this ritual. Visualise burning away the winter season and, with it, all that is past and needs to be released, saying: "Let us burn away winter." Meditate on the past—and negativity—being burned away.

February 4: SNOWDROPS

While snow covers the ground, the seeds are stirring in the earth, responding to the increased light levels. When the thaw comes, they will push green into the light, and already the first snowdrops (*Galanthus nivalis*) are poking their drooping white heads from the frozen earth in my garden. I always await their coming eagerly, the first brave flowers in a barren plot, and some of their folk names—such as Candlemas Maiden, Candlemas Bells, and Fair Maids of February—reflect their flowering period. Snowdrops are a sign that life is returning, and in folklore they represent new beginnings, youth, and purity. I have often read that snowdrops were sacred to the goddess Brighid, but this is simply not true. The plants are not native to Britain and Ireland, and were not introduced until late in the sixteenth century CE from southern Europe.

Snowdrops and their bulbs are poisonous to humans, so it is perhaps not surprising that they were also called the Death Flower and thought to be unlucky if taken indoors. Consequently, they are not used by Hearth Witches medicinally, though the pharmaceutical industry is investigating some of their compounds for treating Alzheimer's disease and HIV. However, I do place the first ones on the altar and take their appearance as a cue to perform a personal ritual of purification that echoes the renewal of the goddess by bathing in a sacred pool.

Snowdrop Purification Ritual

Prepare a cauldron or large bowl of pure water and float some snowdrop flowers (or other early flowers) on its surface. Lay beside it a small crystal ball or spherical representation of the earth. Have some towels ready.

Light a white candle and say:

> *Like the Goddess of spring, I wash in the cauldron of transformation*
> *so that I may be purified and renewed.*

Wash in the cauldron, visualising washing away negativity and letting things you need to be rid of dissolving in the water.

Then wash the crystal ball (representing the earth) in the cauldron and say:

> *As I wash this crystal in the water of this vessel, so may the spring rains cleanse*
> *the face of the earth and make it ready for planting. I beseech the Goddess that the*
> *earth may be cleansed of pollution, negativity, and evil, and I pledge to play my*
> *part in this endeavour.*

Spend some time meditating on this, and when you have finished, close the ritual by saying:

> *Let this ritual end with love and blessings.*

Put out the candle. Take the cauldron of water outside and empty it on the earth, if possible.

February 6: DOROTHY'S DAY

According to weather lore, St. Dorothy's Day is reputedly the snowiest day of all, when the ground is frozen and no spade or plough can turn it. Actually, the sun has come out today, so I'm going to prune my fruit trees and bushes this morning before the apple and pear trees begin to bud. I also need to trim the soft fruit bushes, shortening the side shoots and removing the centre stems to create an open goblet shape. The summer fruiting raspberries will be shortened and the autumn fruiting ones cut down to a couple of inches. The hazel trees will be trimmed, and I will keep the long shoots for sticks to support peas and for making hurdles (fencing).

It was customary to bless fruit trees on St. Dorothy's Day, which is perhaps why she is the patron saint of gardeners. No evidence for her actual existence has ever been discovered, and she was consequently removed from the Catholic liturgical calendar in 1969. She may have been invented as a piece of Christian propaganda (a Christian virgin martyred for refusing to marry a Pagan) or perhaps to serve as a Christian replacement for the Pagan fruit tree customs associated with early February.

Fruit Tree Blessings Ceremony

I think it a nice idea to bless my fruit trees and bushes after pruning them. As I give each one a good top dressing of potash-containing wood ash from my bonfires, I say:

> Lord and Lady, bless these trees
>
> Grant us sunshine, warm breezes, and gentle rain
>
> So that the flowers may blossom
>
> And the fruits may come to ripeness
>
> In the fullness of time.

If you don't have fruit trees of your own, you can send out a general blessing to all the fruit trees in your area.

Mid-February

At this time of year, there is little left growing on my vegetable patch apart from a few remaining carrots and leeks and the members of the *Brassica* tribe—cabbage, kale, brussels sprouts, and broccoli. The Anglo Saxons even called February "Kale Month" (*kele monath*). But by the middle of February, the sun is starting to warm the soil on my vegetable plot. I need to prepare it for planting in March by digging it over, incorporating lots of vegetable matter from the compost heap. I'm also putting my seed potatoes to "chit," or sprout some short shoots. I put the potatoes in old egg boxes with their eyes facing upwards. They need to be placed where they will get some light, but not in direct sunlight. I will be planting out my garlic and shallot sets immediately, though, weather permitting.

All through the dead time of winter, in the warmth of my kitchen, I make plans for the gardens and vegetable patch. What to plant where, what to grow, where the air will be perfumed with roses and lavender, where the earth will be turned for potatoes, where the poles will be raised for the beans. I remember that it won't just affect me and my table, but that the local wildlife depends on it and there must be flowers for the bees, safe places for the insects, perches and nesting places for the birds. I'm willing to share my produce with the mice and small mammals and the fruit with the birds; my plans will have consequences for hundreds of little lives.

The garden is starting to come alive, and I can see bulbs pushing through the ground. According to local folk wisdom, it is time to start work on the garden when the crocuses appear. In preparation for planting seeds, I've been cleaning down the greenhouse and washing all my seed trays, pots, and cloches with warm, soapy water.

The Blessing of the Garden Tools

The garden tools are brushed off, cleaned, and sharpened, and I like to bless them before the real gardening begins. You can do this even if you only have houseplants and a little watering can for them.

> Lord and Lady, bless these tools
> Which I have prepared in your honour.
> Bless my endeavours this year.
> May there be plenty;
> May there be abundance.
> Lord and Lady,
> Blessed be.

February 11: THE DAY THE BIRDS BEGIN TO SING

The birds start to prepare for nesting this month, and already they are claiming their territories. According to tradition, this is the day when the birds begin to sing. They have certainly been pretty quiet over the winter, but as this month progresses, the dawn and dusk choruses increase in volume and complexity, with new voices being added. It reminds me that the birds sometimes need our help during the winter, so I am making fat cakes to give them a much-needed energy boost, which will help protect them from the cold.

NB: Please remember to wash your bird feeders often, as accumulated dirt and bacteria can make the birds ill.

Homemade Bird Cake

Just mix up some birdseed—or even kitchen leftovers like currants, oats, breadcrumbs, cheese, and peanuts—with melted lard, suet, or coconut oil (two parts dry mix to one part fat). Take an old yoghurt pot and put a hole in the bottom and push a piece of string through it. Pack the pot with the mixture and pop this in the fridge to set overnight. Take it out, cut away the pot, and tie a knot in the string to secure it. Then just hang it in your garden and watch the birds come along for a treat!

NB: Never use leftover fat from frying or roasting, as this can coat the birds' feathers and prevent them flying.

February 14: VALENTINE'S DAY

Valentine's Day has its roots in the rites of the Roman mother goddess Juno and the Lupercalia festival (see February 15). The Lupercalia celebration featured a lottery in which young men would draw the names of young girls from a box. What happened afterwards varied from place to place; in some areas a girl was assigned to each young man and would be his sweetheart during the remaining year. In others it was the single women who drew the lot with a single man's name on it. In an attempt to stamp out Lupercalia rites, the church replaced them with the feast of St. Valentine. Under the church, instead of drawing out lovers' names from the box, young people could draw out saints' names and sermons. They were then expected to meditate on their saints and emulate their qualities during the year. However, not surprisingly, this didn't prove very popular. The practice of sending love letters on Valentine's Day appeared in France and England in the fourteenth and fifteenth centuries.

St. Valentine is an amalgamated figure with several conflicting and confused biographies. During the reformations of the 1960s, the Roman Catholic Church, embarrassed by the nebulous nature of the saint and finding no evidence of his existence, dropped St. Valentine's Day from the official calendar.

The custom of choosing a lover on this day may relate to the commonly held European belief that birds select their mates for the year on February 14. In *Parlement of Foules*, Chaucer wrote: "For this was on St. Valentine's Day, when every bird cometh there to choose his mate." In February, activity amongst birds increases, and they begin to nest this month. Perhaps stemming from this belief, a later superstition was that the type of bird a woman first saw on this day was an omen of the type of man she would marry:

- blackbird: a clergyman

- bluebird: a happy man

- crossbill: an argumentative man

- dove: a good-hearted man

- goldfinch: a rich man

- hawk: a soldier or brave man

- owl: a man who would not live long

- sparrow: a farmer

- woodpecker: the girl would remain single

Naturally, Valentine's Eve and Valentine's Day lend themselves to love divinations. One old method is to take five bay leaves washed in rosewater and pin them on your pillow on Valentine's Eve, one in each corner and one in the middle, then dress in a clean nightgown turned inside out and whisper: "Good Valentine, be kind to me/ In dreams let me my true love see."[51] Or you could try a method used by English girls a couple of centuries ago and write the names of prospective lovers on slips of paper, roll them in balls of clay, and drop them in a bowl of water. The first to rise to the surface will be your valentine.[52]

February 15: LUPERCALIA

In ancient Rome February 15 was the Lupercalia, an archaic pastoral rite that persevered into classical times and commemorated the passage of young men into manhood to the god Lupercus. He was a fertility deity, often identified with Faunus or the Greek god Pan, especially worshipped by shepherds, who invoked powers to promote fertility among sheep and protection from wolves. A special group of priests called Luperci were responsible for conducting the rituals.

The celebration began in the Lupercal cave on the Palatine Hill in Rome where Romulus and Remus, the twin founders of Rome, were said to have been nursed by a she-wolf. Two naked young priests, assisted by Vestal Virgins, made offerings of a sacred grain mixture called *mola salsa* and sacrificed a dog and a goat. Blood from the animals was spread on the two priests' foreheads and wiped off with some wool dipped in milk. The priests then ran about the city, scourging women with strips of skin taken from the sacrificed goat called *februa* ("purification"). The Romans believed that this flogging would purify them and assure their future fertility and easy child-

---

51   Long, *The Folklore Calendar*.
52   Ibid.

birth. Being struck by these whips was considered especially lucky for women who wanted to become fertile.

The rituals of February echo the interconnected themes of purity and fertility, with one being reliant on the other—in order to obtain fertility, abundance, blessing, or, moreover, to be worthy of the mysteries, one must be purified within and without.

Sound Cleansing

I have a bodhrán drum that I use to shift blocked energy in my house. It is made of goatskin, which rather fits in with the theme of fertility and purification of the Lupercalia. The goat is reputedly a lusty animal that is associated with fertility in many parts of the world. I am a terrible drummer and can't keep a rhythm to save my life, but it doesn't matter in this instance. Drums have been used to chase away spirits and negative energy in many parts of the world. You can also use bells and singing bowls for this, or even just clap loudly. Start at the top of the house and walk through, drumming into all the corners and visualizing the stagnant areas shifting, allowing the energy to flow.

Movable: LENT

Many of the folk traditions of February focus around the moveable Christian season of Lent, the forty-day period of fasting, penitence, and purification that comes before Easter, which echoes the earlier Pagan customs of purification at this time of year. In 325 CE the Council of Nicaea established that Easter would be held on the first Sunday after the first full moon occurring on or after the vernal equinox, which was approximated to March 21. That means that the beginning of Lent can fall as early as the second week in February or as late as the second week in March.

Before Lent began on Ash Wednesday, for Christians there was one last chance to eat, drink, and be merry on Shrove Tuesday, indulging in rich foods such as meat, sugar, eggs, and butter that were forbidden during Lent. In Britain, Ireland, and some Commonwealth countries, Shrove Tuesday is still called Pancake Day, and elsewhere it is known as Fat Tuesday or Mardi Gras. *Shrove* comes from the word *shrive*, meaning "absolve," since it was customary to go to confession and obtain absolution before the start of Lent. The church bell was rung to call people to confession and became known as the "pancake bell."[53] In Britain the day was a holiday, and children would chant: "Pancake Day is a very happy day/If we don't have a holiday, we'll all run away!" In some places the first three pancakes were sacred, marked with a cross, and set aside.[54] In others it was customary to give them to the chickens,[55] perhaps in an act of sympathetic magic to show them what to do.

. . . .

PANCAKE RECIPE

It was always traditional to have them with a squeeze of lemon juice and a sprinkling of sugar when I was a child, and this is still my favourite way to eat them, but you can use your own preferred topping.

100 GRAMS PLAIN WHITE FLOUR

2 LARGE EGGS, BEATEN

300 MILLILITRES MILK

VEGETABLE OIL

1 LEMON

SUGAR

Put the flour, eggs, and milk into a bowl and whisk to make a smooth pouring batter. Rest the mixture for 20–30 minutes. Wipe a frying pan with a little vegetable oil and pour in some of the batter. On high heat, cook the pancake for about a minute on each side.

February 17: FORNICALIA

Around February 17 the ancient Romans celebrated the festival of Fornacalia in honour of Fornax, the goddess of ovens, who oversaw the proper baking of bread. Her name is connected with the English word *furnace*. "The oven is the mother" was the adage of the Fornicalia.[56]

---

53 Jones and Deer, *Cattern Cakes and Lace*.
54 Raven, *Black Country & Staffordshire*.
55 Ibid.
56 Pennick, *The Goddess Year*.

Fornicalia Ritual

To honour Fornax or your own Hearth Goddess, clean your oven today. I know it's a job that everyone hates, but it's one that has to be done. Consider it a sacred act that honours the Goddess. Afterwards, make some bread and put it to bake in the oven with these words:

> *Hearth Goddess, Goddess of the oven, Lady of fire,*
>
> *You are a goddess of transformation,*
>
> *Taking raw ingredients and transmuting them into nourishing food.*
>
> *On this day I honour you and bake this bread in tribute.*

Share the bread with friends, and be sure to put the crumbs out for the wild birds.

. . . .

HOMEMADE OVEN CLEANER

100 MILLILITRES LIQUID CASTILE SOAP

240 GRAMS BICARBONATE OF SODA (BAKING SODA)

60 MILLILITRES WHITE VINEGAR

WATER

Mix together, adding enough water to turn the mixture into a paste. Spread over your oven and leave for at least 8 hours. It will foam a little. Wash off with clean water.

February 19: HOUSE CLEANING

I'm going to do a spiritual cleansing of my house today. It is a good idea to do this at least once a year, and the month of purification is the perfect time to do it.

House Purification Ritual

In each room of your house, place a dish with a peeled clove of garlic ringed with salt to absorb negative energies. Leave them for an hour. Take the dishes of garlic and salt outside and burn the contents completely. Open all the windows and doors. Carry a dish of cleansing incense (see recipe below) around the house, starting at the top and working your way down, and in each room allow the smoke to go in each corner.

Say:

> *In the name of the God and Goddess,*
>
> *I command all evil and negativity to be gone.*
>
> *This do I will.*
>
> *So mote it be.*

Close the doors and windows. Using a protection oil, dip your finger in and draw it round the edges of all the doors and windows, saying:

> *In the name of the God and Goddess,*
>
> *I seal this place so that no evil may enter.*
>
> *This do I will.*
>
> *So mote it be.*

Light a white candle on your altar or hearth and say:

> *Lord and Lady,*
>
> *Grant me your protection*
>
> *As I give you my thanks and my service.*
>
> *So mote it be.*

House Cleansing Incense

2 PARTS FRANKINCENSE

2 PARTS MYRRH

1 PART CRUSHED JUNIPER BERRIES

1 PART ROSEMARY

FEW DROPS ROSEMARY ESSENTIAL OIL

Quantities are by volume, not weight, so you might use two spoons frankincense and one of rosemary, for example. All ingredients should be dried. Mix together and burn on a charcoal block. If you intend to carry this around your house, place it securely on a fireproof dish on top of a heat-resistant mat.

· · · · · · · · · · · ·

PROTECTION OIL

30 MILLILITRES OLIVE OIL

3 DROPS ROSEMARY ESSENTIAL OIL

4 DROPS GERANIUM ESSENTIAL OIL

4 DROPS CYPRESS ESSENTIAL OIL

Combine and keep in a dark glass bottle.

Late February

We enter Pisces, the faint constellation of the fishes, considered to be the last sign of the zodiac. In Greek mythology, the gods of Olympus had defeated the Titans, the elder gods, but the Titaness Gaia (Mother Earth) coupled with Tartarus, the lowest region of the underworld, where Zeus had imprisoned the Titans, and from this union came Typhon, a hideous monster. Fleeing from him, the goddess Aphrodite and her son Eros took cover among the reeds on the banks of the Euphrates. Pan saw him coming and alerted the others with a shout. Aphrodite and Eros, calling to the water nymphs for help, leapt into the river. In one version of the story, two fish swam up and carried Aphrodite and Eros to safety on their backs, although in another version the two refugees were themselves changed into fish.

By late February, spring is really stepping up a gear. On sunny days I've even seen a few bumblebees and early butterflies basking in the light. In the woods the leaves of the bluebells and wild garlic are starting to emerge, and catkins have blossomed on the hazel and alder trees.

I've been weeding, pulling up lots of fresh green chickweed (*Stellaria media*) from the garden. It is a common weed in most parts of the world and not hard to find. Its botanical name, *Stellaria*, means "little stars," a description of its tiny white five-petalled flowers. My chickens love it (it is not called chickweed for nothing), and it makes a nourishing spring addition to their diets. The leaves can be eaten by humans too, used fresh in a salad, in a soup, cooked like spinach, or even made into a pesto with pine nuts, garlic, and olive oil. Medicinally, chickweed is useful for cooling skin inflammations. Every spring I make chickweed salve.

· · · · · · · · · · · ·

Chickweed Salve

HANDFUL OF CHICKWEED (*STELLARIA MEDIA*) AERIAL PARTS

OLIVE OIL

BEESWAX

Put the chickweed together with just enough oil to cover it into a double boiler. Heat very, very gently for 2 hours. Strain the oil off and discard the plant material. Add some grated beeswax (the more you add, the harder the set) and when the wax has melted, pour into small jars.

The Return of the Frogs

Though in some years we get snow at this time of year, the weather has been mild here and the frogs are returning to my garden pond, having overwintered on land, where they spend most of their time. They are croaking loudly to attract mates, which they only do in early spring. In several cultures this croaking of the frogs was thought to call down the spring rains that cleanse and renew the face of the earth after winter, regenerating and transforming it, watering the sleeping seeds so that they can burst into life. Frogs are associated with creation all over the world for this reason.

Frog Meditation

This annual return of the frogs reminds me to meditate on the powers of water and on the frog as an animal guide. Light a candle and sit quietly while you meditate on the following:

Frog represents the creative power of the waters, the primal source of all life; she has a moist skin, which contrasts with the dryness of death. Water flows, nourishes, and replenishes the earth. The power of frog is concerned with cleansing, purifying, and the free-flowing of emotional energies. Emotional cleansing is another aspect of purification this month. Do you conceal your feelings? Tears are water, too, and have a power of their own. Call on the power of frog to teach you how to nourish your emotions.

February 22: FEAST OF FORGIVENESS

In ancient Rome this was the festival of the *Caristia* ("pardoning"), a day to renew ties with friends and family and settle disputes. Families gathered to dine together, give each other small tokens of appreciation, and offer food and incense to the house-hold gods.[57] The emphasis was on love and accord. Concordia, the goddess of harmony, was invoked, along with Janus, the god of new beginnings; Salus, the goddess of health; and Pax, the goddess of peace.[58]

I really like this idea, so I've incorporated its inspiration into my practice. On this day, offer incense to your household gods to show your appreciation. This is a day of forgiveness, so take the opportunity to mend quarrels: this is another act of purification, removing the toxicity of bad relationships from your life. If you wish, you could cook a meal for family and friends, including any you might have fallen out with, to show them how much you value them.

Put four candles on the table and light them with the invocations; you can do this silently if all the people present are not Pagan.

> *Goddess of harmony, be with us and bless us.* (light the pink candle)
>
> *Goddess of peace, be with us and bless us.* (light the white candle)
>
> *Goddess of health, be with us and bless us.* (light the blue candle)
>
> *God of new beginnings, be with us and bless us.* (light the green candle)

Then just share the meal together and have fun! If for any reason you can't get family and friends together, you can still light the four candles.

February 24: ST. MATTHIAS'S DAY

In the Roman Catholic Church this is St. Matthias's Day. He is called the thirteenth apostle, chosen by the apostles to replace Judas. It's a strange day as it is a leap day, affected by the change of the calendar in leap years—the feast of St. Matthias is moved from February 24 to the following day every leap year.

In Slavonic myth St. Matthias's Day is one of the days on which the *vesna* were said to gather. These are female spirits or fairies associated with youth and springtime. In several Slavic languages, the word for spring is *vesna*, while in Slovene the month of February is called *vesnar*. During the month of February, the *vesna* were able to leave their mountain palaces and travel down to the valleys below in order to return fertility to the land. In Pagan times Vesna was the goddess of youth and spring, daughter of the summer goddess Lada. Her appearance banished Morena, the

57 Peck, *Harper's Dictionary of Classical Literature and Antiquities.*
58 Blackburn and Holford-Strevens, *Oxford Companion to the Year.*

winter hag goddess of death, in much the same way Bride banished the Cailleach in Scottish lore. She represented the victory of spring, light, and life over winter, cold, and death. The season of the Crone is ending.

February 28/29: OUT WITH THE SHVOD

On the last day of February, the old Armenian peasants performed a curious ritual called "Out with the Shvod." The Shvod was one of the guardian spirits, who often appeared as serpents, which variously inhabited fields, woods, and houses. Armed with sticks and old clothes, they struck the walls of their houses and barns, crying "Out with the Shvod and in with March!" to drive the field spirits, which had been sheltering in the house over the winter, into the fields and orchards to begin work on the land.[59] Then the dish of water placed on the threshold the evening before was overturned, the doors closed tightly, and the sign of the cross made to prevent their lazy return to the warmth of the hearth.[60]

Out with the Shvod Ritual

It's not just the land spirits that need to be shaken out of winter lethargy and all thoughts of hibernating inside—it's us too. This is a spring wake-up call. I'm not inclined to go around hitting the walls of my house with sticks and ruining the paint-work, but starting at the top of the house, I flick a feather duster into all the corners, calling "Out with the Shvod and in with March!"

I take this as an opportunity to declutter and get rid of all the clothes, knick-knacks, and other unused stuff that has accumulated over the winter and just sits there, unused, taking up space and sapping energy.

Once all this is done, I place a dish of water on the threshold and overturn it to indicate that the matter is finished, and those items and that laziness will not return this spring. I close the door and make the sign of a protective pentacle on it to seal the business.

Now we have finished with the purifications of February, we are prepared and ready to welcome the work of March.

---

59   *Funk & Wagnalls Standard Dictionary of Folklore, Mythology, and Legend.*
60   Fox, *The Mythology of All Races.*

THE GREEN SHOOTS MONTH

March

• • • • •

The Romans called this month Martius after the god Mars, who was the god of war and agriculture alike since March opened the season for both farming and fighting. As a warrior god, Mars also protected the crops, so "it was to Mars that the Roman husbandman prayed for the prosperity of his grain and vines, his fruit trees and his copses."[61] From this we get our name "March." In the oldest known Roman calendar, the year began in March, though this was later shifted to January with the reforms of Julius Caesar.

In the UK we still say that March comes in like a lion and goes out like a lamb, beginning with cold and blustery winds and ending with longer, brighter days. The winds of March perform an important function and were considered by the old

---

61   Frazer, *The Golden Bough.*

farmers to dry out the fields and make the soil right for planting. March was even called H*lyda* or L*ide* in Old English, which is a reference to the loud winds.

We can feel energy building in the natural world as it responds to the increasing light during this month. Vigorous life is returning to the land; everywhere shoots push up through the earth, trees bud, flowers blossom, and animals and birds begin to mate—the earth is waking up. It is a time of renewal, of promise, of hope when the Sun God gains strength, when the Vegetation God emerges from the earth, and the Maiden Goddess is wreathed in flowers.

In ancient Greece, the festival of the Anthestêria was celebrated in honour of the god Dionysus Anthios (Dionysus the Blossoming), as the first flowers heralded his return in spring.[62] It fell when the fermentation of the wine made in the autumn was complete and it was ready to sample, reminding everyone that life and the seasons are cyclical, that what is born will die and be reborn again. All the temples of the gods were closed except the Limnaion ("in the marshes"), the temple of Dionysus that contained a sacred spring, a passageway to the underworld. The temple was only opened on this one day of the year, and its opening unlocked the way between the worlds of the living and the dead, enabling Dionysus, who had been dwelling in the underworld during the winter, to return, along with the shades of the dead attracted by the scent of the opening of the *pithoi* (large wine jars) left fermenting over winter, half buried in the earth, and now ready to taste. Swaying Dionysus masks were hung in the trees, sending good luck and fertility wherever they looked.

The Hieros Gamos, the ritual marriage of the Basilinna ("queen") to the god Dionysus, was celebrated. In this ceremony she represented Ariadne, the Cretan princess and daughter of Minos who helped Theseus defeat the Minotaur and guided him out of the labyrinth. Theseus abandoned Ariadne on Naxos, where she was found by the god Dionysus, who married her. In one version of the myth, she later hanged herself from a tree and was rescued from the underworld realm of the dead by Dionysus. The themes here are all of emergence from the underworld, like the seed sprouting from the ground, like the Vegetation God in spring. On the last day of the festival, it was necessary to purge the city of the spirits of the dead ancestors, so a meal was prepared for the dead and for the god Hermes Chthonios, their guide, who would take them

62   Federica Doria and Marco Giuman, *The Swinging Woman: Phaedra and Swing in Classical Greece*, ojs.unica.it/index.php/medea/article/download/2444/2053, accessed 27.11.18.

back to the underworld. With this banishing of the dead, the god Dionysus and the year could finally be resurrected.

In ancient Rome, a ten-day festival in honour of the vegetation god Attis, son and lover of the goddess Cybele, took place. A young pine tree representing Attis was carried into the city like a corpse, swathed in a linen shroud and decked with violets, then placed in a sepulchre in Cybele's temple, which stood on what is now Vatican Hill, near where St. Peter's stands.[63] On the Day of Blood, also called Black Friday,[64] the priests of the cult gashed themselves with knives as they danced ecstatically, sympathizing with Cybele in her grief and helping restore Attis to life. That night was spent holding a vigil over the tomb. The next morning, a priest opened the sepulchre at dawn, revealing that it was empty and announcing that the God was risen. This day was known as Hilaria, or the Day of Joy, a time of feasting and merriment.[65] The worshippers cheered as the priest announced, "Be of good cheer, neophytes, seeing that the God is saved; for we also, after our toils, shall find salvation!"[66] The longer, warmer days of spring had come, and vegetation was emerging from the earth.

In an echo of the rites of Attis, in Western Christian tradition, Easter often falls during this month. It marks the death and resurrection of Jesus Christ, sacrificed on a cross, but when his tomb was opened after three days, it was found empty, and he was declared to have risen.

The sun, reborn at the winter solstice, has gradually been gaining strength, and at the vernal equinox (around March 21), the light finally overcomes the darkness and the days become longer than the nights. The Saxons called March *Lentmonat,* "lengthening," referring to the lengthening of days, a word the Christians adopted as "Lent," the days leading up to the festival of Easter.

It is not surprising that many places of the ancient world celebrated New Year at the spring equinox, when the sun entered Aries, the first sign of the zodiac, and the natural world renewed itself. The Babylonian New Year, for example, began after the vernal equinox with the twelve-day festival of Akitu. It commemorated the defeat of the dragon goddess of chaos, Tiamat, by the god Marduk, and the beginning of creation with the emergence of order out of chaos. To mark this, New Year was celebrated

---

63   Rufus, *The World Holiday Book.*
64   https://www.ancient.eu/Cybele/, accessed 15.3.19.
65   Frazer, *The Golden Bough.*
66   Bouyer, *The Christian Mystery.*

with a temporary subversion of order,[67] reminiscent of the customs of misrule in later western Europe, when the king was stripped of his jewellery, sceptre, and crown before kneeling at the altar of Marduk and praying for forgiveness on behalf of himself and his subjects before all his emblems of authority were restored, symbolising the annual renewal of his authority and nature alike. Influenced by these ancient rites, Iranians, Zoroastrians, the Parsis in India, the Kurds, and members of the Bahá'í Faith still celebrate New Year at the spring equinox with the festival of Nowruz ("new day"), and this has taken place in Iran for at least 2,500 years. It proclaims the triumph of light over darkness, good over evil, order over chaos, and the rejuvenation of the world as the warmth of the spring conquers winter.

Out of the winter comes spring. Out of the darkness comes light. In the midst of despair is hope. The world is renewed with youth and vitality, freshness and vigour. The themes of this month are the emergence of the Vegetation God with the green shoots as the youthful Green Man, the Maiden Goddess as the Lady of Flowers, birds nesting, and animals mating, all promising us that life will be renewed and continue.

The folk customs of the season reflect these themes. New clothes were often bought for Easter, particularly gloves and new bonnets for women.[68] With the increase in light, wild and domestic birds start laying, a symbol of renewal and fertility. Forbidden during the fasting of Lent, eggs could now be eaten for luck or given as gifts. In many districts, eggs were coloured or eaten for good fortune at Easter, and there was (and in some parts of England still are) egg-rolling competitions down the hillsides, perhaps to reflect the passage of the sun or perhaps just for fun, and the winner is the egg that rolls the farthest. The Pace Egg mumming troupes go out, performing mumming plays in return for eggs and beer.[69] In Germany it is important to eat something green, and fire wheels are rolled down hills (straw stuffed into large wooden wheels, set on fire, and rolled down a hill at night—again, perhaps symbolising the passage of the sun). If all wheels released roll straight down the hill, it is said to bring a good harvest.[70]

---

67   http://www.payvand.com/news/12/mar/1176.html, accessed 12.2.19.
68   Day, *Chronicle of Celtic Folk Customs*.
69   Ibid.
70   https://www.thelocal.de/20190415/how-to-celebrate-easter-just-like-a-german-list-traditions -customs, accessed 12.1.20.

The energies of this month are about warmth, hope, potential, planting, seeding, youth, growth, renewal, and promise.

♣♣♣♣♣♣♣

Early March

In the woods the stream is still swollen with the winter rain. On the woodland floor, primroses and dog's mercury are flowering, and beneath the hazel trees, fallen catkins lie on the ground. The blackthorn is in full flower, great swathes of starry white blossoms in hedgerows otherwise bare. It flowers before its leaves appear and so is called "the mother of the woods" because it is the first tree to bloom. There is a common superstition that it is always cold when the blackthorn flowers, something country folk called a "blackthorn winter" and refrained from planting anything out until after the blackthorn winter was over.

My thoughts turn to starting work on the garden at the beginning of March. An old rhyme instructs:

> Upon St. David's Day
> Put oats and barley in the clay and
> Sow beans and peas on David and Chad
> Be the weather good or bad.

Folk custom says that sowing sweet peas between the feasts of St. David (March 1) and St. Chad (March 2) will produce larger and more fragrant flowers, so I'll be sure to plant my sweet peas.

March 1: THE MOTHER OF LIGHT

In keeping with this month's theme of life emerging from the darkness into the light, in ancient Rome the first day of March was the Matronalia, celebrating the goddess who watched over pregnancy, childbirth, and mothers, Juno Lucina or "Juno the light-bringer," who brings children into the light. She was depicted veiled, with a flower in one hand and a child in the other. It was a day that celebrated motherhood and women in general, when men gave presents to their wives of sweets, flowers, and jewellery, as well as offering prayers for them, and children would give gifts to their mothers. Women provided feasts for their female slaves, who were given the day off and would go to the temple of Juno Lucina with their hair loose and with no knots or ties in their clothing to offer a cake out of very fine white flour (*simila*).[71]

As the church did with many Pagan feasts and customs, the Matronalia was adopted and evolved into Mothering Sunday in Europe, its day remembered by counting the Sundays of Lent—"Mothering Sunday, Care Away, Palm Sunday, Easter Day." It was meant to honour "Mother Church," and some Anglican churches still keep up the old custom of "clypping (greeting) the church" on Mothering Sunday, walking around the church in a big circle and singing a hymn.[72] However, Mothering Sunday was also a permitted break from the Lenten fast, so servants were given the day off to visit their mothers, taking flowers and a basket of treats that often included a simnel cake, the name perhaps dating right back to the Roman simila cake. This is still Mother's Day in Europe, when mothers are given flowers and chocolates, and simnel cake is traditional.[73]

In Bulgaria the first of March is Baba Marta's Day (Grandmother March's Day), when people tied *martenitsas*, protective charms made from red and white wool tassels, around wrists, trees, doors, and young animals. These were worn until the first stork returns from the south, signalling the beginning of spring.[74]

Goddess of Light Ritual

Honour the Goddess who brings life into the light—this can be all life, from the greenery of spring to young animals and human children—and ask her protection. Decorate your altar with spring flowers, such as daffodils, primroses, and violets, and as many candles as you wish, saying:

> *Come, our fairest Lady, I call you.*
> *You gave me the light of life,*
> *You created me, you gave me birth.*
> *You nourish and support all life.*
> *Your light blazes in the flames around me*

---

71 Bogle, A *Book of Feasts and Seasons*, and Ovid, *Fasti*.

72 Bogle, A *Book of Feasts and Seasons*.

73 This day should not be confused with the peculiarly American Mother's Day, which is held on the second Sunday in May and was initiated by Anna Jarvis in the nineteenth century to reunite families that had been divided during the Civil War.

74 www.b-info.com/places/Bulgaria/BabaMarta/, accessed 7.3.19.

Illuminating the darkness

Uncovering what is hidden

With the light of knowledge

Showing me the beauty of this world.

Come, Goddess,

Bless that which is newly born,

Bless the emerging shoots

As they strive towards the light.

I honour you, Mother of Light.

Come, Lady, and bless all mothers.

If you like, you can place an offering of a slice of simnel cake on the altar (put it out for the birds tomorrow). Honour all mothers today, and share simnel cake with them.

. . . .
Simnel Cake

The twelve marzipan balls on the top represent the twelve months of the year.

350 GRAMS MIXED DRIED FRUIT

250 MILLILITRES BOILING WATER

150 GRAMS UNSALTED BUTTER, SOFTENED

150 GRAMS SOFT BROWN SUGAR

3 LARGE EGGS, BEATEN

200 GRAMS SELF-RAISING FLOUR, SIFTED

2 TEASPOONS GROUND MIXED SPICE (UK) OR
    PUMPKIN PIE SPICE (US)

454 GRAMS MARZIPAN

2 TABLESPOONS APRICOT JAM

Put the dried fruit in a heatproof bowl and pour boiling water over the fruit. Soak for 15 minutes. Strain the fruit through a sieve, then spread it on a tea towel to cool. In a bowl, cream the butter and sugar together. Gradually add the eggs, a little bit at a time. If the mixture curdles, add a

. . . . .

little flour. Fold in the remaining flour and mixed spice gently into the cake mixture. Add the fruits. Spoon half the cake mixture into a greased 20 centimetres/8-inch deep-sided round cake tin that has the base lined with parchment. Roll a third of the marzipan into a circle the same size as the tin and lay the marzipan disc on top. Cover with the rest of the cake mixture. Bake at 170°C/325°F/gas mark 3 for an hour, then turn the oven temperature down to 150°C/300°F/gas mark 2 and bake for a further 50 minutes. Remove from the oven. Leave the cake to cool slightly in the tin, then turn out onto a wire rack to cool. Warm the apricot jam and sieve to remove any lumps. Brush it over the top of the cake. Roll out half the remaining marzipan into a circle and cover the top of the cake. Make 12 balls out of the rest of the marzipan and place on top of the cake. Place the whole cake under a medium grill for about 2 minutes to make the marzipan turn golden.

March 5: THE GREEN MAN

This is the time when the God returns as the Green Man, the spirit of vegetation, unfurling in the leaves on the trees. Many Pagans have sculptures and masks that represent him as a face surrounded by leaves, and they were often a feature of architecture, including churches, in the mediaeval period here in England. Most mythologies have some kind of representation of the vegetation spirit, a god who represents new growth in spring.

Coming of the Green Man Ritual

In an echo of the masks of the God hung in the trees at the Anthestêria, I am putting out my Green Man masks in the garden, as I do every year. Some of these are resin, some concrete, and some ceramic. These foliate faces represent the spirit of vegetation we call back to the land at this time of year, asking for his blessing. (If you don't have a garden, you can place a Green Man mask on your altar.) The invocation in this ritual is based on a poem written by a late friend of my hearth, Paul England, who loved to wear the Green Man mask in our springtime ceremonies.

Say:

Your mask, it is a magical world
Your name, it is constantly changing
You're a breath of the wind, you're the son of Pan
You're the greenwood prince, you are the Green Man
You dance all day to your father's tune
Then sleep by the light of the moon.
You never speak a word to the plants and trees
But your heart belongs to the growing
You live in the spring and all summer long
And sleep when the weather is snowing
Come breath of the wind that seeds all the flowers
In the bright summer sun that shines for hours
Dance all day to your father's tune
Then sleep by the light of the moon.

March 9: RETURN OF THE BIRDS

In Slavic countries birds were thought to bring the spring with them when they returned on March 9, the holiday of Strinennia. Special cakes are made in the shape of birds, which are thought to ensure their return. They are carried around the village amidst the singing of *Vesnyanki* (invocations to spring). Children are given pastries shaped like birds to toss into the air while they say "The rooks have come!"

Here in England most of our summer bird visitors don't arrive till next month, but the rooks have been with us all year, and in the garden I've seen signs that our native birds are preparing to nest and breed, gathering moss and twigs, singing in the trees and bushes for mates.

Mid-March

I've seen hares running in the bottom field this week. They are usually nocturnal creatures that remain hidden during the hours of daylight, and it is only during the mating season they are abroad in daylight. It is a magical sight. The expression "mad as a March hare" refers to their wild behaviour during March when they may be observed boxing or leaping into the air as they prepare to mate. Hares are prolific breeders, producing two to four litters a year, and a female hare can even conceive while she is still pregnant. It is not surprising that hares are associated both with the season and with fertility. Even now we have the idea of the Easter Bunny delivering eggs, a tradition imported into Britain from America via Germanic immigrants, who had their own traditions of the Easter Hare who comes at night to lay eggs for the Easter egg hunt.[75] So where did the idea come from that hares lay eggs at Easter? Unlike rabbits, hares do not burrow into the earth but live their entire lives above ground, creating a shallow depression, known as a "form," as a nest. Ground-nesting birds, such as plovers and lapwings, also build their nests on open grassland or arable farmland at this time, and people coming across eggs in a nest that looked rather like a hare's form may have jumped to that conclusion. Finding such eggs in spring was probably the origin of the Easter egg hunt.

Wild birds all around are mating and nest building, while my chickens are starting to lay regularly again, responding to the increased levels of daylight. Eggs are a welcome symbol of the spring and new life, an emblem of potential in the way that a seed is an emblem of the potential life of a plant. Decorating eggs and giving them as gifts in the spring, especially at Easter or the vernal equinox, was and is a custom in many countries.

Dyed Eggs
Hen's eggs can be dyed using natural colourings; boil eggs with the following:

- orange: onion skins
- pink: beetroot and vinegar
- yellow: turmeric
- blue: red cabbage leaves and vinegar
- yellow: carrot tops
- violet: beetroot
- green: bracken
- purple: blackberries

---

75 Simpson & Roud, A *Dictionary of English Folklore.*

- yellow-green: daffodil flowers

- rust: cayenne pepper

You can also paint your eggs, and if you do, consider the symbols and the energies of the season. Here are some suggestions:

- snake: regeneration

- sun wheels: health and vitality

- leaves and flowers: growth and renewal

- four-leaf clover: change of luck

- paisley: the Goddess's womb

- lines, horns, and pillars: the God

- circles: eternity, the Wheel of the Year, the whole

- yin and yang: the balance

- hares and rabbits: fertility

- use relevant runes and ogham signs too

Spring Branch

Cut a branch that is budding with green leaves. Using strands of sewing thread, suspend blown and coloured hen's eggs from it or papier-mâché eggs painted and coloured in ways that symbolise the energies at this time of year to you.

March 17: THE GOD AND GODDESS OF SPRING

On this day the ancient Romans honoured Liber and Libera as spring fertility deities. Liber was another name for Bacchus/Dionysus, while Libera was another name for the goddess Ariadne. The statues of the gods were garlanded with ivy, and it was a day of liberty and license, when slaves were permitted to speak freely. Old women called *Sacerdotes Liberi* (priestesses of Liber and Libera), crowned with ivy, tended portable altars along the streets and charged a small fee to sacrifice oily honey cakes called *liba*.[76]

---

76 Carol Field, *Celebrating Italy* (William Morrow, 1990).

In Russian myth the spring fertility god and goddess, Lado and Lada, were worshipped along with the springtime cult of the *rusalki*, nymphs who brought fertility to the land. They are spring fertility deities similar to the Norse Freyr and Freya and the Roman Liber and Libera.[77]

In the Christian calendar, March 17 is St. Patrick's Day. Patrick was born in Britain but was carried off by raiders to serve as a slave in Ireland. After escaping, he became a Christian priest, gaining the reputation of battling Paganism in all its forms, banishing the "snakes" from Ireland—since there were never any actual snakes in Ireland, this probably referred to Pagans. In the Highlands and islands of Scotland, his feast is considered the real first day of spring:

> *On the high day of Patrick*
> *Every fold will have a cow-calf*
> *And every pool a salmon.*[78]

Curiously, St. Patrick also has a partner. The day after St. Patrick's Day was called Sheela's Day in rural Ireland, bringing the festivities of St. Patrick's Day to an end with dropping the shamrock worn all day into the final glass of drink. No one knows who Sheela was. Some say she was a relative of St. Patrick, perhaps his mother or even his wife.[79] Others make a connection with the sheela-na-gigs, the grinning images of naked old women with open vulvas carved on churches throughout Ireland, England, France, and Spain from the eleventh to the sixteenth century CE.[80] The name "sheela" in connection with these figures is a mystery. It is generally thought to be the Irish form of the Anglo-Norman name Cecile or Cecilia, since most of the images in Ireland are found in areas where the Normans invaded. "Gig" is an old English slang term for a woman's private parts.[81] In Ireland, though, sheelah was a

---

77 Joanna Hubbs, *Mother Russia: The Feminine Myth in Russian Culture* (Bloomington: Indiana University Press, 1988)

78 Kightly, *The Perpetual Almanack of Folklore.*

79 https://www.yourirish.com/traditions/sheelahs-day, accessed 27.2.19.

80 Rufus, *The World Holiday Book.*

81 https://www.bbc.co.uk/news/uk-england-45116614?ocid=socialflow_facebook&ns_ campaign=bbcnews&ns_mchannel=social&ns_source=facebook&fbclid=IwAR2f4-wSXsYolaVege7ttX5mBTK5nBDiuh_s86C9TDAO9u7HMjN5OMoJgH0, accessed 26.2.19.

term applied to elderly women.[82] It is not known what these figures represent. They may be grotesque representations of female wantonness to warn people against the sin of lust. Alternatively, since they generally appear above doorways, they may be protective figures. They could be fertility symbols since in some places brides were required to look at and perhaps touch the sheela before weddings.[83] Modern Pagans often choose to see them as pre-Christian representations of an earth or hag goddess similar to the Scottish Cailleach, who rules the winter and changes place with the maiden Bride (Brighid) in spring. I have a little sheela-na-gig figurine made for me by a friend, which sits on one of my altars.

Lord and Lady of Spring Ritual

I will be dressing my altar with ivy and offering honey cakes to the God and Goddess of spring with these words:

> Know that this is the time that the Goddess is renewed in all her glory. She is beauteous and young once more. Tall and graceful, she walks amongst us as a maiden and our beloved one. Come, our fairest Lady, grant blessing unto the seeds which become the flowers of tomorrow. Come, O gracious Lady, and protect that which is newly born, that children and animals grow strong beneath thy hands. Let the seeds be blessed in thy name, O Goddess.

> Come, our gentle Lord, grant blessing unto the seeds which become the flowers of tomorrow. Come, O gracious Lord, and protect that which is newly born, that children and animals grow strong beneath thy hands. Let the seeds be blessed in thy name, O Lord.

> Let this ritual end with love and blessings.

---

82 https://hyperallergic.com/396030/mapping-the-mysterious-ancient-carvings-of-naked
    -women-across-ireland/?utm_campaign=coschedule&utm_source=facebook_page&utm
    _medium=Hyperallergic&utm_content=Mapping+the+Mysterious+Ancient+Carvings
    +of+Naked+Women+Across+Ireland, accessed 27.2.19.

83 Georgia Rhoades, "Decoding the Sheela-na-gig," *Feminist Formations* 22.2 (2010): 167–196.

. . . .

ROMAN HONEY CAKE

Honey was the only sweetener the ancient world had, and this ancient recipe might not be to modern tastes. I use them for offerings.

3 EGGS

200 GRAMS RUNNY HONEY

60 GRAMS PLAIN FLOUR (ALL-PURPOSE FLOUR)

Whisk the eggs and slowly add the honey. Fold in the flour, a little at a time. Pour into a 20-centimetre tin (8 inches) and bake at 180°C/350°F/gas mark 4 for 40 minutes.

Late March

We enter the sign of Aries the ram, considered the first sign of the zodiac since it is nominally the time when the spring equinox occurs as the sun crosses the celestial equator from south to north in Aries.[84] In ancient Egypt this led to Aries being called the "Indicator of the Reborn Sun," connected with the ram-headed god of fertility, Amun Ra.[85] In Mesopotamia it was called "the hired labourer" and associated with the god Dumuzi the shepherd and his ram.[86] In Greece it was linked with the Golden Fleece of Greek legend, sought by Jason and the Argonauts, which was nailed to an oak tree in a grove in Colchis, guarded by a dragon. It must have been seen like a heavenly reflection of earthly matters at the very time when new lambs were in the fields and life renewed itself.

Life is certainly renewing itself in the garden and the land around me. There are butterflies on sunny days and early bees lazily looking for nectar in the early flowers. There are English daisies (*Bellis perennis*) in the lawn, cheerful little flowers rayed like the sun that flower roughly equinox to equinox and that I use to make salves for bruises. There are yellow primroses and cowslips all over the garden, golden celandines, violets, and wood anemones. The hedgerows are covered in a fresh green haze

---

84   Because of the precession of the equinoxes, the sun now appears in Aries from late April to mid-May.

85   Staal, *The New Patterns in the Sky*, and Olcott, *Star Lore*.

86   Krupp, *Beyond the Blue Horizon*.

of new leaves on the elder, hawthorn, and dog roses. The daffodils are all out in the garden and along all the road verges, sunny flowers that tell me spring has arrived in full force. They are potent symbols of cheerfulness, rebirth, and new beginnings that are said to bloom from Ash Wednesday and die on Easter Sunday.

Some of my perennial herbs are pushing their way into the light: the frothy green sweet cicely and spears of chives. I've been picking coltsfoot (*Tussilago farfara*), one of the earliest flowers of the year, the sun-coloured flowers appearing before the leaves, hence its folk name Son-afore-the-Father. I use coltsfoot tea for coughs and bronchitis at this time of year. I've also found the fresh green shoots of cleavers (*Galium aparine*), which we called sticky buds when I was a child. It makes a great spring tonic, cleansing for the lymphatic system, in the form of a tea, eaten, or juiced.[87] This is the time when I make nettle soup, full of vitamins and minerals, after the dearth of wild fresh greenery in the winter months.

NETTLE SOUP

2 ONIONS

1 CLOVE GARLIC

2 POTATOES

LEAVES STRIPPED FROM 10 NETTLE STEMS

1½ (3½ CUPS/850 ML) PINTS VEGETABLE STOCK

SALT AND PEPPER TO TASTE

½ PINT (1 CUP/284 ML) MILK OR SOYA MILK

FRESH PARSLEY TO GARNISH

Peel and chop the onion, garlic, and potatoes, then fry gently in some oil until soft. Add the nettle leaves and the stock. Boil for 20 minutes. Liquidise, then return to the pan, add the salt, pepper, and the milk, and reheat. Garnish with parsley to serve.

---

87   Julie Brunton-Seal and Matthew Seal, *Hedgerow Medicine* (Ludlow: Merlin Unwin, 2008).

The Vernal Equinox

The vernal equinox occurs around March 21 but the dates can vary, so please check your almanac. It is a moment of balance, when night and day are of equal length, but the light is gaining, and with that increased light, the world revitalises itself. This is a time of great energy, with high tides and floods. As we feel the vitality of spring coursing through our veins, we can take the opportunity to renew ourselves, our dreams, and our aspirations. It time to sow the seeds of new projects and spiritual inspirations under the auspices of the youthful God and Goddess in the vernal equinox rite.

Nowadays, most modern Pagans call the spring equinox Ostara. It was given this name in the 1970s by the writer Aidan Kelly, who explained that

> We have Gaelic names for the four Celtic holidays. It offended my aesthetic sensibilities that there seemed to be no Pagan names for the summer solstice or the fall equinox equivalent to Yule or Beltane—so I decided to supply them. The spring equinox was almost a nonissue. The Venerable Bede says that it was sacred to a Saxon Goddess, Ostara or Eostre, from whom we get the name "Easter."[88]

We actually know nothing about the goddess Eostre. There is only one reference to her in early literature, and this by the seventh/eighth century English monk Bede in his *De Temporum Ratione* ("The Reckoning of Time"). He wrote that during *Eosturmonaþ* (the lunar month of March/April), Pagan Anglo-Saxons had once held feasts in Eostre's honour, but the tradition had died out by his time. Based on this single source, folklorist and recorder of fairy tales Jacob Grimm attempted to reconstruct a possible Germanic equivalent goddess, calling her Ostara, arguing that since Germans called April *ôstarmânoth* while most countries retained the biblical *pascha* for Easter, the word must relate to *áustrô*, from the Old High German adverb *ôstar*, which "expresses movement towards the rising sun," concluding that the putative deity would have been a goddess of dawn.[89]

Given the lack of any direct evidence for Ostara or Eostre, scholars have dismissed the goddess as a pure invention of Bede,[90] concluding that the Old English word *eas-*

---

88 Aidan Kelly, blog, May 2017, https://www.patheos.com/blogs/aidankelly/2017/05/naming -ostara-litha-mabon/, accessed 20.2.2020.

89 Grimm, *Teutonic Mythology*.

90 Karl Weinhold, *Die Deutschen Monatnamen* 1869 (Whitefish: Kessinger Publishing, 2010).

tre is simply an approximation of the Latin *albae* ("white"), a word sometimes applied to Easter.[91] It has to be said that this doesn't mean the goddess Eostre/Ostara didn't exist—it is unlikely that Bede made her up—but we have one very brief mention of her name, and Jacob Grimm made a connection between her name and the word for east, the direction of the rising sun. We certainly know nothing at all about her worship, and there is most definitely no mention of hares and eggs as cult symbols, as I sometimes read. Neither is there a linguistic connection with the Latin word *oestrus* (relating to ovulation and eggs), nor with the Middle Eastern goddesses Ishtar and Astarte. Nevertheless, the name resonates with modern Pagans, and as long as we don't make up fake histories for it, we can happily call the vernal equinox "Ostara" if we wish.

Our ancestors certainly celebrated the spring equinox, whatever they called it. Like them, we take our cue from nature itself and celebrate the vernal equinox as the time when the light gains over the dark and the world rekindles in response, bursting forth from its winter sleep in a flurry of growth and new birth. The Green Man is young and vital, bringing the trees and plants to greening. The youthful Goddess is wreathed in flowers, and the two begin their courtship. The sun warms the earth, ready for planting. Like the earth, we too plant our own seeds at this time; seeds we literally plant in the garden, but also seeds of goals that we will make into reality.

Ostara Ritual

Decorate your altar with yellow flowers (I use daffodils, forsythia, tansy, and coltsfoot from the garden). A bowl of seeds and a bowl of decorated eggs are placed on the altar (you can use papier-mâché eggs if you don't want to use real ones). A candle is placed in the cauldron; if you can work outside, have ready an unlit bonfire or brazier and some wine and bread.

Have ready a plant pot, a seed, and some compost. This will be used to plant a seed during the ritual, which will symbolise a hope or project for the coming year. This is a magical act and a practical lesson—care for the plant, water it regularly, and it will produce fruit. Neglect it, and it will shrivel and die.

---

91   Shaw, *Pagan Goddesses in the Early Germanic World*.

Say:

> I come to celebrate the festival of spring, Ostara,
> when the Lord and the Lady meet as youth and maid,
> when all about us life renews. The Sun strengthens,
> moving towards summer and his time of glory…
> I invoke and call upon thee, fair Goddess of spring,
> Lady of Flowers; thee I invoke. I call to thee.
> Mighty one, our green Lord, all honour to thee,
> consort of the Goddess; come, I call thee.

Take up the seed and say:

> Know that this is the time that the Goddess is renewed in all her glory.
> Fairest Lady, gentle Lord, grant blessing unto the seed that becomes the flower of
> tomorrow. Let the seed be blessed in thy name. Let the seed be cast to the earth.

Plant a seed in the pot, thinking about what goal it symbolises for you.

> Let the fire of joy be lit that is the light of the
> growing sun and the light of the year.
> The fire [or candle in the cauldron]
> is lit in token of the equinox sun.

Pause and consider what this symbolises.

Take up the egg. Hold it in your hands and think about what it represents: potential, life, and rebirth. Place it in the quarter that most fits the goal you have for it: earth for health and practical matters, west for emotional matters, south for spiritual goals, or east for study and inspiration.

Take up the wine and say:

> Let the wine be blessed, which is the wine of spring and the wine of the Lady.

Drink. Take up the bread and say:

> Let the bread be blessed in the name of the God, our Lord;
> It is the bread of life and the bread of the Lord.

Eat. When all is finished, say:

> Let the candles be put out, but let me remember the lessons of this night.
> The rite is over. Blessed be.

March 25: LADY DAY

From the twelfth century to 1752, Lady Day (which was the official date of the spring equinox) was counted as the first day of the legal year in Britain. In Christian lore it marks the Annunciation, when an angel ("messenger") visited the Virgin Mary and announced that she would bear the saviour of mankind. When the angel left, she found that she was pregnant. Her son, called Jesus Christ, sacrificed himself to redeem the world and was crucified wearing a crown of thorns. There was a superstition that if Easter should fall on Lady Day, then some disaster will shortly follow:

> When my lord falls in my lady's lap
> England beware of some mishap.

Last Three Days of March: THE BORROWED DAYS

Lore has it that if it's not stormy and windy the first three days in March, the bad weather is saving itself for the three borrowed days at the month's end. It was the Romans who gave these days a bad reputation. They believed they were dangerous days, fraught with taboos and the spectre of bad weather, and there are various weather sayings concerning them:

> March borrowed from April
> Three days and they were ill
> The first was snow and sleet
> The next was cold and wet
> The third was such a freeze
> The birds' nests stuck to trees.

THE MONTH OF OPENING

• • • • •

Our name for this month comes from the old Roman name for it, Aprilis, gener-ally thought to be derived from *aperio*, a verb meaning "to open," in the sense that the earth is opening up and flowering. As the Roman poet Ovid said, "Because Spring opens everything and the sharp/Frost-bound cold vanishes, and fertile soil's revealed."[92] However, he himself believed that the name derived from Aphrodite, the Greek goddess of love, whom the Romans called Venus, saying that while the first month (March) was dedicated to fierce Mars, the second month was granted to Venus because love rules the whole world, bringing together human and animal partners to mate and give birth to young, especially at this time of year.

---

92   https://www.poetryintranslation.com/PITBR/Latin/OvidFastiBkFour.php, accessed 6.3.19.

April showers bring a flurry of new growth, and everywhere flowers are opening, leaves unfolding, the birds are busy nest building, and animals are mating. According to British folklore, adders (one of our few native snakes) begin mating on April 4.

This is the month when the summer birds return to Britain, such as the swallow and the cuckoo. For the Norse April was *Gaukmonad*, "cuckoo month," and in many places when the bird's distinctive call is heard, then spring is really deemed to have arrived. In Sussex it was said that spring began when "the old woman" (the hag of winter) shook the cuckoos from her apron. The cuckoo is a summer visitor to Britain, arriving in April and leaving in August. Special cuckoo fairs were once held all over the country during April to welcome it. Sadly, much of its habitat has been destroyed in recent years, and the call of the cuckoo is a much rarer sound now.

Cuckoos bring good luck or bad luck, depending on what you are doing when you first hear them. It is lucky to hear them if standing on grass but bad luck if on barren ground. If the call comes from the right, it is good luck for the year—make a wish and it will be granted—but it is unlucky if it comes from the left. If you are looking at the ground, you will be dead within the year; the Scots say the number of calls it makes indicate the number of years you have left. Moreover, whatever you are doing, you are fated to do for the rest of the year, so if you are in bed, you will become ill and bedridden, and if you have no food in your stomach, you will be poor for the rest of the year. However, if you turn over the money in your pocket or spit on it, it will last the year.

Another European harbinger of spring is the swallow. In ancient Greece returning swallows were thought to usher in the safe return of Dionysus, the vegetation god. In the second century CE, boys in Rhodes went from house to house, singing: "The swallow is here and a new year he brings/As he lengthens the days with the beats of his wings."[93] But as Aristotle cautioned, "One swallow does not make a summer,"[94] meaning that the appearance of one bird doesn't indicate a trend, though the appearance of flocks of them do. From early times swallows have made their nests in the eaves of buildings, and for the Romans they were sacred to the Penates, the household gods, so it is lucky if they nest on your house, offering protection from

---

93   Miller, *Animals and Animal Symbols in World Culture*.
94   https://www.stmarys-ca.edu/sites/default/files
      /attachments/files/Nicomachean_Ethics_0.pdf.

lightning, fire, and storms. Destroying a nest or killing a bird meant disaster for the house and its inhabitants.

In ancient Rome the whole month was dedicated to Venus, originally a goddess of gardens, and also contained festivals in honour of other agricultural deities since work on the land was in full swing—such as Ceres, the goddess of grain crops, and Flora, goddess of flowers. The honouring of female deities of agriculture and fertility continued with sacrifices to placate Tellus, goddess of the earth.[95] Her Greek equivalent is Gaia, and we often use the name Gaia for Mother Earth in connection with environmental movements, which was suggested by James Lovelock's book *Gaia: A New Look at Life on Earth*, in which the earth is viewed as a single organism with self-regulatory functions.

The Romans also remembered new animal life with the Parilia festival in honour of Pales, a woodland and pastoral deity. It was mainly observed by shepherds for the protection of their flocks. The sheep pen was decorated with green branches, and at dawn the shepherd would purify the sheep by driving them through the smoke of a bonfire composed of straw, olive branches, laurel, and sulphur. Millet cakes and milk were offered to Pales, after which the shepherd would wet his hands with dew, face east, and pray four times for protection for the flock.

The Romans held the Floralia at the end of April and the beginning of May, which gave rise to many of the May Day customs we still practice today. Flora is a goddess of the spring and flowers and blossoms in general, as well as youth and its pleasures in this youthful season of the year.

The energies of April concern the opening up and blossoming of the year and the earth. The magic of the season reminds us to open ourselves to new things and to love, beauty, and grace.

Early April

April 1: APRIL FOOL'S DAY/VENERALIA

As schoolchildren we celebrated April 1 as April Fool's Day, with pranks and practical jokes that had to be played before midday. The origins of this custom are

---

95   Fowler, *The Religious Experience of the Roman People.*

unknown. Some think it dates back to the Roman Hilaria (see March), others that it arose from the joyful and jokey customs of carnivals celebrated around Easter time, Lord of Misrule traditions, or just by people being confused by the sudden change to the Gregorian calendar in 1752, when eleven days were removed. It is still a day of fun in many parts of the world. In Scotland the first day of April is Huntigowk Day, a *gowk* being a cuckoo, or the person being sent up as the April fool.

In Rome it was also a day of joy, consecrated to Venus Verticordia ("Venus the heart-turner"), the goddess of love, harmony, and beauty. At her temple women washed her statue, replaced her golden necklace and other jewellery, and offered her roses and other flowers. Women bathed in myrtle-scented water and wore crowns of myrtle,[96] a traditional women's plant that it is said only women can grow, associated with many goddesses of love.

Every Pagan mythology has a goddess of love—the Egyptian Hathor, the Mesopotamian Ishtar, the Irish Aine, the Norse Freya, the Slavic Lada, among many, many others. The Greeks had Aphrodite. At her birth the seas bubbled and turned rosy, and she arose, full grown and standing on a seashell, in all the surpassing glory of her loveliness and arrayed in the panoply of her irresistible charms. She floated to Cyprus, arriving in April, and as soon as her pearly white feet touched the shore, grass and flowers sprang up at her feet, a goddess of love associated with the flowering of the earth and the mating of humans and animals.

Goddess of Love Ritual

The altar is set in the centre of the room with a statue of the Goddess, a pink candle, and a goblet of water. The room can be decorated with tealights placed in shells and lit before the ritual. Each person is given a flower; if you are doing this alone, just hold a single flower.

Light the pink candle and say:

> *Goddess of love, opener of the year,*
> *You are the softness of the primrose*
> *And the lingering scent of violets.*
> *Where you walk, the earth blossoms.*

---

96   *Plutarch's Lives* (The Dryden Translation; New York: Modern Library, 2001).

In the gentle April rain you open like a flower

Ready to receive the embrace of the God.

Your touch fills our souls with fire

And none can resist your power

For you are the source of all.

Goddess of love, be with me (us).

Each person puts their flower by the statue of the Goddess. Say:

This is a month of fire and water: the warmth of the sun, the fall of the rain,
the fire of love, and the flow of creation.

If fire is the divine spark that gives vitality to the world, the power of water
allows the soul to receive it and nourish it into growth.

Water is a living thing and honoured as sacred. It nurtures and sustains life,
cleanses, and regenerates. Love flows throughout creation, underpinning all life
and giving it meaning.

Drink from the cup and say:

Goddess of love,

Open my spirit to joy and my heart to love.

Bless me with compassion and kindness.

Let your goodness flow through me.

Surround me with love.

Take a moment to reflect and feel this, then say:

This rite is ended. Blessed be.

Blow out the candles.

April 2: THE GRACES

According to Greek legend, after Aphrodite, the goddess of love, arose from the
sea and arrived at Cyprus, the Three Graces bedecked her with golden ornaments
and escorted her to the divine halls of Olympus. Her attendants are Thalia ("joy"),
Euphrosyne ("mirth"), and Aglaea ("splendour"), the Three Graces of life who inspire
poets and artists and bring joy, charm, and beauty to gods and men. They preside
over all banquets, dances, and happy social events. Don't forget to honour them, by

whatever name you call such deities, for without love and friendship, fun, grace, beauty, and art, all striving is meaningless and the wonder of the world is lost.

Three Graces Ritual

Decorate the altar with spring flowers. To 20 millilitres of sunflower oil add 3 drops of cardamom essential oil. Set up three pink candles. Anoint each one with the oil.

Light the first candle, saying:

> Goddess of joy, hear me. May there be joy in my life.
>
> May there be love, friendship, and wonder at the beauty of creation.

Light the second candle, saying:

> Goddess of mirth, hear me. May there be mirth in my life.
>
> May there be laughter with friends.

Light the third candle, saying:

> Goddess of splendour, hear me. May there be splendour in my life.
>
> May there be beauty, grace, and creativity.
>
> Let this ritual end with love and blessings. Blessed be.

Allow the candles to burn out.

April 6: SELF-BLESSING

In the month of love and opening, it is important to love and honour your relationship with the gods. Prepare a sacred space to work in by cleaning it thoroughly and decorating it with flowers. On a low table place a clean white cloth, a white candle, some flowers, and a phial of olive oil. Say:

> This is the time of opening, when all about us blossoms and we open ourselves to
> the joy of the world. I call upon the Lord and Lady to witness my acts tonight and
> bless me that I may walk in their ways.

Light the candle. Take the oil and anoint your feet:

> Blessed be my feet that shall walk the sacred paths.

Anoint your knees:

> Blessed be my knees that shall kneel before the sacred altars.

Anoint your breast:

> *Blessed be my heart that shall be filled with love for the Lord and the Lady.*

Anoint your mouth:

> *Blessed be my lips that shall speak the sacred words.*

Anoint your forehead:

> *Blessed be my self. Let me walk in love and blessing. Fill my heart with rejoicing,*
> *with beauty and strength, power and compassion, humour and humility,*
> *reverence and mirth. Sacred pair, bless your servant.*

Let the candle burn out.

Mid-April

The natural world is certainly opening up and blossoming. I go out into the fields and woods with my collecting basket to find seasonal treats and wild herbs for medicines. This is the best month for dandelion (*Taraxacum officinale*) flowers; traditionally, you should pick them on St. George's Day (April 23) to make your dandelion wine. I collect violets (*Viola* sp.) in the woods, which I use in moisturisers and face creams; alexanders (*Smyrnium olusatrum*), one of the best wild vegetables of spring; and the first early leaves on the brambles (*Rubus fruticosus*). Most people know the blackberry fruit that comes later, but the astringent leaves are full of antioxidants and vitamin C and make a medicinal tea for sore throats and mouth ulcers. On the edge of the fields I discover Jack-by-the-hedge (*Alliaria petiolata*), which has a mild peppery-garlicy flavour, which I put in salads and sandwiches. My favourite seasonal treat is the ramsons or wild garlic in the woods (*Ullium ursinum*). They have a very strong garlic scent, and the leaves and flowers can be used for a garlic pesto, infused in oil, or added to soups and salads.

This is a busy month in the garden too. As I'm planting my seeds, I'm aware of the old gardener's advice and plant "one for the mouse, one for the crow, one to rot, and one to grow," and put plenty in. Dwarf beans are sown under cloches outside, and beetroot, carrot, kale, kohlrabi, lettuce, parsnips, peas, spring onions, rocket, spinach, and chard are sown directly into the ground. In the greenhouse I am making up the hanging baskets I put outside the kitchen in summer, though I won't be able to put them out until late May, when all chance of frosts are past here.

. . . .

RAMSON PESTO

170 GRAMS RAMSONS (YOU CAN USE THE LEAVES,
STEMS, AND FLOWERS)

270 MILLILITRES OLIVE OIL

65 GRAMS PINE NUTS (WALNUTS ALSO WORK WELL)

70 GRAMS PARMESAN CHEESE, GRATED

PINCH OF SALT

The ramsons will need careful washing to remove any insects, especially if you are using the flowers too. Place on a cloth to dry. Put everything in a food processor and blitz. This is best used fresh but will keep for 2–3 days in the fridge or you can freeze it.

April 20: LORD OF THE ANIMALS

At this time we also look to the young animals born in spring, both wild and domesticated, and ask the Lord of the Animals to protect them. In Rome they celebrated the Parilia in honour of Pales, a woodland and pastoral deity.[97]

Lord of the Animals Ritual

Prepare a bowl of water and have ready a sprig of rosemary or bay. Prepare an incense of frankincense and pine oil. If you are working outdoors, you can light a bonfire or brazier in the centre of the ritual space. If you are working indoors, place a white candle on a low table in the centre of the work area, with a heatproof dish and lit block of charcoal beside it. Have some honey cakes or bread and wine ready.

Sprinkle the ground with water to sanctify the space, then throw the incense on the fire or charcoal. Sprinkle yourself with water using the sprig of herbs as an act of purification. Say:

---

97 James L. Butrica, "Propertius on the Parilia," *Classical Quarterly* (Memorial University of Newfoundland, 2000) and Ovid, *Fasti* IV, https://www.poetryintranslation.com/PITBR /Latin/OvidFastiBkFour.php#BkIVintro, accessed 20.4.19.

I call upon the lord of the animals, protector of flocks and herds,
protector of the wild creatures of the woods and forests.

Go to the east of the working area. Offer one of the cakes and some wine by putting them on the ground and saying:

Lord, bless the animals and the farmers, bless the bees and insects, bless the birds
of the air, bless the fish in the waters, bless the plants and the gardeners, and
protect them from harm. If I have offended you and your wild places with my
loud voice and heavy footsteps or if I have cut branches from a tree sacred to
you, forgive me. Lord, grant blessing to the animals. Let them grow strong and
healthy. May my prayers be granted.

Repeat this in the south, the west, and finally the north. Go back to the centre. Wash your hands and face in the water as a final act of purification. Eat some of the bread and drink some of the wine. Say:

O kindly lord of the animals, I honour you. I have sprinkled myself with water,
I have offered cakes and wine. May my prayers be heard and answered.
This rite is ended. Blessed be.

Late April

We enter the zodiac sign of Taurus the Bull, one of the largest constellations, which contains the clusters of stars that form the Pleiades (which nestles on the bull's shoulder) and the Hyades cluster (which forms its face). Its bright red eye, the star Aldebaran, seems to glare at Orion the Hunter. Taurus is one of the oldest recognised constellations and may even have been identified as such in the Upper Palaeolithic age, as depicted in the cave paintings of Lascaux (c. 15,000 BCE).[98] The Babylonians called it "The Bull of Heaven," which the goddess Ishtar sent to kill Gilgamesh for spurning her advances.[99] In Greek mythology Taurus was identified with the Cretan

---

98   Dr. David Whitehouse, BBC News, 9 August 2000, http://news.bbc.co.uk/1/hi/sci
      /tech/871930.stm, accessed 18.9.19.

99   https://www.ancient-origins.net/opinion-guest-authors/ancient-epic-gilgamesh-and
      -precession-equinox-003957, accessed 18.9.19, and Hines, *Gilgamesh*.

bull captured by the solar Herakles as one of his twelve labours (his journey around the zodiac). According to the tale, King Minos of Crete prayed to the god Poseidon to send him a snow-white bull as a sign that he had the right to rule. Poseidon duly sent the bull, but with the provision that Minos would sacrifice it to him. Minos decided to keep the lovely bull and substituted an inferior animal for sacrifice. Angered by this, Poseidon asked Aphrodite to cause Minos's wife Pasiphaë to fall in love with the bull, and the woman subsequently gave birth to the half man, half bull Minotaur.

The bull is an ancient symbol of the fertility, virility, and vitality of the season, associated with several gods such as the Sumerian Dumuzi, the wild bull who is sacrificed and dies for his people; the Egyptian corn god Osiris; and the "bull-footed" Dionysus of Greece, vegetation gods who were sacrificed with the harvest and reborn in spring so that life could continue.

April 22: SPUD PLANTING DAY

This was traditionally Spud Planting Day in Sussex. In the evening Tater Beer Night was celebrated to toast the crops. I shall be putting in my main crop potatoes today.

April 23: ST. GEORGE'S DAY

In Christian lore St. George is the patron of soldiers and farmers, said to have been born either in Turkey, Syria, or Palestine and to have served in the Roman army before being martyred for refusing to spurn Christianity. Despite being the patron saint of England, there is no connection at all to Britain. He is first mentioned in the fifth century CE, and the dragon-slaying legend was added in the eleventh century and popularised in the late thirteenth century by Jacobus de Voragine's *The Golden Legend*. The story goes that St. George rode into Silene (modern-day Libya) to free the city from a dragon, saving the daughter of a king of Asia Minor who was being sacrificed to it. After defeating the dragon, he refused to kill it but asked the princess to wrap her girdle round the monster's head and lead it through the town. He told the inhabitants he would dispatch it if they all converted to Christianity. The story is very similar to the Greek myth of Perseus saving Andromeda from the sea monster, and it is tempting to think the chronicler stole this to spice up George's story. The Roman Catholic Church, finding no evidence of his actual existence, removed him from the official list of saints in 1969.

It is an interesting myth, however. George is also honoured throughout the Middle East, where his story is somewhat different. Here, Jiryis—or Girgus, as he was known—was martyred under the rule of Diocletian, being killed three times but springing back to life each time. In the Iranian version, he also resurrected the dead and made trees bud and pillars sprout flowers. After one of his deaths, the world was covered by darkness that was lifted only when he was resurrected.[100] Sometimes he is identified with al-Khidr, the "green one" or "verdant one," a prophet or angel who guards the sea and teaches secret knowledge.

George may well have originated in an ancient vegetation god. He is considered a patron saint of farmers, with a feast day in the planting season of spring. *George* means "cultivator of the land" or "ploughman." *Jiryis Baqiya* translates as "George, the resurrected one."[101] The motifs of deaths and resurrections are repeated in the mythologies of gods such as Tammuz, Dionysus, and Adonis, seasonal myths that represent the conflict of summer and winter (the dragon) and who restore fertility to the land.[102] In England the old mummer's play featuring George's battle with the Turkish knight is still performed at Christmas and in spring. There are many versions of the play, but in all of them George is killed and returns to life. It is possible to see him as a pre-Christian form of a fertility icon in the foliate head (Green Man) in churches.[103]

The importance of George in Eastern European countries cannot be understated. The Russians say "George will bring spring" and "There is no spring without George." Finnish proverbs of "St. George comes with his fish basket" alternate with others that indicate he brings grasses. George is fertility. This is no more evident than in France, where statues of St. George were carried through the cherry orchards of Anjou to ensure a good crop.

Eastern European lore also states that the earth of winter is poisonous and cannot be sat or walked upon before St. George's Day. On St. George's Day, the earth is

---

100   *The Encyclopaedia of Islam.*
101   Ibid.
102   J. Mackley, "The Pagan Heritage of St. George," paper presented to International Medieval Congress (IMC), University of Leeds, 11–14 July 2011.
103   Ibid.

reborn and alive once again.[104] Folklorist James Frazer, in *The Golden Bough*, recorded that

> amongst the Slavs of Carinthia, on St. George's Day…the young people deck with flowers and garlands a tree which has been felled on the eve of the festival. The tree is then carried in procession, accompanied with music and joyful acclamations, the chief figure in the procession being the Green George…[105]

Other rituals of St. George's Day included the blessing of crops in the Ukraine, where, after the blessing given by a priest, couples lay down in the fields and rolled several times over the newly sprouted shoots.[106]

Today is the traditional day to make dandelion wine, and indeed, this is usually the time when the dandelions are in full flower, sunny golden flowers covering the fields and verges. I will be gathering flowers for wine, which should be kept at least two years before it is drunk.

. . . .

DANDELION WINE

6 PINTS DANDELION FLOWER HEADS

1 GALLON WATER

3 POUNDS SUGAR

2 LEMONS, SEPARATED INTO RINDS AND JUICE

1 ORANGE, SEPARATED INTO RINDS AND JUICE

1 CUP BREWED BLACK TEA

YEAST AND NUTRIENT

1 POUND RAISINS

Gather the flowers when you are ready to use them fresh. Boil the water and pour over the flowers; let this stand for two days, stirring daily. Boil with the sugar and citrus fruit rinds for 60 minutes. Put it back in the bin and add the citrus fruit juice. Cool to lukewarm and add the tea (leaves or

---

104 Mall Hiiemäe, "Some Possible Origins of St. George's Day Customs and Beliefs," *Folklore* 1 (June 1996), published by the Institute of Estonian Languages, Tartu.

105 Frazer, *The Golden Bough*, 166.

106 Frazer, *The Golden Bough*.

teabag removed), yeast, and nutrient. Cover the bin and leave in a warm place for three days, stirring daily. Strain into a demijohn and add the raisins. Fit an airlock.

April 25: ROBIGALIA

In Rome this was the Robigalia,[107] a festival that beseeched Robigus, the personification of mildew or blight, to leave the growing crops alone.[108] The name implies a reddish colour, as is found in wheat rust. According to Ovid, the priest, carrying a bowl of wine and a cask of incense, prayed:

> *Thou scaly Mildew, spare the sprouting corn,*
> *And let the smooth top quiver on the surface of the ground.*
> *O let the crops, nursed by the heaven's propitious stars,*
> *Grow till they are ripe for the sickle.*[109]

I think this is a good time to bless the seedlings in the greenhouse and vegetable garden, as the tiny little plants are vulnerable until they get stronger. As well as literally blessing seedlings, you can ask for help with the seedlings of new ideas and projects.

Seedling Protection Ritual

I go to the seedlings, light a green votive candle, and say:

> *Lord and Lady, protect my seedlings, whether of plants or new ideas.*
> *Let them grow freely, nursed by the earth and the sun, until they are ripe.*
> *Blessed be.*

April 30: WALPURGISNACHT/BELTANE EVE

In Celtic tradition, the last night of April was thought of as the darkest of the year. The transition between winter and summer is a liminal point, a time between times, and therefore surrounded by danger and supernatural forces. It was believed that malevolent spirits and witches flew to frighten people, spawning evil throughout the land. The bad fairies of mischief and the winter spirits make a last foray, for at dawn

---

107 Ovid, *Fasti*.
108 Rhiannon Evans, *Utopia Antiqua: Readings of the Golden Age and Decline at Rome* (Routledge, 2008).
109 Ovid, *Fasti*.

tomorrow, the good fairies will emerge and claim the land for summer completely.[110] In Britain and Ireland people pounded on kettles, slammed doors, cracked whips, rang church bells, and made all the noise they could to scare off the corruption they imagined to be moving on the air. They lit bonfires and torches and hung primroses or rowan and red thread crosses on the barns and byres to protect the animals. Such vigils were kept throughout the night until the rising of the May dawn, when the forces of bane would have been finally defeated and the summer safely delivered.

In Germany, April 30 is Walpurgisnacht, named after St. Walpurga, an eighth-century Englishwoman who became the abbess of a German monastery. She was renowned for battling pests, sickness, and witchcraft, so it is not surprising that people called upon her intercession to protect them from evil spirits and pestilence on this, one of the most dangerous nights of the year. It is said that for nine nights before the first of May, Walpurga is in flight, chased by the Wild Hunt, going from village to village. People left their windows open so she could shelter behind the cross-shaped windowpane struts from her enemies. In thanks, she laid a little gold coin on the windowsill and fled further.[111] One farmer described her as a white lady with long flowing hair, a crown upon her head, and shoes of fiery gold, while in her hands she carried a spindle and a three-cornered mirror that showed the future. A troop of white riders chased and tried to capture her. Walpurga begged another farmer to hide her in a sheaf of grain. No sooner was she hidden than the riders rushed by overhead. The next morning the farmer found grains of gold instead of rye.[112] The stories would seem to be an analogy of summer fleeing from winter at this time of year. The Walpurga processions enacted around the villages and fields in Germany and France are supposed to protect the lands against strong winds and bad weather in the coming month.

It is safe to assume that the folk practices around St. Walpurga's Eve predated the saint and were subsequently associated with her, meaning the real Walpurga took on the attributes of an earlier fertility goddess or possibly the combined characteristics of several. Churches in Germany and at Antwerp, and an eleventh-century manuscript from Cologne, show St. Walpurga with ears of grain, like earlier mother

---

110   Anna Franklin, *The Illustrated Encyclopaedia of Fairies* (London: Paper Tiger, 2004).

111   E. L. Rochholz, *Drei Gaugöttinen: Walburg, Verena und Gertrud, als deutsche Kirchenheilige. Sittenbilder aus germanischen Frauenleben* (Leipzig: Verlag von Friedrich Fischer, 1870).

112   Ibid.

goddesses.[113] She is represented with a dog, like the Celto-Germanic fertility goddess Nehalennia,[114] as well as Frau Gode and Frau Frick (Frigga). There may be some connection with the Windhound, a mysterious dog connected to fertility that is left behind by the Wild Hunt, which must be fed in order to ensure good crops. Other illustrations show her with a staff. The Gothic word *walus* appears to be an epithet of someone (usually female) who carries a magic staff of office, such as a sybil or diviner. The historic Waluburg of 500 years earlier was a woman of the Germanic Semnonii tribe who served as a mystic adviser to a Roman governor of Egypt in the second century CE.[115] It is possible that there was originally a goddess called Walburga, Waldborg, or Walburg, as several Pagan websites and books suggest, though there is a distinct lack of direct evidence for it.

Walpurgisnacht is also known as *Hexennacht* or "witches' night" in Germany, when witches are abroad, many flying up to revel on the Brocken, the highest peak in the Harz Mountains, an eerie place featuring two rock formations called the Devil's Pulpit and the Witch's Altar, as well as the Brocken Spectre, which are weird halos of light seen around the mountain. According to Grimm, some mountains were once the residence of Dame Holda, the crone of winter, and her host, the "night-women" who rode through the air on certain nights and did men kindnesses. It was Holda herself who led the revels on the mountains to dance the snow away.

Tomorrow summer will have arrived, but tonight the forces of winter try to make their final assault and have to be fought back. May Day festivals traditionally included a fierce battle between the forces of winter and summer.

May Eve Ritual

It was traditional to burn all worn-out household items such as brooms, cloths, and wooden implements in the Walpurgis Night fires. Life-size (or smaller) strawmen were made and "loaded" with the ill health and ill luck of the past, then burned in the fires on Walpurgisnacht. This is the forcible casting-out of winter, illness, and that which is worn out so the May King and May Queen and their green-bedecked and licentious troops can bring in the fertility of crops, beasts, and humankind.

---

113   Nigel Pennick, personal communication.
114   Hilda Ellis Davidson, *Roles of the Northern Goddess* (Routledge, 1998).
115   Jones and Pennick, A *History of Pagan Europe.*

Prepare a figure of paper or straw and load it with worn-out items to represent the old season and things you wish to be rid of to be burned on the bonfire or brazier. If you can't do this, take an old piece of paper, perhaps something on which you have written old ideas and things you no longer believe in. Write on it other things you wish to be rid of, and this can be burned in a candle flame.

Say:

I cast out winter, I cast out illness, I cast out ill luck,

I cast out all that has passed its time.

Let it be gone so I may greet the summer anew.

THE MERRY MONTH

• • • • •

The extended hours of daylight are very noticeable here in England by May, and the weather is getting much warmer, so the month has brought a full flush of fresh green growth and a plethora of wildflowers. All the hedgerows become white and fragrant with hawthorn blossoms, the grass in the fields is lush and tall, and the woodlands are carpeted with bluebells. It is a month of blue skies and cotton wool clouds, of bonfires, maypoles, and May Queens, of fairies and enchantments, of milk and honey, fledgling birds and the buzzing of the bees. In the solar calendar, May marks the real coming of summer, and all the folk customs and rituals of May reflect this.

The Romans called this month *Maius*, meaning "mother" or "nursing mother," named after the Greek goddess Maia, the eldest of the Pleiades, one of the seven sisters represented by a bright cluster of stars in the constellation of Taurus the Bull. For the Romans, Maia embodied the concept of growth, as her name was thought to be related to *maius* and *maior*, meaning "larger" or "greater," identifying her with the earth goddess Terra and Bona Dea, the good goddess. The Pleiades were important seasonal markers in the ancient world, rising heliacally (with the sun at dawn) in early May after being invisible for forty days, and again appearing on the western horizon at the beginning of November. This twofold division of the year, according to the position of the Pleiades, heralded the seasonal work on the land of planting and harvest, as well as safe summer sailing and the coming of the winter rains and storms, closing channels of navigation on the Mediterranean.[116] Indeed, the Pleiades were important seasonal markers in the cultures of both the northern and southern hemispheres.[117]

In England, the customs and games of May Day were called going "a-maying" or "bringing in the May" and reached their heights during the Middle Ages. There are records of towns and councils spending significant amounts of money on public celebrations.[118] Villagers would go out into the woods and fields to collect armfuls of flowers and greenery for decoration, a custom Kipling described in his poem A *Tree Song*:

> *Oh, do not tell the Priest our plight,*
> *Or he would call it a sin;*
> *But—we have been out in the woods all night,*
> *A-conjuring Summer in!*
> *And we bring you news by word of mouth—*
> *Good news for cattle and corn—*
> *Now is the Sun come up from the South,*
> *With Oak, and Ash, and Thorn!*[119]

Maypoles, usually made of stripped birch trees, were cut and set up on the village green and hung with ribbons, ready for dancing.[120] Many communities elected a young girl to become the May Queen to preside over the festivities. Sometimes she was accompanied by a May King. In Elizabethan times the king and queen were called Robin Hood and Maid Marian. There might be a Jack in the Green, a man wearing a wicker cage covered in fresh greenery, to represent the opulent growth of

---

116 Krupp, *Beyond the Blue Horizon*.
117 Ibid.
118 Hutton, *The Stations of the Sun*.
119 http://www.kiplingsociety.co.uk/poems_treesong.htm, accessed 15.1.20.
120 Hutton, *The Stations of the Sun*.

the season. We can speculate that he is connected to the foliate heads (green men) found on architecture, and that he perhaps represented a vegetation or woodland spirit.

May Day bonfires blazed across the hilltops, and jumping the fire was thought to offer protection, blessing, and fertility. Even the ashes of the fires had special powers and were spread on the fields to protect them and bring fruitfulness. In Ireland cows were driven through the ashes to guard them from the attentions of fairies.[121]

The Puritans were outraged at the immorality that often accompanied the drinking and dancing, and Oliver Cromwell's parliament banned maypoles altogether in 1644, describing them as "a heathenish vanity generally abused to superstition and wickedness."[122] Condemning the custom of going out into the woods to feast and gather greenery, Christopher Featherstone declared, "Men doe use commonly to run into woods in the night time, amongst maidens, to set bowers, in so much, as I have heard of ten maidens which went to set May, and nine of them came home with childe."[123] Philip Stubbes complained that, of the girls who go into the woods, "not the least one of them comes home again undefiled."[124]

The birth of summer obviously means the death of winter. Death and rebirth is a theme enacted in many seasonal mumming plays and in the May Day dance of the Padstow Obby Oss (hobby horse) in Cornwall, England. The evening before the dance, the village is decorated with green branches and flowers. The sinister black Oss, led by the Teaser, parades through the town to the accompaniment of drum and accordion. Now and then the drum falls silent, and the Oss gradually falls to the floor, only to rise again. At midnight the Oss dies, to be reborn again next summer.

As the death of winter takes place, so did many European festivals of the dead, in order to make a purification before the summer began.[125] For the Romans May was generally an unlucky month, when marriage was forbidden. It was also the time of the Lemuria, a festival to placate the Lemures, the wandering spirits of the dead, which St. Augustine described as evil and restless manes that tormented and terrified

121 *Cormac's Glossary.*
122 *The Retrospective Review* VIII (London: Charles Baldwyn, 1823).
123 Quoted in Hutton, *The Stations of the Sun.*
124 Ibid.
125 Ronald Hutton, *Halloween? It's more than trick or treat,* https://www.theguardian.com/commentisfree/2014/oct/28/halloween-more-than-trick-or-treat-origins?fbclid=IwAR13rqBx1oqclv4giBmWmYstGVhsyM9GxrOxP8Q8Jo7eo_j3zBs2xsZoo6U, accessed 18.8.20.

the living.[126] The Lemuria was a three-day festival (May 9, 11, and 13) when the head of the household rose at midnight and cast black beans behind him for them to feast on, saying: "These I cast; with these beans I redeem me and mine." This had to be said nine times without looking back.

As the Wheel of the Year turns to summer, we honour the Goddess as the flower bride who seeks her groom, the Green Man, in the greenwood. Their passion and fire will bring in the summer and dispel the forces of winter and bane, and the Goddess will become the fertile mother. Now is the time of growth, for the blossoming of the earth, for warmth and celebration. So we kindle the Beltane fires, raise the maypole, and dance!

Early May

May 1: MAY DAY/BELTANE

May begins with the modern Pagan festival that is usually called Beltane. We know that in Pagan Ireland, the first of May was called *Bealtaine* or *Beltene*, though we don't much about how they celebrated it. The earliest reference to it is believed to be in the tenth century CE *Samas Chormaic*, or *Cormac's Glossary*, which describes cattle being driven between two fires the Druids made for luck:

> Belltaine i.e. May Day i.e. "lucky fire" i.e. two fires which the Druids used to make with great incantations, and they used to bring the cattle (as a safeguard) against the diseases of the year to those fires, they used to drive the cattle between them.[127]

Cormac derived the name Beltane from "lucky fire," though elsewhere in the text he speculated it might come from "Bial, an idol god."[128] While *tene* means "fire," *bel* could be translated as "bright" or "lucky," or it could be connected to the Gaulish sun god Bel or Belenos whom Julius Caesar identified with the Greek/Roman sun god Apollo. We can safely assume that bonfires played a part in the celebrations, a continuing custom well documented in succeeding centuries, well into the 1800s.

---

126 St. Augustine, *The City of God*, 11.
127 *Cormac's Glossary.*
128 Ibid.

Though the Pagan Irish left no written records, the Christian chroniclers tried to record earlier customs and myths (though often not without inserting Christian messages and classical legends). From these we know that the early Irish had a twofold division of the year. In the fifteenth- or sixteenth-century CE manuscript *Tochmarc Emire* ("The Wooing of Emer," probably transcribed from an earlier tenth-century source), the hero Cúchulainn explains: "For two divisions were formerly on the year, namely, summer from Beltane the first of May, and winter from Samhain to Beltane," making it clear that Beltane was considered the start of summer. In the early 1500s, a quatrain says this of Beltane, describing it as a time of increase and plentiful milk:

> I *relate this to you, a surpassing festival,*
> The *privileged dues of Beltane:*
> Ale, *roots, mild whey,*
> And *fresh curds to the fire.*[129]

Beltane certainly seems to have been the Pagan feast that the Irish church feared most. The Book of Armagh described Beltane as "an idolatrous ceremony," featuring "the Druids, singers, prophets," and attended "with manifold incantations and magical contrivances." Beltane was also the first Pagan festival to have been suppressed, according to *The Life of Saint Patrick*, where the fires of Beltane and the Easter fires were said to be in direct opposition until the Pagan ones were defeated.[130]

Many of our present May Day customs come from the Roman Floralia, such as fetching in armloads of greenery and flowers. It lasted several days, spanning the end of April and the beginning of May, and was a feast of joy and unrestrained merriment, with the whole city bedecked in blossoms and people wearing flowers in their hair and wreathing their animals in garlands. Offerings of milk and honey were made to Flora, the goddess of flowers and blossoms, youth and its pleasures, with prayers for the prospering of the ripe fruits of the field and orchard.

As always, with our spiritual practice, we look to nature for our inspiration and direction. At the beginning of May, we celebrate the Lady of Flowers and the Green Man coming together in love, the most powerful force in the universe, which binds spirit and matter together, creating the world from opposites. This union is the God

---

129   Kuno Meyer's translation as found in Kenneth Hurlstone Jackson's *Studies in Early Celtic Nature Poetry* (Cambridge: University Press, 1935).

130   J. B. Bury, *The Life of St. Patrick and His Place in History* (Freeport, NY: Books for Libraries, 1971), 104–106.

and Goddess at the point of their sacred marriage, an act which brings about all of creation with the reconciliation of duality.

Beltane Ritual

Two pillars of wood are set up in the centre of the circle, three feet apart. One is decorated with a green lady mask and flowers, the other with a green man mask and oak leaves. A small green candle in a glass jar stands atop each. In the north the altar has a single red candle.

Take three breaths: together with the earth beneath you, together with the sky above you, and together with the circle around you.

Say:

With Beltane we celebrate the coming of summer,

When life is in full flow and the primal forces of creation join in union.

Go to the Goddess pillar and light the candle, saying:

I honour the Goddess and open myself to the Goddess within.

Go to the God pillar and light the candle, saying:

I honour the God and open myself to the God within.

Here burn the twin fires of Beltane, male and female,

God and Goddess, sky and earth, sun and moon,

Body and spirit, each flame burning in each one of us.

This is the time of purification by fire. As you pass between the pillars with their candles on top, know that you leave behind winter, negativity, and pain. Step forward between the flames, saying:

I leave winter behind and move forward into the work of summer.

Pause for a while as you reflect on this, then say:

We now celebrate the most ancient of magics, the magic of joining.

The Lady of the Land takes the hand of the Green Lord,

And their marriage brings life to the world.

Pick up the God candle:

This is the fire of the Lord.

Pick up the Goddess candle:

This is the fire of the Lady.

The two candles are used to light the single red candle on the altar.

> *United in life and abundance. Blessed be!*
> *Lord and lady, illuminate me from within.*
> *Fill me with the light of creation. Help me radiate light upon the world.*
> *I ask this in the name of the Lord and Lady. Blessed be.*
> *I take with me the energy of Beltane, when the spirit fully manifests*
> *within the material world, and we are blessed.*
> *This rite is ended. Blessed be.*

Don't forget to wash your face in the May Day morning dew, as this traditional rhyme advises:

> *The fair maid who, the first of May*
> *Goes to the fields at break of day*
> *And washes in dew from the hawthorn tree*
> *Will ever after handsome be.*

May 6: MILK A PUNCH DAY

Cattle were turned out to their summer pastures at the beginning of this month. The Anglo Saxons called May *Thrimilce*, or "thrice milking." Because of the richness of grass, the milk was of finer quality and the cows yielded much more abundantly and had to be milked three times each day, so it was in May that the Anglo-Saxons began making cheese. On May 6 Alderney farmers celebrated Milk a Punch Day, when they drank fresh milk as a toast to the season of plenty.

May 8: FLORA DAY

In Helston, Cornwall, today is the Furry Day, otherwise called Flora Day or the Floral Dance. It is one of the oldest surviving early summer festivals in Britain. There are several explanations for word *furry*, even that it derives from the goddess Flora and the Roman Floralia or the Latin word *Feria*, meaning a fair or holy day.[131] The festivities, as Marian Green says, echo "the idea of the dance of life, and now at the very beginning of summer, the dancers welcome the strength of the returning sun."[132]

---

131 Green, *A Harvest of Festivals*.
132 Ibid.

Preparations for the big day begin in mid-April when gatherers cut branches of sycamore, beech, and other greenery used to decorate the town. Furry Day itself starts after sunrise when the dancers take to the streets and circle the old town. This is followed by the mummers' play known as the Hal-an-Tow, when Robin Hood, Friar Tuck, St. George, and St. Michael, along with several other characters, act out battles in which good defeats evil (i.e., summer defeats winter) and sing the ancient Hal-an-Tow song, which includes the chorus:

With Hal-an-Tow! Jolly Rumble, O!

For we are up as soon as any day, O!

And for to fetch the Summer home,

The Summer and the May, O,

For Summer is a-come, O,

And Winter is a-gone, O.[133]

Afterwards, around 1,000 children dressed in white take part in the children's dance. At midday the Furry Dance itself takes place, led by the mayor, driving out the memory of winter and bringing with them the warmth and blessings of summer.[134] At the final dance of the day, the many visitors from all over the world are invited to join in, and the whole town is filled with dancers.

Flower Goddess Ritual

Decorate your altar with as many seasonal flowers as you can. Light two green candles and say:

Come, Lady of Flowers, so that I may honour you and sing your praises.

In your season every tree is clothed with leaves;

The grass grows high in the pastures.

You wear a thousand colours, a thousand different forms.

You are also the goddess of the fields,

For if the crops have blossomed well, the harvest will be good;

If the vines have blossomed well, there will be wine.

---

133 Roy Palmer (ed.), *Everyman's Book of English Country Songs* (Littlehampton, 1979).

134 https://www.timetravel-britain.com/articles/history/helston.shtml, accessed 27.3.19.

Honey is your gift; you call the bees to the violet
And the clover and the wild thyme.
Let me use life's flower while it still blooms.
I pray you, goddess, bless me.

Allow the candles to burn out.

Mid-May

This really is the birds' month. Bird activity is intense in May, and they seem to sing all day and most of the night. There are more insects flying in the warmth too, with many bees and butterflies on my herbs now.

There are blossoms on my apple and pear trees, the vegetable garden needs more time but is producing a greater choice of fresh foods, with spring cabbage, rhubarb, early lettuce, spring onions, radishes, and even early new potatoes. We can still get frosts in May, and the weather is still changeable; it can be warm and sunny or cold and wet. I won't be putting in any tender plants until June, but I'm sowing more lettuce, radish, parsley, basil, and peas directly into the ground so that I can crop throughout the summer. In the greenhouse I'm sowing annual flowers and herbaceous perennials, marrows, courgettes (zucchini), autumn cauliflower, calabrese, and kohlrabi.

The herb garden is keeping me busy too. I collect the early fresh green growth of comfrey (*Symphytum officinale*) to make salves that heal cuts and small wounds, sprains, and arthritic joints. I also collect the leaves of the common mallow (*Malva sylvestris*), a soothing plant with a high mucilage content, which is useful for stomach ulcers and dry coughs in the form of a tea or to use as a poultice to reduce inflammations such as insect bites and boils. The fresh young leaves even make a lovely addition to a salad. The woodruff (*Galium odoratum/Asperula odorata*) is coming up everywhere, and I pick the flowers to make a May-time drink called May Bowl. The sweetly scented leaves can be dried or pressed between the pages of a book to scent drawers and linen cupboards.

· · · · · · · ·

May Bowl

12 SPRIGS YOUNG SWEET WOODRUFF, CHOPPED

5 OUNCES (1¼ CUPS/140 GRAMS) POWDERED SUGAR (ICING SUGAR)

2 BOTTLES DRY WHITE WINE

2 PINTS SPARKLING WINE

CHOPPED STRAWBERRIES

Place in all the ingredients except the sparkling wine and strawberries in a bowl. Cover for 30 minutes. Remove the herbs. Add the sparkling wine and strawberries. NB: Avoid woodruff if pregnant or breastfeeding.

Busy Bees

The bees are busy pollinating the flowers in the garden, the orchards, and the fields, and I am reminded that we are reliant on this precious insect for most of our crops. Without the bee, a great many (though not all) plants and crops could not be pollinated and would die out, affecting great swathes of ecosystems and agriculture alike. The ancients understood this and associated the bee with the Mother Goddess herself, the queen bee who rules the hive. She streams with honey, the sweetest substance in the world at the time,[135] which the Greeks believed was the food of the gods themselves.[136] Many goddesses were associated with the bee, including Artemis, Aphrodite, Demeter, Cybele, Diana, Rhea, and Aphrodite, the nymph goddess of summer who was served by priestesses called *Melissae*, or bees.

Bees and honey have been important throughout history as the only source of sweetness. Before sugar was known, honey was required for making beer, wine, and mead, as well as cakes and desserts. Bees have collected a great deal of myth and folklore. One of the most charming is the custom of telling the bees, whereby a beekeeper must keep his hives informed of important news, such as a death in the family, a wedding, or someone leaving home. If the beekeeper failed in this duty, the bees would find out about it anyways and go into mourning, which would mean they might leave their hive, stop the production of honey, or die.[137]

---

135 Hilda Ransome, *The Sacred Bee* (London: George Allen & Unwin, 1937).
136 Ibid.
137 Steve Roud, *The Penguin Guide to the Superstitions of Britain and Ireland* (London: Penguin Books, 2003).

Goddess of the Bees Ritual

Have ready some mead and honey cakes (or vegan wine and cake if you wish) and a yellow candle.

Mother Goddess, you are the queen bee,

The lady of honey, the sweetness of life;

Come to my rite.

Light the candle:

You call the bees to the flowers

To pollinate them and make them fertile

So that we shall have fruit and seeds,

So that we shall live.

Without you the earth is barren.

You are the sweetness of life.

You are life itself.

Offer the mead by pouring it on the earth (or into a bowl, which can be taken outside and put on the earth later) and the cakes by placing them on the ground.

I make you this offering, Melissa, lady of the bee,

In thanks for your messengers, the insects.

In thanks for their work,

I will honour them.

Let blessing be.

Let the candle burn out.

May 11: MAY EVE OLD STYLE/BELTANE EVE OLD STYLE

When the Gregorian calendar was adopted to replace the Julian calendar in 1752, eleven days had to be dropped from the calendar, thus drawing all the dates forward by eleven days, which is why the hawthorn does not blossom now on May 1. This makes today May Eve Old Style, when the Manx fairies and witches are supposed to be particularly active. In Ireland the Lunantishees, or fairies, guard the blackthorn trees and will punish anyone who tries to cut its wood on this day.

Solitary hawthorns growing on hills or near wells were considered to be markers to the world of the fairies; any human who slept beneath one, especially on May Eve, was in danger of being taken away to the land of the fairies. The flowering of the hawthorn marked the opening of the summer season, the time when people could get out and about and when young men and women could meet up, so it is not surprising that May was often considered the month of courtship and love. Moreover, the scent of hawthorn blossom is supposedly redolent of sex,[138] and the hawthorn is associated with love-making. In ancient Greece girls wore hawthorn crowns at weddings.

However, while in some circumstances it was considered to be a tree of love, like other fairy trees, it was very unlucky to bring it indoors, except on May Day, when the taboo is lifted:

> Hawthorn bloom and elder-flowers
> Will fill a house with evil powers.

Ritual for Contacting the Goddess Within

Prepare an infusion of hawthorn blossoms by putting a half ounce of blossoms in a pot and pouring a pint of boiling water over them. Infuse for 10 minutes and strain into a cup. Hawthorn is wound about with the mysteries of the Goddess and should be treated with great care. For women who seek contact with the sexual side of the Goddess within themselves, hawthorn tea may be employed. It may be used by men to gain deeper understanding of this aspect of the Goddess and their female partners.

Go outside (if possible) to your garden or wild place early in the morning, beneath a hawthorn tree, if possible, and inhale its scent. Set up a stone for an altar. If you can't go outside, decorate your altar with seasonal wildflowers. Put the infusion in your cup on the altar and light two green candles. Say:

> Goddess, Lady, White Queen:
> I come to you in the soft warmth of May
> Beneath boughs jewelled with flowers.
> Your perfume loads the air
> With the scent of love and magic.

---

138   Geoffrey Grigson, *The Englishman's Flora* (Phoenix House, 1956).

Take up the cup of hawthorn blossom tea, saying:

I bless this cup and ask that as I drink of it

I may learn more of the wisdom of the Goddess

Who is manifest within me.

I ask that I may learn more of her ancient ways

And feel her love for all creation as my own.

When you are ready, drink from the cup and feel the sacred flower spirit of the summer Goddess contact your spirit within and become one with you. Gaze at the wildflowers and feel the earth blossoming and growing around you. Feel your spirit grow and blossom within you and become one with the current of the year, the manifest love of the summer Goddess.

Pour the remaining liquid onto the earth as an offering to the earth Goddess, saying:

White Queen, I thank you for being with me this day

And ask that I may recognise that you are within me as I dwell within you.

Let me feel your presence in all things, visible and invisible.

This rite is ended. Let blessing be.

May 12: May Day Old Style/Beltane Old Style

The children of the Dorset fishing village of Abbotsbury still "bring in the May" on the old day. Carrying garlands made by a local woman, each one constructed over a frame and supported by a stout broomstick, they go about the village from door to door, and receive small gifts in return. Later, the garlands are laid at the base of the local war memorial. At one time this was an important festival marking the beginning of the fishing season, when wreaths were blessed, carried down to the water and fastened to the bows of the fishing boats. After dark, the fishermen rowed out to sea and tossed the garlands to the waves with prayers for a safe and plentiful fishing season. It is tempting to see a carry-over from Pagan times, when sacrificial offerings were made to the gods of the sea.

⧼⧼⧼⧼⧼⧼⧼

Late May

We enter the zodiac sign of Gemini, the Twins. Two bright stars called Castor and Pollux appear relatively close together in the night sky, forming the heads of the Twins, while the other stars of the constellation drop in two parallel lines from them, providing the bodies. In Greek myth, the heliacal rising of Gemini marked the period of calm summer seas and was associated with the twins Castor and Pollux, hatched from an egg after their mortal mother Leda was seduced by the god Zeus in the form of a swan. Though Pollux was immortal, his brother Castor was not. Such was their love for each other that when Castor died, Pollux appealed to Zeus, who placed them together in the stars. They spend their time alternately in the heavens and the underworld (when they can't be seen) as the seasons change.

In Babylonian astronomy the constellation was known as the Great Twins, a pair of minor gods who were perhaps twin aspects of Nergal, god of the dead and the underworld.[139] They were named Meshlamtaea ("the one who has arisen from the underworld") and Lugalirra ("mighty king") and were guardians of doorways in general but, moreover, defenders of the summertime entrance to the realm of the dead.[140] In Babylonian tradition the two solstices were the two entrances to the underworld, the winter one (located in the region of Capricorn) used by souls journeying to the afterlife and the summer one (located in the region of Cancer, the Crab) used by souls incarnating or visiting earth.[141] The Twins guard the entrance to the summer solstice next month.

May 25: MOTHER EARTH

In summer the spring Maiden becomes the Mother Goddess, who begins to bear. On this day the Greeks celebrated the festival of Gaia, the deity representing earth, the fruitful power that sustains universal life and the ancestral source of all life.

---

139   Nicole Brisch, "Lugalirra and Meslamtaea (a pair of gods)", *Ancient Mesopotamian Gods and Goddesses*, Oracc and the UK Higher Education Academy, 2016, http://oracc.museum.upenn .edu/amgg/listofdeities/lugalirraandmeslamtaea/, accessed 19.9.19.

140   White, *Babylonian Star-Lore*.

141   Ibid.

Mother Earth Ritual

Light a green candle on your altar and say:

> Listen to the words of the earth mother. Know me. I have had many names. Some call me Gaia and others Rhea or Cybele, while to many I am simply known as the Mother, for I am the earth. I am the bringer of fertility, and I preside over the whole cycle of being: planting, growth, and harvest; birth, growth, decline, death, and rebirth.
>
> I am the great matrix of nature and my spirit flows throughout it, connecting it into a unified, sacred whole.
>
> My magic flows throughout the world—every uncurling oak leaf in spring, every humming summer bee, every rutting stag, every misty shore.
>
> The land beneath your feet is not merely dirt but a fountain of energy that sustains animals, plants, and people. All space is sacred space because it is my body.
>
> I am the mother of all living, and my love is poured out upon the earth. All life, all creation is sacred. This is a truth that you cannot challenge or change without diminishing yourself. You are not separate from nature or above it but part of it. All life is equal; if the deaths of animals and plants are meaningless, then so is yours. You must learn to honour the divinity in all things if you are to honour the divinity in yourself.
>
> Honour your spirit but know that you are also a physical being, alive and vital in my beautiful creation, able to see, hear, touch, taste, and feel. Life is not a punishment or a fallen state in which the soul has become imprisoned in matter but a wonderful gift to be explored and enjoyed. Powerful forces have united to make a gateway for your spirit to incarnate, grow, and transform.
>
> I am the all-encompassing source of life. Within me there is no separation, no judgement; one being is not better or superior to another. I exist within you and without you, and my nurturing flow of life is always available to heal, balance, and vitalise, for you are my own child.

Finish the ritual by saying:

Mother Earth, I hear your words and will honour them.
Blessed be.

May 29: GARLAND DAY

In Castleton, Derbyshire, this is Garland Day, when the Garland King rides on horseback at the head of a procession of musicians and young girls, who perform a dance similar to the Helston Floral Dance. The garland the king wears is actually an immense beehive-shaped structure that fits over his head and shoulders, covered with greenery and flowers and crowned with a special bouquet called the "queen."

He is yet another representation of the spirit of increase and blossoming this month, like Jack in the Green or the Green Man. As Pagans, we think of the Green Man as a very real force of nature. We imagine him walking the land and kindling all he touches with his life force. As he mates with the Goddess, he co-creates the world.

Jack in the Green

Light a green candle on your altar and say:

Jack in the Green, our garland king
Clad in your summer crown
You kindle the land
With the touch of your hand
And dress its summer gown
Blessed be.

THE MONTH OF GLORY

• • • • •

June comes and light blazes across the land. Now is the time of brightness and warmth, when the Sun God stands in all his glory, with long days and short nights. According to the early chronicler Bede, the Anglo Saxons called the month *Litha*,[142] which probably means "light." Basking in the light of Father Sun, Mother Earth is in the full flush of her maturity, soft and ample; foliage is lush, and the perfume of flowers fills the air. The crops have been planted and are growing nicely. The young animals have been born. The hay fields stand tall, shivering in the summer breeze, ready for haymaking. Winter seems far away. Unsurprisingly, we feel more joyful and want to spend more time in the open air—it is a natural time of celebration.

The name "June" comes from Juno, the Roman goddess of women, marriage, and childbirth, wife of the sky god Zeus. Her name is derived from the Latin name *iuvenis*

---

142 Kightly, *The Perpetual Almanack of Folklore.*

(as in juvenile), which was used to indicate a young woman ready for a man and probably refers to the ripening of the crops. This month the sun and earth consummate their union as the seed of fire kindles the earth to swell with fruit so that autumn and harvest can come in turn. In Scots Gaelic, it was *An t'Og mhios*, the young month, while in the Slavonic languages it was named as the linden month and the rose blossoming month.[143]

In the northern hemisphere, the summer solstice falls this month. It marks the zenith of the sun, the longest day. The word *solstice* is derived from Latin and means "sun stands still." For three days around the winter and summer solstices, the sun appears to rise and set at almost exactly the same place, so it seems to be standing still on the horizon. However, while the date of the solstice varies between June 19–23, the official calendar "Midsummer" is pegged to June 24, which is St. John's Day in the Christian almanac and to which the earlier Pagan festivities of the solstice were appropriated.

Every ancient religion had its own customs and traditions associated with the summer solstice, and they date back into prehistory. Midsummer was—and still is—an important festival for those who live in the far north. There are many folk customs associated with it, most of which celebrate the light and encourage the power of the sun with sympathetic magic in the form of bonfires, rolling wheels, circle dances, and torchlight processions.

Midsummer fires once blazed all across Europe and North Africa and were believed to have the power to protect the revellers from evil spirits, bad fairies, and wicked witches, as well as ward off the powers of blight, disease, and death. In England every village would have its own fire, while in towns and cities the mayor and corporation actually paid for its construction, and the jollities accompanying it were often very elaborate. Large bonfires were lit after sundown, and this was known as "setting the watch" to ward off evil spirits. Men and women danced around the fires and often jumped through them for good luck, and afterwards a smouldering branch was passed over the backs of farm animals to preserve them from disease. As late as 1900 at least one old farmer in Somerset would pass a burning branch over and under all his horses and cattle.[144] The Cornish even passed children over the flames to protect them from sickness in the coming year.

---

143 Nilsson, *Primitive Time-Reckoning*.
144 Tongue, *Somerset Folklore*.

Torches would be lit at the bonfire, and these would be carried inside the milking parlour to keep milk and butter safe from evil magic, then around the fields and growing crops as a protection and blessing. The ashes of the bonfires were scattered in the corn as an aid to fertility.[145] Some of these torchlight processions reached lavish proportions. Garland-bedecked bands of people, sometimes called a marching watch, carried cressets (lanterns on poles) as they wandered from one bonfire to another. Often Morris dancers attended them, with players dressed as unicorns, dragons, and hobby horses.

Midsummer was a potent time for magic and divination. The twelfth-century Christian mystic Batholomew Iscanus declared, "He who at the feast of St. John the Baptist does any work of sorcery to seek out the future shall do penance for fifteen days."[146] More recently, young girls would use the magic of the season to divine their future husbands. According to one charm, a girl should circle three times around the church as midnight strikes, saying: "Hemp seed I sow, Hemp seed I hoe/Hoping that my true love will come after me and mow." Looking over her shoulder, she should see a vision of her lover following her with a scythe.

The raising of the midsummer tree, identical to the maypole, is a custom found in many areas, including Wales, England, and Sweden. It was decorated with ribbons and flowers, and topped by a weathercock with gilded feathers, the cockerel being a bird of the sun.

It was the tradition for people to watch the sun go down on St. John's Eve, then stay awake for the entire length of the short night and watch the sun come up again. In the sixteenth century, John Stow of London described street parties where people set out tables of food and drink that they invited their neighbours to share, made up their quarrels, lit bonfires, and hung their houses with herbs and small lamps.[147]

In Britain it was the custom to visit holy wells just before sunrise on Midsummer's Day, when the light would infuse the water with magical and healing powers. The well should be approached from the east and walked round sunwise three times. Offerings such as pins or coins were thrown into the well and its water drunk from a special vessel.[148]

---

145 This has a scientific basis: wood ash provides a high potash feed for plants.
146 *Mediaeval Handbooks of Penance*, ed. J. T. McNeill & H. M. Garner (New York, 1938).
147 A *Survey of London*, ed. C. L. Kingsford (Oxford, 1908).
148 McNeill, *The Silver Bough*.

The magic of June is concerned with light, fire, warmth, and growth, the heat and light of Father Sun bringing Mother Earth to bear fruit.

Early June

June 1: THE GODDESS OF FERTILITY

In ancient Rome the first day of June marked the birthday of Juno, queen of the gods, and the whole month was sacred to her. She is the guardian of women, so the month was considered the most propitious month for marriage, and in some places it still is. She is a complex goddess with many facets, but she is connected with the idea of vital life force, fertility, and eternal youthfulness. In this aspect she had her counterparts in other pantheons, such as the Greek Hera, the Norse Freya, and the Avestic Anahita.

Mother of Fertility Ritual

Consider the Goddess at this time of year by whatever name you know her. She is the earth beginning to bear, responding to the light of the Sun God at this time of long hours of daylight and greater warmth. In this short ritual, we address her as the vital life force that flows throughout the world and throughout us.

Light a red candle on your altar and say:

> Goddess, your vital force flows throughout the world,
>
> Pushing up with every shoot
>
> Each fledgling bird
>
> Each opening flower.
>
> You are the life giver
>
> The woman of power
>
> Who rejuvenates the earth.
>
> Flow through me too
>
> And let me know your touch.

Reflect on this for a while, and let the candle burn itself out.

June 5: DAY THE BIRDS STOP SINGING

In some early medieval calendars, this is listed as the date the birds stop singing until later in the year. The birds are busy with their parenthood and the woods are full of fledglings, which means their songs change before falling silent this month. The cuckoo's note falters and the nightingale's voice becomes harsh.

June 7: THE HEARTH GODDESS

Almost every pantheon contains a Hearth Goddess, including Vesta, Hestia, Brighid, Gabija, and Svasti. The flame of the hearth represented her in every house and stood for the Goddess herself. In Greek myth Hestia was worshipped as the centre, whether the centre of the city, the house, even the centre of the world, the *omphalos* ("the navel") at Delphi. As the domestic hearth is the sacred centre of the home, the hearth of the gods is the centre of the cosmos. According to Plato, the twelve Olympian gods, who represent the twelve constellations of the zodiac, circle the House of Heaven, while Hestia remains still at the centre, tending the hearth, which is called "the Everlasting Place." Her name, according to Plato, means "the essence of things"—a formless essence symbolised by the flame, which flows through everything that has life.

Her Roman equivalent is Vesta, and the Romans celebrated the Vestalia in her honour this week. This was a seven-day celebration for women only, when they walked barefoot to make offerings to the Goddess. Her priestesses, the *Vestales*, made hard-baked cakes, using water carried in consecrated jugs from a holy spring and sacred salt. These were cut into slices and offered to the Goddess. After the festival, the temple was cleaned and the refuse thrown into the Tiber River.[149]

Celebration of the Hearth Goddess

Since the Hearth Goddess represents the purity of fire and the security and prosperity of the home, safeguarding the wellbeing and security of the inhabitants as well as its wealth and supplies, I think it is important to honour her even during the summer months. I never forget that she is the essence of life and the hearth keeper of the gods. Though there is no fire in the hearth in summer, I keep a candle burning on

149 Mike Dixon-Kennedy, *Encyclopedia of Greco-Roman Mythology* (Santa Barbara, CA: ABC-CLIO, 1998).

the mantelpiece (you could do this on your altar if you don't have a hearth) and make regular offerings.

Today I will put flowers on the hearth and make an offering of incense to the Hearth Goddess.

Mid-June

In my garden pond, the tadpoles are acquiring their legs but still have their tails. This will be absorbed into the body, and by the end of June the young frogs will be ready to leave the pond.

My vegetable plot is yielding plenty of salad vegetables and soft fruits now, and I'm having to water the greenhouse copiously. This is my busiest time of year in the herb garden, when most of my herbs are at their best. As well as using fresh herbs for cooking, I am industriously collecting and drying leaves and flowers, as well as preparing tinctures, oils, vinegars, and salves. Mother Earth is in full bearing, and the Sun God pours his energy into the plants so that this is the time when they are filled with power. This is why the Sun God in every mythology is the patron of healing. This is the most potent time of year to collect many herbs for magical purposes too, and I will be trying to lay in a good enough supply of herbs to last the year.

I collect mint (*Mentha* spp.) for tea and for ritual cleansing, oregano for spells of love and friendship and to add to skin-care products, St. John's wort to make macerated oil and tincture, fennel (*Foeniculum vulgare* syn. *Anethum foeniculum*) to honour the Sun God and for protection, and dill (*Anethum graveolens* syn. *Peucedanum graveolens*) for upset stomach and protection spells.

Elderflowers, sacred to the Mother of the Elves, are gleaming white in the hedgerows, and I make sure to collect and dry a good supply of these to use for fevers and hay fever as well as skin lotions, elderflower cordial, and elderflower champagne.

· · · · · · · · · · · · · · · · · · · ·

ELDERFLOWER CHAMPAGNE

This is a very hit and miss old recipe: sometimes it works and sometimes it doesn't. If there is no sign of the natural yeast working after a day or two, try adding a little champagne yeast.

1½ POUNDS SUGAR

1 LEMON

4 PINTS ELDERFLOWER HEADS

2 TABLESPOONS WHITE WINE VINEGAR

1 GALLON COLD WATER

2 CAMPDEN TABLETS

Warm a pint of the water and dissolve the sugar in it. Allow it to cool. Squeeze the juice from the lemon and chop the rind roughly. Place the flowers in a bowl and add the vinegar, pour on the rest of the water, sugar, and lemon rind, and add the Campden tablets. Steep for 4 days. Strain the infusion well so that all trace of matter is excluded and bottle in screw-top bottles. The elderflower champagne will be ready to drink in 7 days.

June 11: HAYSEL

This is the date when haysel (haymaking) traditionally begins, which is on the feast of St. Barnabas, who is often pictured carrying a hay rake:

Barnaby bright, Barnaby bright
Light all day and light all night.

On his day it was customary to deck churches and houses with Barnaby garlands of roses, sweet woodruff, and pink ragged robin. Another tradition rhyme about this is as follows:

When Barnabas smiles both night and day
Poor ragged robin blooms in the hay
At St. Barnabas, the scythe in the meadow.

June 13: FEAST OF THE THUNDER GOD

Water becomes very important at the height of the summer when the growing crops need irrigating. According to an old saying, A dry May and a dripping June/ Brings all things in tune.[150] However, the hot weather often brings thunderstorms, and this is the season the thunder god was honoured and sometimes placated. He has had many names, and the oak was usually sacred to him since lightning was often believed to strike the oak more than any other tree. In Greece he was called Zeus, and it was said that thunderstorms raged more frequently around his sacred oak grove at Dodona than anywhere else in Europe. The oak was also sacred to Thor, the Norse thunder god whose famous hammer caused thunder; during the conversion of the Germans, St. Boniface felled an oak in which Thor was believed to reside. Oaks also figured in many representations of Taranis, the British thunder god. The Finnish god of thunder was Ukko ("oak"). In Russia the oak god was called Perun, "thunderbolt." The Lithuanian god of the oak was Perkaunas or Perunu ("thunder"); if lightning struck a tree, a rock, or a man, they were believed to hold some of his sacred fire. In Latvia, even today, oak wreaths are worn by men named Janis (John) at Midsummer. Small oak branches with leaves are attached to cars in Latvia during the festivity.

Thunder God Ritual

Have ready a bowl of water and a twig of oak in leaf. Using the oak twig, sprinkle some of the water on the earth. Light a red candle. Say:

> Thunderer: your roar causes the sky and earth to tremble
>
> You spark the fire of lightning
>
> Your light rends the clouds
>
> I honour you and offer you praise.
>
> Be gentle with us
>
> Send us rain in time of need
>
> To nourish the earth
>
> Blessed be.

Put out the candle to signify the end of the rite.

---

150 Blackburn and Holford-Strevens, *Oxford Companion to the Year.*

Late June

We enter the zodiac sign of Cancer the Crab, a small constellation and the faintest in the entire zodiac; if you live in a light-polluted city, you probably won't be able to see it at all. In Greek mythology Cancer was identified with the crab that appeared while Herakles fought the many-headed Hydra (represented by the constellation Hydra). It bit him on the foot, and Herakles stamped on it and killed it before turning back to his task. The goddess Hera placed the crab among the stars but made the stars really faint in token of the fact it had failed to distract the hero.

The summer solstice is said to occur when the sun enters the first point of Cancer the Crab, though because of the precession of the equinoxes, the sun is actually in the sign of Taurus when the summer solstice occurs. However, the mythology is based on the system extant in classical times, when, on its annual journey around the zodiac, the sun spent forty days wandering in the mysterious realm of darkness that is Cancer. The Egyptians associated the constellation with Anubis, the jackal-headed god of the dead, viewing it as a gateway to the netherworld. In Babylon it also had magical connections with the dead and ghosts, and to the Chinese it is a lunar mansion called "Ghosts" and has links with the dead and the afterlife. The constellation of Cancer was known to the Chaldean and Platonist philosophers as the Gate of Men, though which they believed that the souls of people came down from heaven and were incarnated at the summer solstice, as opposed to Capricorn, which was the Gate of the Gods, where departed souls returned to the heavens at the winter solstice and though which the Sun God was reborn.[151]

The Summer Solstice

It has been raining on and off for most of the day, and it still is as we arrive at the site of our Midsummer vigil. The willow-fringed lake is hazy and the oak trees dripping. We set up beneath the ancient linden, and the perfume of its blossoms fills the air. Then, as we are about to begin, the sky clears and a rainbow forms over the lake, a full bow arched across the sky. We stare at it in wonder. It hangs for a long time. Our ritual begins with the words "open wide the ancient gateway," and here the gateway

---

151   White, *Babylonian Star-Lore.*

is in the sky before us over the lake and our ritual site, inviting us in. As we reach the lake, the rainbow fades. We have passed the gateway and entered the liminal place and time. We speak the sacred words, watch the sun go down, and begin our vigil through the night, feasting and telling stories around the fire, watching the stars through the short hours of darkness. Venus, the morning star, rises, and the birds begin, one by one, to sing, heralding the dawn.

As the sun rises over the horizon, Dave plays a swan bone flute, gilded in gold, a gift of the lake itself a year and a day ago, a year and a day in the making. A gleam of light shimmers along its edge as it is played only once, at that moment, then Dave smashes it and returns the pieces to the lake, an offering to the gods. Swan veils of mist swirl across the surface of the water, gathering and dispersing, running in from both sides to a single point, where they rise, forming the shape of a white figure, the Lady of the Lake herself come to give us her blessing before the strengthening sun burns off the mist and bathes us in a golden dawn.

Summer Solstice Ritual

This ritual is performed at the rising of the sun on the day of the solstice. A glass vessel full of water is placed on the ground, a sprig of rosemary beside it. Sit and wait until the sun starts to rise, then say:

> This is the time of greatest light. The powers of winter are far away, the powers of darkness a story for children. We celebrate in this time of brightness. We honour the Lord of the Sun and the Lady of the Earth, whose marriage causes the grain to grow, the vine to ripen, the herbs to become imbued with power. Without their gifts, we would not be.
>
> Mother Earth, you are life, you are abundance
> You produce everything in nature
> You produced me, your child
> You are first in all things, you surround me
> You are beneath my feet.
> You give me the food I eat, the water I drink
> From you comes all I see, all that breathes.

Father Sun, you are the bright and shining light

You are the eye of the sky

You see right through to the limits of the darkness

You behold everything; even into the realm of chaos

Your blessings fall upon the earth and cause the crops to grow.

Wait for the sun to rise and illuminate the vessel and charge the water with solstice power.

Take the glass vessel and say:

As I drink, I embrace the light within me.

Drink and say:

Let the light grow within me.

Take the sprig of rosemary, dip it in the water, and sprinkle it over yourself. Say:

I give thanks to the Great Goddess of the earth. Mother, grant us your blessings. Grant us full orchards and fields of ripening grain. Be with us in our lives, as you once were to those of old. Grant us your love and blessings. Let blessing be!

O Lord of the Sun, great eye of the heavens! Grant your light and your blessing to this land; protect us from the powers of blight and darkness. Be with us in our lives as you once were to those of old. Grant us your wisdom and your blessings. Let blessing be!

Let this ritual end with love and blessings. Blessed be.

June 23: MIDSUMMER EVE/ST. JOHN'S EVE

While the solstice date varies, Midsummer's Eve is fixed on the calendar as June 23, pegging a moveable feast to a fixed date, and the folk customs of the solstice moved with it.

Midsummer Eve was believed to be one of the great fairy festivals[152] when fairies are abroad, moving amongst humankind, frolicking around the Midsummer bonfires

---

152 According to the folklore, good fairies start to come out around the vernal equinox, are very animated by Beltane, and at the peak of their activities by Midsummer. By Halloween, most of the good fairies have disappeared from sight and the bad fairies, such as goblins, rule the winter period.

and playing all sorts of tricks, ranging from stealing human brides and performing innocent pranks to inflicting horrible curses and even death.[153] In the Shetlands the mysterious selkies come ashore. They normally look like gray seals, but on this night they shed their skins to become human and dance on the shoreline. If they are disturbed, they will grab their skins and run back to the sea, though if a man can steal and hide the skin, he can force a selkie maid to marry him—if she ever finds her skin, she will put it on and be off back to the sea. In Russia the green-haired Rusalka fairies walk the land at Midsummer, and where they tread flowers appear, and their movement through the grain causes it to grow. The mischievous Robin Goodfellow or Puck is about in English woodlands, playing tricks on unwary travellers and leading them from their paths. Certainly we had a strange experience in the coven one solstice when we turned away from the circle and couldn't find our way back, even though it was only a few yards away and we knew the woods intimately. Eventually, after walking just a few paces, we found ourselves at the other side of the woods, at least a mile away, so I do believe it happens!

According to fairy lore, if you want to see fairies, then you will need the aid of certain magical herbs such as thyme. In Shakespeare's A *Midsummer Night's Dream*, Oberon tells Puck "I know a bank where the wild thyme blows/Where oxlips and the nodding violet grows" because at midnight on Midsummer's night, the King of the Fairies dances with his followers on wild thyme beds. It was an ingredient of many magical potions, dating from around 1600, which allowed the user to see fairies. One simple charm was to make a brew of wild thyme tops gathered near the side of a fairy hill plus grass from a fairy throne. It was also an ingredient of the fairy ointment that was applied to the eyes of newborn fairy babies to enable them to see the invisible. Like other fairy flowers, wild thyme is unlucky if brought indoors. It is one of the best herbs used to attract and work with the fairies and is utilised in offerings and spells.

Midsummer's Eve Fairy Ritual

Prepare a garland of lavender flowers, rosemary, violets, and thyme sprigs, all of which you must pick yourself. Go to a fairy-haunted place at dawn, taking with you a bottle of homemade wine, a cup, some cakes that you have made yourself, and a garland of flowers.

---

153   W. B. Yeats (ed.), *Folk and Fairy Tales of the Irish Peasantry* (London, W. Scott, 1888).

Put on the garland. Say:

> *Spirits of this place, I call to you.*
>
> *Spirits of this place, I honour you.*
>
> *Attend me now and witness my intentions.*

Pour some of the wine into the cup. Pour a few drops on the ground, saying:

> *Spirits of this place, I make this offering to you.*

Drink some of the wine.

Take the cakes and crumble one onto the ground, saying:

> *Spirits of this place, I make this offering to you.*

Eat one of the cakes. Say:

> *Spirits of this place, draw near and listen to my words. I come to honour you,*
> *to pledge to you that I shall honour the sacred earth on which we both live;*
> *I shall not pollute or harm it. I shall honour the wild places and hold sacred*
> *the creatures of the earth, my brothers and sisters of fur and fin, of leaf and bark.*
> *I shall hold sacred the cycles of the seasons and be part of the dance of the earth.*
>
> *Like you, spirits of this place, I shall be brave and compassionate, humble*
> *and honourable, taking no more than I need and treading softly on the earth.*
> *I shall be wild; I shall be free. Test my words, and if you find them truthful,*
> *spoken from my heart, then accept me as your friend. If you find them false, then*
> *treat me accordingly.*

Sit quietly for a while and listen to the world around you. You may see evidence of spirit presence or hear voices in the trees or whispering in the wind.

When you are ready to leave, get up and leave the rest of the cakes, pour the wine onto the ground, and say:

> *Spirits of this place, you have listened to my words and weighed my intentions.*
>
> *I go now, but I shall hold you in my heart. Spirits of this place, hail and farewell.*

It is important to build up a relationship with the place that you work and the spirits that inhabit it over a period of time. It would be foolish to descend on a spot and demand its energies; it takes a long time for the spirits to get to know you and trust you. It is beneficial to carry out most of your magical work in the same place. Over the years it will become more and more powerful, and you will gain the trust of its spirits.

. . . . .

June 24: MIDSUMMER'S DAY/ST. JOHN'S DAY

The date for celebrating the moveable summer solstice became fixed on the day of St. John the Baptist, thus enabling the Catholic Church to associate many of the ancient summer solstice customs with his worship. The solstice fires became the fires of St. John, whom Jesus called "a bright and shining light." The early Christians had a deliberate policy of transforming Pagan celebrations into church occasions. Some of the representations of John are rather strange for a Christian saint. He is often depicted with horns, furry legs, and cloven hooves, like a satyr or woodwose. His shrines too are often of a rustic nature, ostensibly because John was fond of wandering in the wilderness. It is possible that John not only took over a Pagan Midsummer festival for his feast day, but also the attributes and shrines of an earlier green god. Other Midsummer symbols accumulated around St. John, and he was made the patron of shepherds and beekeepers.

In the Middle Ages, Christian mythographers declared that St. John was born at the summer solstice at the time of the weakening sun, announcing his own power would wane with the birth of Christ at the winter solstice, the time of the strengthening sun,[154] associating them with the oak and holly respectively, perhaps drawing on earlier myth and folklore. The evergreen holly persists through the winter death-time and so was identified with Christ, the white flower emblematic of his purity, the prickles his crown of thorns, and the red berries the drops of his shed blood: "of all the trees that are in the woods, the holly bears the crown," in the words of the old carol.[155]

The Midsummer Wand

The most propitious time in the year to make a magic wand is at Midsummer, and whether you count this as the solstice or the calendar day is up to you, but for magical use, you should cut your own wand from living wood. Go out before dawn on Midsummer Day and seek your chosen tree as the sun rises. The wood should be virgin—that is, of one year's growth only—and the wand should be cut from the tree at a single stroke. It should measure from elbow to fingertip. If you wish to, you can smooth and polish the wand with glass-paper, but do not varnish it. Make a small

---

154 Walter, *Christianity.*
155 Williamson, *The Oak King, the Holly King, and the Unicorn.*

hollow in the end that you will hold in your hand and insert a piece of cotton thread with a drop of your own blood into it before sealing it with wax.

June 29: ST. PETER AND ST. PAUL'S DAY

In many places the solstice/Midsummer festivities begun on St. John's Eve went on until St. Peter and St. Paul's Day.

A French proverb states that if it rains today, it will rain for thirty more days. Alexander Carmichael in the *Carmina Gadelica* recorded this Scottish fishermens' saying:

> *Wind from the west, fish and bread;*
> *Wind from the north, cold and flaying;*
> *Wind from the east, snow on the hills;*
> *Wind from the south, fruit on the trees.*

Between Midsummer and this day, many rush-bearing customs take place in England, when rushes or new-mown hay (this is the hay-making season) are brought in to be laid on the floors of churches.

June 30: ROSE DAY

June is the month of roses, when they are at their most abundant. Armenians celebrate Rose Day seven weeks after Pentecost. Originally this was a summer festival of the goddess Anahid, who was offered roses and doves. Roses are sacred to many gods and goddesses of love, including Isis, Aphrodite, Venus, Eros, Cupid, Inanna, and Ishtar.

Like other flowers with rayed petals, they are an emblem of the sun. Like the sun, which dies each night and is reborn each day at sunrise, the rose is an emblem of renewal, resurrection, and eternal life, which is why the Celts, Egyptians, and Romans used them as funeral offerings.[156] I collect them to make rose vinegar, rose water, and oils and infusions to add to skin creams. Some petals I dry for tea or adding to incense.

Today, to honour the Goddess, I decorate my altar with roses.

---

156 Green, *Gods of the Celts*; Roger Phillips and Martyn Rix, *The Ultimate Guide to Roses* (London: Macmillan, 2004); and Laurie Brink and Deborah Green, *Commemorating the Dead: Texts and Artifacts in Context; Studies of Roman, Jewish and Christian Burials* (Berlin: de Gruyter, 2008).

THE GOLDEN MONTH

July

· · · · ·

July is high summer. In Gaelic it was called *an mios buidhe*, the golden month, referring to the standing wheat fields. In Bulgaria it was "the hot month."[157] The Anglo-Saxons named July mead-month, referring to the blossoming meadows. The Welsh call it *Gorfennaf*, the month of completion, or the end of summer. July is a pause before the busy harvest month comes to the farms in August.

The hot, brazen skies of July fill the air with a dreamy, sultry light. We are in the dog days of summer, the hottest part of the year. The name comes from the Roman belief that they are tied to the heliacal (i.e., with the dawn) rising of the Dog Star, Sirius ("scorching star"), the brightest star in the sky, which lies in the constellation of Canis Major, which follows the constellation of Orion the Hunter across the sky. They thought that Sirius was a distant sun that, during the dog days, rose with our

---

157 Nilsson, *Primitive Time-Reckoning.*

sun to add its own heat,[158] creating a period of desiccating hotness when rainfall was at its lowest level, summer growth and moistness draws to an end, and the sun begins to dry the grain ready for harvesting.

In Norse myth the Dog Star, Sirius, was called *Lokabrenna* ("the burning of Loki" or "Loki's brand"), associating it with the trickster god. In one seasonal tale, Sif ("relative") was the wife of Thor, the god of thunder. She had beautiful golden hair until Loki cut it all off for a prank. Thor was so angry that he wanted to kill the trickster, but Loki was able to persuade the dwarfs to make some magical hair for Sif that would grow like her own hair once it touched her head. Sif's hair is the golden grain; her husband is the thunder god who brings the fertilizing rain to make it grow. Loki, usually described as a god of wildfire and heat, is associated here with Sirius and the heat of the dog days, which causes the ripening and subsequent cutting of the grain.

The dog days signal the beginning of the departure of the vegetation god, the Green Man, as the grain dries out, ready for the harvest. This was marked in ancient Greece with the Adonia festival[159]—as Theophrastus said, "when the sun is at its most powerful" to mark the death of the vegetation god Adonis. Women would plant small gardens—called gardens of Adonis—in clay pots or wicker baskets. These were composed of wheat, barley, fennel, and lettuces. These would be placed on the roof, or as close to the sun as they could get. During this time of year, the great heat gives an impetus to a plant's growth, but this can become spindly, with the plant outgrowing its strength and the young shoots just withering in dryness, a symbol of the god's imminent departure. After eight days, the dying gardens of Adonis were cast into the sea or into springs, and the occasion was one of communal mourning. According to the poetess Sappho of Lesbos: "Delicate Adonis is dying, Kytherea; what should we do? Beat your breasts, maidens, and rend your garments."[160]

July was known as the hungry month in Ireland because though the grain stands ripening in the fields, the harvest could not begin until the first day of August, counted as the first day of autumn. It was considered unlucky to harvest grain, gather fruits, or dig potatoes until Lughnasa (August 1).

---

158 Pliny, *Natural History*, II.
159 Marcel Detienne, *The Gardens of Adonis* (Princeton University Press, 1977).
160 https://www.sacred-texts.com/cla/usappho/sph60.htm, accessed 21.1.20.

Early July

The humming of the insects is the music of the meadows and woodlands, the drowsy bee buzzing among the clover flowers, and the grasshoppers and crickets chirping in the lawn. Most birds are silent now, and many are preparing for migration at the end of the month.

The perfume of the linden tree and the elderflowers drench the air, the lavender is flowering, and in the hedgerows purple foxgloves stand proud. It is a time of little harvests in the garden. My fruit bushes have to be covered with netting to protect the crops from birds. Shining purple blackcurrants, golden gooseberries, ruby raspberries, and swelling peas, beans, and salads stand ready to be picked. I spend my mornings hoeing, watering, and weeding.

There is plenty for me to do in the still room, where I make my herb simples, with garden and foraged plants—meadowsweet (*Filipendula ulmaria*), which is often called the "herbal aspirin," is made into tea for arthritis and into a salve for pain; mullein (*Verbascum thapsus*) tea for coughs and mullein oil for earache; raspberry fruit (*Rubus* spp.) vinegar for sore throats; vervain (*Verbena officinalis*) tincture for anxiety and stress; wood betony (*Betonica officinalis*) tea for headaches and ointment for bruises; wild red poppies (*Papaver rhoeas*) for insomnia; plantain (*Plantago major*) for insect bites; and self-heal for cuts and grazes. Linden (*Tilia* spp.) is one of my favourite herbs collected this month, used for stress and anxiety; it usually starts flowering around the solstice, and it is in full bloom now:

. . . .

LINDEN TEA

2 TEASPOONS FRESH NEW LINDEN FLOWERS

1 CUP BOILING WATER

Put the flowers into a teapot and pour on the boiling water. Infuse for 5 minutes and strain. This is good to drink when you are stressed and need to wind down.

NB: Do not use over a period of more than four weeks. Do not take if you are on lithium.

July 1: THE WAITING HARVEST

Around me, the golden fields of grain are ripening in the summer light and heat, but they are not ready to harvest yet. It's an anxious time for the farmers, as drought or storms might still ruin the crops.

The Corn/Grain God is an important figure in Craft lore, and we follow his story around the year in ritual. The old folksong "John Barleycorn" tells his story. John Barleycorn, the spirit of the grain, is cut down and buried in the earth, seeming to be dead, but when the spring rains come he is resurrected and grows with the summer sun. With the late summer he begins to wither and weaken, and his head droops. He ages as autumn comes, and his enemies cut him down. They tie him up on a cart (the sheaves of grain are gathered, tied, and carted away), they beat him up (flail the grain), wash him, toss him about (winnow the grain), roast the marrow from his bones (scorch the grain), and grind him between two stones (mill the grain), then drink his blood (the alcohol brewed from the barley).

Grain was probably the most vital crop for our ancestors, and it remains one of our most important foods. It could be made into bread—the "staff of life," as the Bible calls it—or into beer. In myth it was often seen as a god in itself, the son/lover of Mother Earth who shoots in spring, grows to maturity in summer, is harvested in the autumn, and is buried in the earth (in the form of seed) and dwells in the underworld during the winter, before the whole cycle starts again. It stands as a metaphor for the spiritual cycle of birth, life, death, and rebirth. In the Craft we call this cycle the Eternal Return.

Blessing of the Waiting Harvest Ritual

This is a ritual to bless not only the standing crops in the field and garden, but also the creative and spiritual seeds you have planted, which are yet to mature. If you want to get the right results with a garden, you need to plan it well in advance, plant the seeds, and nurture them before you can expect a harvest. So it is with life; so it is with the spirit. What you nurture will grow; what you neglect will die. What spiritual seeds have you planted this year? How have you nurtured them? What drought, storm, or neglect threatens their harvest? Spend some time meditating about this.

If you have a garden, you can perform this ritual there and make it a blessing of both crops of spiritual aims. If not, you can perform this ritual in your sacred space, setting up your altar with a candle and representations of the harvest to come, such as wheat ears or long grasses to stand for them. Have ready a gold or yellow candle, a goblet of wine, and loaf of bread.

Light the candle and say:

> The sun stands high in the sky, and all begins to ripen and come to maturity.
> The fields grow golden in the sun with ears of ripening grain, and the trees bow
> under the weight of their fruit, but the time of the harvest has not yet come.
> The fruits of our labours are within sight, but the harvest is not yet complete,
> for heat, drought, or storms may still destroy it.

Think for a moment about what harvest you wish for. Say:

> Lady, Queen, Earth Mother, grant that our efforts increase and flourish,
> grant us shining harvests. Hail to thee, Earth Mother of Men;
> bring forth now in the God's embrace, filled with good for the use of man.

> Lord of the Sun, heat, and fire, send your shafts of light to inspire and protect us,
> to fill us with your vitality and warmth.

Take the goblet of wine, saying:

> I drink, yet it is not wine I drink but the blood of the God.
> I drink and salute the God, praying that the Lord and Lady
> will guard us until our harvest is complete. May it be good!

Drink. Take the bread, saying:

> I eat, yet it is not bread I eat but the body of the God, sprung from the womb of
> the Earth, ripening under the Sun. I eat and salute the Sun, consuming the body
> of the God. I pray to the Lord and Lady that they will guard our work until our
> harvest is complete. May the crop be good!

Eat, then say:

> This night I (we) have asked the Lord and Lady to protect our waiting harvests,
> to give us plentiful crops. Let us remember their bounty and thank them for their
> gifts. Let this ritual end with love and blessings on all. Blessed be.

Mid-July

July 15: ST. SWITHIN'S DAY

English folklore has it that if it rains today, then it will rain for the next forty days:

St. Swithin's Day if thou be fair
For forty days 'twill rain no more.
St. Swithin's Day if thou bring rain
For forty days it will remain.

Farmers once anxiously watched the skies on St. Swithin's Day, as too much rain at this time of year would ruin the harvest. St. Swithin was a ninth-century English bishop. When his bones were removed from the churchyard into the cathedral, he seems to have objected, as a thunderstorm broke and went on for forty days; he was weeping at the moving of his grave.

This is a month that celebrates many patron saints and deities of water, wells, grottoes, and shrines. The feast of Sul (or Sulis), the patron goddess of the famous mineral springs at Bath in England, fell this month, while in ancient Rome the Neptunalia was held in honour of Neptune as god of waters, along with festivals of Salacia, goddess of salt water and inland mineral springs, and the goddess Furrina, patroness of freshwater springs. In Britain many holy wells, which once would have been dedicated to a local deity, were assigned to St. Anne, the mother of the Virgin Mary. (Her feast day is celebrated just before Lammas on July 26.) The similarity of her name to that of the goddess Anu or Danu may have made it to easier to Christianise these ancient holy places. One of the best-known wells dedicated to her is that of the spa town of Buxton in the English Peak District, previously dedicated to Arnemetiae, the local water goddess.

Goddesses of Water Ritual

We need water: it is a source of life, fertility, nourishment, cleansing, and healing. For the ancients it was sacred, and water has often been considered to be a living thing, with individual wells, streams, springs, seas, and rivers worshipped as living deities. It flows and moves like life itself, like our emotions.

Take a large glass bowl of water and a large seashell to drink from. Say:

Spirits of water,

Come to my aid.

Pour forth your healing power into this vessel.

Let us be filled with vital health and life

In body, mind, and soul.

Protect me from all ill.

Spirits of water,

Come to my aid.

Put your hand over the bowl of water and say:

Wellspring of creation, ocean of dreams,

The universe drinks from your source.

You are the Lord and Lady, whose life-streams drink of intermingling oneness,

Your fountains are the gods, the waters of life and death

Your tides are our lives and stories, your eddies our dreams.

Here are your waters and your watering place.

Lord and Lady, unite our personal rivers with the original sea

That in this fractured world we may drink from the source

That quenches the thirst of longing; drink and be whole again

As in the long ago when we dreamed the gods and they dreamed us.[161]

Step forward, dip the shell into the water, and drink from it. Pause for a while; absorb the power of water and understand its sacred nature. When you are ready, say:

Let this ritual end with love and blessings.

Blessed be.

---

[161] Poem written by Pamela Harvey and published in *The Wellspring* by Anna Franklin and Pamela Harvey (Capall Bann).

✿✿✿✿✿✿✿

Late July

We enter the zodiac sign of Leo the Lion, the constellation which lies between Cancer the Crab to the west and Virgo the Virgin to the east. The lion's mane and shoulders are formed from a cluster of stars called the Sickle, echoing the beginning of the harvest theme of the constellation, while the bright star Regulus ("little king") forms his heart. Leo was one of the earliest recognised constellations, with the Persians, Turks, Syrians, Jews, and Indians all calling it the lion.

In Greek myth it was identified with the Nemean lion, killed by the solar hero Herakles as one of his twelve labours (his journey around the zodiac). The lion had captured some women and held them as hostages in a cave. It could not be killed by any weapon, so many warriors died trying to free the captives. Herakles fought it barehanded and strangled it, afterwards wearing its pelt as a cloak. Zeus then placed the lion in the sky as the constellation Leo.[162]

The Babylonians called the constellation the Great Lion and portrayed it with wings. It was a symbol of the ferocious nature of high summer, when the scorching sun desiccated the fields, dried up the rivers, and caused drought. The regent of the Lion was the minor god Latarak, a protective deity, but it was also associated with the warlike goddess Inanna, who was titled the Lioness of Heaven.[163]

July 25: ST. JAMES'S DAY

St. James was one of the twelve apostles, and his shrine at Santiago de Compostela in Spain attracts pilgrims from all over the world. In mediaeval times they often wore his badge, the scallop shell. However, this symbol was probably appropriated from the earlier Roman festival of Salacia, held this month to honour the wife of the sea god Neptune: her symbol was the seashell. Like many Christian churches, Santiago de Compostela was built over a Pagan site, with excavations revealing a Roman temple and an even older Celtic well. The shell was associated with other goddesses too, such as the sea-born Aphrodite/Venus.

---

162   Janet Parker and Julie Stanton (eds.), *Mythology: Myths, Legends & Fantasies* (Global Book Publishing, 2007).

163   White, *Babylonian Star-Lore*.

On St. James's Day in the poor districts of London, children used to construct, at the edge of pavements, small grottoes of sand and earth, decorated with oyster shells, broken glass, stones, flowers, and moss. They would stand besides these grottoes and ask for contributions: "Penny for the grotter" or "Please, sir, remember the grotter." This went on at least until 1957, the year in which *The Times* described them as a "nuisance."[164] It's tempting to think that they may have been performing a rite that went back to ancient Pagan times.

A grotto is a natural or artificial cave, and they were used in antiquity as shrines of the gods, particularly those that had naturally fed springs. When I was a child, on a seaside holiday I was taken to the shell grotto in Margate in Kent, with its 21 meters of winding passages decorated with 4.6 million shells creating images of gods and goddesses, trees of life, and patterns made of whelks, mussels, and oysters. This grotto is a mystery, and no one knows whether it is an ancient Pagan site or a Regency folly. Whichever it is, I remember being struck by its atmosphere, its numinous quality, the sense of the imminence of the sacred.

Making a Goddess Grotto

Today I am going to make a goddess grotto to honour the lady of the waters. If you want to do this, you will need:

- a plant pot

- soil

- stones

- moss

- shells

Put the soil in the pot, and arrange the stones and moss to form a hollow shape. Arrange the moss around this, and lastly add the shells. I have seen such grottos planted with bonsai trees and placed in gardens to make a beautiful permanent shrine.

---

164   www.schooloftheseasons.com, accessed 3.7.19.

THE HARVEST MONTH

• • • • •

The intense heat of the dog days has brought summer growth to its end, and the crops have ripened, ready for cutting. For the ancient Romans, August fell under the protection of Ceres, the grain goddess. The Anglo-Saxons called it the harvest month,[165] Ruthenia the sickle month, Moravia the cutting month, Bulgaria the fruit month, while in Denmark it was the corn month.[166]

For the farmers, this is the most important time of year, the harvest—the gathering of the golden wheat and the silver oats, the root crops and the fruit—when they warily scan the skies and sniff the wind for the scent of rain. In the past all the village would assemble to help, and itinerant labourers would be drafted in. Factory and school holidays were timed to coincide with the period so that more people would be free to assist. However, where once lines of reapers crossed the fields with scythes

---

165   Kightly, *The Perpetual Almanack of Folklore*.
166   Nilsson, *Primitive Time-Reckoning*.

and sickles, now there is a hum of machinery, often late into the night, as the farmer tries to beat the weather. Sheltering and nesting mice and rabbits dash from the fields, and the face of the countryside changes from golden fields to dusty stubble.

Until the Industrial Revolution in Britain, Europe, and the USA, most of the population worked on the land in a way that had changed little since ancient times. Even at the end of the nineteenth century, much of the grain was cut by hand, with the farmer and his labourers working side by side, mowing down the grain, then using sickles to gather it up into sheaves bound with straw, which were left to dry before being threshed with hand flails to separate the grain from the chaff. Labourers, both local and itinerant, would gather at the appointed day at a given farmer's field and begin work, fuelled with beer and cider and given dinner by the farmer's wife. In some places the workers elected a foreman to negotiate with the farmer for wages and terms, and he was addressed as "my lord," was the first to eat and drink, and imposed fines and punishments on workmen who broke his rules. His deputy was the Lady of the Harvest.

According to the Irish, Lughnasa (August 1) is the last day of summer and the start of autumn, and therefore the correct day on which to begin the harvest. To begin the harvest before Lughnasa was thought to be wrong and even shameful, and only a very needy man or a bad farmer would do so. The Scots would exclaim "It's lang to Lammas!" in jest when food was late to the table, reflecting the reality of scarcity when waiting for the harvest to begin. People looked forward to the day of first reaping when the hunger would be over. Everything that had been worked for was in reach.

Around the world the first of the harvest, called the first fruits, was offered to the gods, and only after giving the gods their portion were people free to enjoy the rest. In ancient Greece barley was offered as first fruits to Demeter and Persephone at the great temple of Eleusis, where underground granaries stored the produce. In some places the first fruits were believed to contain a spirit. Estonians would not eat bread from the new corn until they had bitten on iron to protect them from the spirit within. In Sutherland, Scotland, when the new potatoes were dug, the whole family had to taste them or the spirits in them would be offended and the potatoes would not keep.[167]

---

167   Frazer, *The Golden Bough*.

The idea that the grain contained a spirit persisted right into the nineteenth century in Britain and even longer in other places around the world, possibly dating back to the ancient belief that the gods of the grain are "sacrificed" and give their lives so that humankind might live, their flesh devoured in the form of bread or wheaten cakes. The followers of the Egyptian Osiris, for example, ate wheaten cakes marked with a cross that embodied the god, and today Christians eat the body of Christ in the form of bread wafers similarly marked with a cross. In Greece such deities were titled *soter*, which means "one who sows the seed" but which we often translate as "saviour."

This month is concerned with the rites at the beginning of the harvest, the offering of the first fruits, and the sacrifice of the gods of the grain so that we might eat. The Mother Goddess now becomes the Queen of the Harvest.

Early August

August 1: LUGHNASA/LAMMAS

August begins with Lughnasa, the modern Pagan celebration of the beginning of the harvest, the bounty of the earth, and the abundance of all that Mother Earth gives us. The modern festival has its roots in both the Irish Lughnasa and the Anglo-Saxon Lammas.

In England the first day of August was known as Lammas, probably from the Anglo-Saxon *hlaef-mass*, meaning "loaf-mass." The *Anglo-Saxon Chronicle* of 921 CE mentions it as "the feast of first fruits."[168] It marked the time when the first of the grain crop was gathered, ground in a mill, and baked into a loaf. This first loaf was offered up as part of the Christian Eucharist ritual. In Ireland, Wales, and England, Lammas was also the day for separating the lambs from the ewes, as it was thought to be luckier to do it on that day. Some even say that this is the origin of the word Lammas, as masses were said for the protection of the lambs on that day. Lammas appears just once in Old English poetry, in the calendar poem known as the *Menologium*. In the section for August, the poem describes Lammas and the coming of autumn:

---

168 King Alfred the Great (trans. Rev. James Ingram), *Anglo-Saxon Chronicle* (CreateSpace Independent Publishing Platform, 2016).

Everywhere August brings
to peoples of the earth Lammas Day.
So autumn comes…
Plenty is revealed, beautiful upon the earth.[169]

Many modern Pagans use the word Lughnasa for this festival. It is an Irish word that translates as "the games/assembly of Lugh," and the only time Lughnasa is mentioned in the Irish chronicles is in connection with the tribal assemblies held for the weeks each side of August 1. It is always stressed that the events were presided over by kings, with the one near Tara headed by the high king of Ireland and the others by local kings. The gatherings included the settling of tribal business matters, horse racing, athletic contests, martial contests, games, and even sometimes real fights for the right to rule and become king. They may have included rituals to ensure a plentiful harvest, though there is no record of this [170] One chronicle does relate, however, that for the old Pagans, holding the fair ensured corn, milk, and full nets, men like heroes, tender women, and good cheer in every household; if it were not held, there would be decay and immature kings.[171] Each assembly was held at the grave of a mythical woman who died clearing land for pasture, perhaps hinting at an earlier harvest celebration. The eleventh-century collection of Irish heroic tales known as the Ulster Cycle gives the four festivals of the old Irish year as Samhain, Imbolc, Beltane, and Bron Trogain, rather than Lughnasa. *Bron Trogain* means "the earth sorrows under its fruits"[172] and suggests the labour of the Earth Goddess in giving birth to the harvest.

Rite for Lughnasa

Lughnasa celebrates the fruition of the year's work with the start of the grain harvest, the weaning of calves and lambs, and the first apples, pears, bilberries, blackberries, and grapes. For your Lughnasa celebrations, gather a basket of assorted ripe fruit and lace it on the altar or decorate the ritual area with fruits and grain. They may be blessed during the course of the ritual and shared out at the end of the evening for

---

169 A *Little History of Lammas*, https://aclerkofoxford.blogspot.com/2017/08/a-little-history-of
-lammas.html?fbclid=IwAR01BbnyJQP1mKPZ8r34JOcV5vA-kHIrcHYerMdjU8lor4eekXm
-byLDtlI, accessed 5.11.19.

170 Hutton, *The Stations of the Sun*.

171 Roger Sherman Loomis, *Celtic Myth and Arthurian Romance* (Constable, 1995).

172 *The Táin: Translated from the Old Irish Epic Táin Bó Cúailnge*, trans. Ciaran Carson (Penguin
Classics, 2008).

luck, if you share the occasion with others. Have ready bread and wine. If you ritually planted a seed in a pot at Ostara, place the fruits of this harvest on the altar too. Place one brown and one yellow candle on the altar.

Say:

> *I come to celebrate the rite of Lughnasa as the time of the harvest is here.*
> *The fields are golden in the sun, with ears of ripe grain. It is a time of rejoicing,*
> *for we see the fruits of our labours. It is a time of sacrifice, when the Corn Lord*
> *gives of himself so that we may have our bread.*

Light the brown candle and say:

> *Come, Great Goddess, Mother Earth,*
> *Whose body supports us,*
> *Lady of life and lady of death,*
> *Be welcome here as Queen of the Harvest.*

Light the yellow candle and say:

> *Welcome, O Corn Lord,*
> *Golden-haired son of Mother Earth,*
> *Lover of the sovereign Goddess of the land,*
> *Sacred king who meets death at the queen's hand.*

Take up the bread and say:

> *The year did spin and spring came round*
> *While our dear Lord lay in the ground*
> *Till rain fell thick upon his bed*
> *And slowly then he raised his head*
> *And grew apace till Midsummer's Day*
> *When with his flowering bride he lay*
> *But the year does spin and he must die*
> *And as a seed must once more lie*
> *We hunt him down with sharpened sickle*
> *To pierce his heart and see blood trickle*
> *To flay his skin from off his bones*
> *And grind him up between two stones*

> *Our dying Lord has lost his head*
> *But with his death we have our bread.*

When you are ready, take up the wine and say:

> *The first of the harvest is always for the gods.*

Pour some wine on the earth or into a dish on the altar, which you can take outside later. Say:

> *The first of the harvest is for the gods.*

Hold the cup and say:

> *I drink and salute the Queen of the Harvest and ask that as I drink, I may know*
> *abundance. Blessed be.*

Drink. Take up the bread and say:

> *The first of the harvest is always for the gods.*

Put a piece on the ground or on a dish on the altar, which you can put outside later. Say:

> *I eat, but it is not bread I eat, but the body of the God, sprung from the womb of*
> *the earth, ripening under the sun. I thank the God for his sacrifice and ask that*
> *as I eat, I may know his compassion.*

Eat some bread.

Take some time for meditation and consider what you have received this year, what you have harvested. How have you used this? What do you need to sacrifice? When you have finished, say:

> *I give thanks to the Goddess of the earth.*
> *Lady, grant me your blessings. Be with me in my life*
> *as you once were to those of old. Grant me your wisdom. Blessed be!*
>
> *Great Lord and consort of the Goddess, grant blessing to this land.*
> *Be with me in my life as you once were to those of old.*
> *Grant me your blessing. Blessed be!*

I have celebrated the rite of Lughnasa. I have witnessed the harvesting of the grain and the sacrifice of the Corn Lord. I have honoured the Lady and her Lord. Let this ritual end with love and blessings. Blessed be.

Mid-August

The lush green growth of early summer is looking frowsy and starting to wear. Tree leaves are spotted with brown and nibbled by insects. The wildflowers are going over a little, though I can still find mugwort, lady's bedstraw, pink clover, and rosebay willowherb in the field margins. A few heads of meadowsweet linger on, while yarrow, nipplewort, yellow hawkweed, and blue skullcap begin to seed. Deadly nightshade and woody nightshade bloom in the hedgerows, and the white trumpet flowers of bindweed rampage throughout the hedges. I can hear the crickets in the grass rubbing their back legs together to make a chirping sound.

Birds such as jays, jackdaws, and finches are swooping down to feast on the gleanings in the harvested fields. The young birds are maturing, and there are pheasant chicks in the woods. The cuckoo is silent now, and the young birds, reared by strangers, will leave soon for warmer climes. This is the month when birds fall silent as they go into moult and gain their new coats to be ready for winter. The only sounds to be heard are a few notes from the goldfinch, though the robin recovers first, and by the end of the month most birds will be back in song.

This is the time of summer ripeness, and I have an abundance of fresh produce from the vegetable garden, including tomatoes, cucumbers, onions, baby carrots, broccoli, cabbage, beetroot, cauliflowers, fresh salad, courgettes, beans, and peppers. It's a time of harvesting and weeding, barbecues and picnics, or just sitting back with a cup of tea and watching all my hard work paying off.

It's a bountiful time for foragers in the fields and hedgerows too. The first blackberries are starting to ripen on the tips of the branches, and there are bilberries, a traditional food of Lughnasa in Ireland. Rosebay willowherb (*Chamerion augustifolium*) flowers pink in the field margins, and it is always a marker of Lughnasa for me. I collect the leaves for tea and the flowers to make a syrup to treat diarrhoea. Another plant I always associated with the festival is borage (*Borago officinalis*), with its bright blue flowers that taste like cucumber, which can be added to salads. The leaves make a tonic that was once thought to promote courage amongst warriors, so it is useful during the Lughnasa games. The yarrow (*Achillea millefolium*) is flowering, and I use it as a first-aid herbal external treatment for cuts and small wounds, as it helps to stop bleeding. The wild camomile, also called scented mayweed (*Matricaria discoidea*), which grows alongside them, makes a calming tea.

Mugwort (*Artemisia vulgaris*) is starting to flower in the hedgerows, as well as opportunistically growing all over my herb garden, so I'll be able to gather plenty. This is an important plant in the British magical tradition, known as the mother of all herbs and called "the oldest of plants…mighty against evil" in the Anglo Saxon *Lacnunga*, or Nine Herbs Prayer.[173] It is added to incense or made into incense sticks and oils, and it is used in a similar way to the way Native Americans use white sage to cleanse, protect, and bring in positive energies, as well as to engender prophetic dreams when it is used in the form of a leaf beneath the pillow or taken as a tea.[174]

. . . .

MUGWORT INCENSE BUNDLE

MUGWORT STEMS AND LEAVES, FRESH

COTTON STRING (IT IS IMPORTANT TO NOT USE
SYNTHETIC MATERIALS)

Gather your herbs and loosely bunch them. Begin wrapping fairly loosely with the string to allow drying; it also burns better when you come to use your bundle. Tie it off and trim any loose edges. Hang up to dry for around 8 weeks.

August 12: LAMMAS OLD STYLE

The season is starting to shift. August 12 is Lughnasa Old Style, when the dog days end, bringing to a close the cycle of growth. In past times it was the beginning of the hunting season. In ancient Rome it was the festival of Vertumnus, god of the autumn winds, a god who brings changes.

---

173   Lacnunga British Library MS. Harley 585, online at http://www.wyrtig.com/GardenFolklore/NineHerbsPrayer.htm, accessed 29.11.19.

174   Julie Brunton-Seal and Matthew Seal, *Hedgerow Medicine* (Ludlow: Merlin Unwin Books, 2008).

Lammas Wool Ritual

The apple harvest also begins in August. The God is honoured with lamb's wool or Lammas wool, a hot spiced drink of cider and ale with toast or pieces of apple floating in it. Each person takes out a piece and wishes good luck to everyone before eating it and passing the cup on.

. . . .

LAMMAS WOOL

4 LARGE COOKING APPLES

HONEY

NUTMEG

4 PINTS (9½ CUPS/2273 ML) ALE

Core the apples and fill the centres with honey. Sprinkle with nutmeg and bake in a slow oven (160°C/300°F) for 40 minutes in a deep baking tin. Remove from the oven and pour the ale over the apples. Heat gently on the hob for a few minutes, spooning the ale over the apples. Strain off the liquid and serve warm. The apples can be served separately.

August 15: MARYMAS

Marymas is the Scottish name for the feast of the Assumption of the Virgin Mary on August 15. In more northerly latitudes the harvest is later, and Marymas, rather than Lughnasa, marked the start of the harvest and was surrounded by its own customs, many of which survived well into the nineteenth century.[175] Mary seems to have absorbed the harvest deity attributes of earlier goddesses. The assumption of Mary into heaven supposedly took place at Ephesus, a famous sanctuary of the goddess Artemis, who was represented there by a many-breasted statue, symbolising the productive and nurturing powers of the earth.

The start of reaping was a day of celebration and ritual. Whole families would go to the fields dressed in their best clothes to hail the God of the Harvest. The father of each family would lay his hat on the ground and face the sun. Taking up his sickle, he would cut a handful of corn, which he passed three times around his head whilst

---

175 Carmichael, *Carmina Gadelica*.

chanting a reaping salutation.[176] The rest of the family would join in praising the God of the Harvest, who provided bread, corn, flocks, wool, health, strength, and prosperity.

The Lammas bannock (a traditional Scottish loaf) made from the new wheat would be dedicated to Mary, mother of God, and elaborate rituals surrounded its preparation. Early in the morning, people would go out into the fields to pluck the ears of the new grain. These would be spread over rocks to dry and then husked by hand. After being winnowed and ground in a quern, the flour was mixed into dough and kneaded in a sheepskin. It was traditional to cook the bannock over a fire of rowan, then the father of the family broke it into pieces to be shared with his wife and children. They would sing the *Ioch Mhoric Mhather*, or "Paean of Praise to the Holy Mother," whilst walking in a procession sunwise around the fire, with the father in the lead and the rest of the family following in order of seniority. The family then proceeded sunwise around the outside of their house, and sometimes around the fields and flocks, while reciting a protection charm.[177]

Ritual for the Queen of the Harvest

This is a celebration of the Goddess as Queen of the Harvest and Lady of the Herbs for my own garden. Fresh herbs or flowers are gathered and made into bouquets or wreaths to be blessed in the ritual and later hung up as a blessing and protection in the house. A loaf of bread is baked.

Go out into the garden. Put the bouquets and wreaths of herbs on the ground. Say:

> Goddess, Queen of the Harvest,
>
> I come to honour you.
>
> You have given of yourself
>
> You have sprouted the seed and nurtured the shoots
>
> You have opened the flowers and set the fruit
>
> I come to give you thanks.

Take up the bread. Proceed sunwise (clockwise) around the plot, laying pieces of bread on the ground around its borders, saying:

---

176   Ibid.

177   Carmichael, *Carmina Gadelica.*

I walk sunways around my dwelling

In the name of the queen

Who did protect me

Who will preserve me

In peace, in plenty, in righteousness of heart.

Take up the herbs and say:

Queen of the Harvest, bless these herbs which I have prepared in your honour.

They are the wind and the rain, the soil and the sun made manifest,

grown from your womb. Bless them, I pray you, as I honour you and

give you thanks. Let this ritual end with love and blessings. Blessed be.

Oatmeal Bannock

This is a very traditional type of bannock and can be cooked outside on a pan or griddle over a fire or barbecue.

1 CUP (¼ POUND/125 GRAMS) MEDIUM OATMEAL

PINCH OF SALT

PINCH OF BICARBONATE OF SODA

2 TEASPOONS MELTED BUTTER

¼ CUP WARM WATER

Mix the oatmeal, salt, and bicarbonate of soda in a basin and stir in the melted butter. Add enough of the water to make a stiff paste. Roll into a ball and knead on a breadboard lightly dusted with oatmeal. Roll the dough out to a ¼-inch thickness and trim to a circle using a plate. Sprinkle with a little oatmeal and cut into quarters. Cook on a warm, lightly oiled griddle until the edges begin to curl. Flip the bannock over and cook the other side. Can be served hot or cold.

August 19: BLESSING OF THE GRAPES

The grapes in the greenhouse are starting to ripen, though the ones outdoors won't be ready until the end of next month. In warmer climes the grapes may well be ready for picking. In Armenia, the blessing of the grapes takes place on the Sunday closest to the Assumption. No grapes are eaten until today, when they are taken to church to be blessed, then distributed to the churchgoers when they leave. Women named Mary have parties in vineyards or their homes because this is considered their name day. In ancient Rome this was the Vinalia, when Venus and Minerva were called upon as patrons of gardens and olive groves respectively, and gardeners were given a holiday. The priests plucked the year's first ripe grapes and asked Jupiter to protect the growing vines.

Though I make various country wines from flowers, herbs, and fruit, I also make grape wine, which has a very special place in mythology. The grape vine (*Vitis vinafera*) is closely associated with the sun. Its name is derived from *viere*, meaning "to twist," referring to its spiral growth and associated with the path of the sun and immortality alike. Far from being introduced into Britain only at the time of the Romans, the vine was well known and propagated before the Bronze Age. The use of wine in magical ceremonies is well known as it changes the consciousness of its imbibers, releasing inhibitions and perhaps allowing instincts greater reign, sometimes even releasing prophetic powers. Intoxication was once seen as a divine state, allowing worshippers to be possessed by their god. The grape harvest begins now, when we celebrate the powers of the Sun God, who has ripened the crops.

Blessing of the Grapes Ritual

I pour a libation of last year's vintage wine onto the roots of my vine, saying:

> *Lord of the sun, bless this new fruit of the vineyard, which you have*
> *ripened by heavenly dew, an abundance of rainfall, gentle breezes,*
> *and fair weather, and have given us to use with gratitude. Blessed be.*

Late August

Virgo is the largest of the zodiac constellations, visualised as a maiden holding an ear of wheat in one hand and a palm branch in the other. She represents the Harvest Goddess presiding over the sky at the time of the grain harvest. Most of the fertility and harvest goddesses of the Mediterranean and Middle East are in some way associated with Virgo, including Ishtar (Babylonian), Isis (Egyptian), Ceres (Roman), Demeter, Persephone, and Erigone (Greek), as well as the Christian Virgin Mary.

Virgo's brightest star, Spica ("ear of grain"), was associated with the Sumerian goddess Shala, entitled Lady of the Field. The heliacal rising of Virgo's third brightest star, Vindemiatrix ("wine gatherer"), similarly announced the time to pick the grapes. Aratus called it the "fruit-plucking herald."[178]

Virgo is only visible from spring to later summer, and many fertility goddesses have myths associating them with a lover or daughter who dies with the harvest and who returns in spring after the goddess has fetched them from the underworld—the seasonal disappearance and reappearance of Virgo may have been seen as a heavenly representation of this. For example, in the story of Ishtar and her consort, the vegetation god Tammuz, Tammuz died in autumn and was taken to the underworld. The grieving Ishtar travelled there to secure his release, but she was taken prisoner. During the period of her absence (i.e., while Virgo is absent from the sky), the earth was unfruitful and barren. When the gods saw this, they secured her release.

August 21: THE GODS OF THE STOREROOM

I've been harvesting, preserving, freezing, and making jam throughout this month, and my storeroom and shelves are starting to fill up. In the ancient world, the harvested grain and produce would be stored in underground vaults, where the temperature would help preserve them. On this day the Romans honoured Consus, the underworld god of stored grain. His altar was subterranean and only uncovered twice a year, once in December and once in August. His wife, Ops Consiva ("wealth from planting"), was honoured a few days later on August 25. Worshippers invoked her by touching the ground. Her altars were heaped with flowers, wine, and fresh-baked bread. They also honoured the *Penates*, or household deities, on a regular basis, as they guarded the *penus*, or storeroom, the innermost part of the house.[179] This seems like a good day to honour my household deities and ask their help in looking after the fruits of my harvest.

Honouring the Gods of the Storeroom Ritual

I am making garlands and using them to decorate the shrine of my household gods. I pour a little wine into a cup and put it into the shrine along with a cake and some incense, and say:

---

178 *Aratus: Phaenomena*, trans. A. W. Mair and G. R. Mair, Loeb Classical Library 129 (Cambridge, MA: Harvard University Press, 1921).

179 Celia E. Schutz, *Women's Religious Activity in the Roman Republic* (University of North Carolina Press, 2006).

I greet you, household gods
Gods of the full storeroom
Protect this harvest as I lay it aside
Bless this house with prosperity
Bless this house with contentment
Bless this house with survival
Let there always be enough
To share with those who need it
Bless that which sustains my body
For as long as I live.
Blessed be.

THE MONTH OF COMPLETION

September

• • • • •

September is a gleaming month of ripeness, when the red apples are ready for picking, branches bending under the weight of their fruit. We collect blackberries and elderberries in the hedgerows, hands sticky with purple juice. The grapes are ripening on the vine. Mushrooms sprout and fruit under the harvest moon. It's a busy month of picking and nutting, preserving and storing, making cider and brewing beer. For the Anglo-Saxons this was *haefest monath* (harvest month); in Gaelic *an sultuine*, the month of plenty[180]; in Welsh *medi*, the month of reaping.[181]

In the modern calendar, September is usually considered to be the first month of autumn, a word that comes from the Latin *autumnus*, which signified the passing of the year. In Germanic countries the season was usually referred to by the term "harvest" (Dutch *herfst*, German *Herbst*). In America it is often called "fall," probably

---

180   Kightly, *The Perpetual Almanack of Folklore.*
181   Nilsson, *Primitive Time-Reckoning.*

referring to the falling of the leaves at this time of year or a contraction of the Middle English expression "fall of the year."[182] The message is clear: the agricultural work of the year, and the harvest, is almost completed; the days are getting shorter; and the weather is getting colder. The year is in decline.

In modern times at the beginning of September, the last of the grain is usually cut, though of course this depends on the weather and latitude. The invention of farm machinery means that the harvest is often gathered in before the end of August, but in earlier times it extended into mid-September in England and even later in Scotland and northern areas. If the harvest had been good, the Harvest Home festival was one of thankfulness, relief, and great joy in all that had been accomplished, as well as looking forward to a period of rest and release. It was a time to celebrate with festivities and feasts and was marked with rituals and customs to ensure that the stored harvest would be safe and that life would return to the fields in the spring.

The last sheaf to be cut obviously marked the successful completion of the work, so it was treated with special attention. The corn spirit was considered "beheaded" when the last sheaf was cut. The sheaf, accompanied by its cutter and all the reapers, was usually taken to the farmer's house and made into a figure or doll. These corn dollies were then kept until the following year, when they were ploughed into the earth on Plough Monday (see January), which marked the new start of the agricultural year. In Wales the seed from it was mixed with the seed at planting time "in order to teach it to grow."[183]

After the harvest came the Harvest Supper. On a small farm, the feast would have been held in the kitchen or on larger farms in the specially decorated barn. It was viewed as a right by the workers and could be a costly business for the host. In Sussex it was traditional to serve caraway seed cake, which was served to the workers throughout the harvesting because it was believed that the seed not only provided strength for them but also increased their loyalty to their employer. After the meal there was usually dancing to the music of the fiddle, with a plentiful supply of beer and tobacco. Songs were sung and the farmer was toasted.

The church disapproved of the overtly Pagan and raucous nature of the harvest celebrations. Many churches have harvest thanksgiving celebrations now, but these mostly date from Victorian times. In 1843 the Reverend R. S. Hawker decided to

182   https://www.etymonline.com/word/harvest, accessed 9.8.19.
183   Owen, *Welsh Folk Customs.*

have a special service in his Morwenstow, Cornwall, parish. The idea spread, and it became the custom to decorate churches with fruit, vegetables, and flowers brought in from gardens (which are later distributed to the poor or used to raise funds) and to sing special hymns written for the occasion, such as "We plough the fields and scatter."

In the northern hemisphere, the month of September contains the autumn equinox. Afterwards the hours of darkness progressively become greater than the hours of light, with dawn getting later and sunset getting earlier each day—a process that will continue until the winter solstice. The sun is in decline on its southward course.

Though the autumn equinox can be celebrated as a simple Harvest Home festival, it contains a much deeper mystery, one that speaks to the central core of our Pagan teachings. The festivals of the year teach us about the great cosmic pattern, showing us the ebb and flow of energy in the manifest world and the spiritual truths that underlie them. At the autumn equinox, we experience the death that comes before resurrection—the death of the year that comes before its rebirth in spring, the physical death that comes before rebirth into another life, and the spiritual death and rebirth that comes with initiation. These ideas were at the core of the ancient Rites of Eleusis held at the autumn equinox in Greece.[184]

The central myth that underlay the mysteries was that of the grain goddess Demeter and her daughter, Persephone, who was stolen away to the underworld at the decline of the year, only to return in spring. According to the story, the mysteries were instituted after Demeter, searching for her missing child, rested at the house of Celeus, king of Eleusis. There she learned from Hecate that Persephone had been abducted by the god of the underworld, Hades, and was held prisoner in his chthonic realm. Demeter asked the people of Eleusis to build a temple for her, then she retreated into it and remained there, brooding on her loss. The following year no crops grew. The trees refused to yield fruit, and the buds withered on the vine. An endless winter descended on the earth. Zeus realised that the whole of creation was doomed unless Demeter lifted her curse, so he sent Hermes into the underworld to fetch her. However, Hades was unwilling to lose his lovely bride and cunningly offered her a sweet pomegranate as she readied herself to leave. He knew full well that anyone who eats the fruit of the underworld is doomed to remain there. Thus it

---

184 Cicero, *Laws* II, xiv, 36.

fell that though Persephone was allowed to visit her mother, she was now bound to return. Persephone could spend two-thirds of the year with Demeter, but the remaining third of the year must be spent with her husband, Hades. With Persephone's return, spring came and the frozen buds blossomed; the earth became green and fertile once more. But when Persephone goes back to the underworld, Demeter decrees that barren winter shall cover the earth. At Eleusis ("advent"), Demeter taught the human Triptolemus the principles of agriculture, which he taught others in turn, and this was how humankind learned how to farm.

The core message of the rites was rebirth after death, as symbolised by the cycle of vegetation. For two thousand years, large crowds of worshippers made the pilgrimage to the rites of Eleusis from all over Greece, and later from all over the Roman Empire. Initiation was open to all—Greeks and foreigners, men and women, freemen and slaves—on the condition that they had not committed the sin of murder.

In the coven we acknowledge that at the autumn equinox, light and darkness stand in balance once more, but the darkness is gaining, day by day, as we move towards winter. We watch the dying fire of the sun and lament the fallen God of the Grain as he travels to the land of the west. The expansive, active part of the year is over, and it is time to turn inwards. Each festival of the year, in its eternal spiral, can be viewed as an initiation into a new mode of consciousness. At the autumn equinox we experience the mystery of the death of the God who enters the underworld, where he will rule as the Lord of the Dead until his rebirth at Yule. Through that death comes transformation, regeneration, and rebirth. The sun's power is waning, but deprived of the external light, we encounter inner illumination. For this is the mystery you must know: for every beginning there is an end; for every end, a beginning. The God's tomb is but the earth-womb of the Mother, and as the wheel turns, the Lord of Death will return to us as the Lord of Life.

Early September

As we slip gently into autumn, we look to finish off the business of summer and prepare for winter, knowing that from the equinox, the darkness and cold will grow. Even at the beginning of September there is a nip in the morning air, and the luscious blooms of summer are starting to go to seed.

This is the time of abundance for me, with a profusion of fresh garden produce and foraged food available. I'm harvesting main crop potatoes, carrots, swedes, turnips, and beetroot, as well as cauliflowers, broccoli, beans, the last of the fresh salads, tomatoes, bell peppers, apples, and pears. This is one of my favourite months for foraging, too, and the hedgerows are bountiful with hazelnuts and sweet chestnuts, berries such as rosehips, elderberries, blackberries, rowan, and hawthorn berries, and mushrooms spring up in the woods and meadows. There are still fresh herbs around, and I preserve them by hanging them in bunches in a well-ventilated space to dry or by freezing them in water in ice cube trays (a cube can then be dropped into a soup or a stew). This is a very busy month. The harvest must be gathered in before the first frosts, and food must be prepared, stored, and preserved for the dead time of winter to come, with freezing, drying, canning, making jam and chutney, brewing wines, beers, and apple and pear brandy, and making my yearly batch of cider vinegar.

Naturally, I also use September's bounty for making herb simples like blackberry vinegar and elderberry glycerite, as well as mulled hedgerow punch.

. . . .

Mulled Hedgerow Punch

3 CUPS MIXED AUTUMN BERRIES (SUCH AS BLACKBERRIES, ELDERBERRIES, AND HAWTHORN BERRIES)

2 LITRES APPLE JUICE

2 STAR ANISE

2 CINNAMON STICKS

3 CLOVES

3 CENTIMETRES FRESH GINGER, GRATED

Put all the ingredients into a pan, bring to a boil, turn down the heat, and simmer for 20 minutes. Strain into mugs and serve hot. Sweeten with honey, if desired.

. . . .

BLACKBERRY VINEGAR

This is very good for coughs, so take a teaspoon whenever you feel the need. Quantities can easily be increased, allowing 1 pound blackberries to 1 pint vinegar.

2 POUNDS BLACKBERRIES (*RUBUS* SPP.)

2 PINTS MALT VINEGAR

Place the washed blackberries in a bowl and break them up slightly with a wooden spoon. Pour the malt vinegar on top and cover the bowl with a cloth. Let stand for 3–4 days, stirring occasionally. Transfer to a saucepan and boil for 10 minutes. Cool, strain, and bottle the resulting liquid.

. . . .

ELDERBERRY GLYCERITE

The same method can be used to make elderberry vinegar. Many people find this very good for colds. Drink a tablespoon of blackberry or elderberry vinegar in hot water with a little honey.

RIPE ELDERBERRIES (*SAMBUCUS NIGRA*)

VEGETABLE GLYCERINE (FOOD GRADE)

Using a fork, strip the berries from the stem. To make a glycerite, put the berries into a clean jar and pour on slightly warmed glycerine until they are completely covered. Seal and keep in a warm place for 2–4 weeks, shaking daily. Strain through muslin and store in a dark bottle in a cool place for up to 2 years. Take a spoonful four times a day for colds and flu.

September 1: AUTUMN SOWING

The end of one harvest or cycle is the beginning of another. Soon the farmers will be making their autumn sowings in the grain fields. The Greek Orthodox Church celebrates New Year on September 1. The culmination and completion of each year comes with the harvest, so the autumn sowing of the seeds was considered New Year. The church prays for good weather, seasonable rains, and an abundance of the fruits of the earth. Greek farmers take seeds to church to be blessed before the autumn sowing, and people make wreaths of greenery and fruit to represent abundance in the coming year. Before dawn the old wreaths are thrown in the sea and the new ones dipped in the water for luck. When the wreaths are hung up, the sowing begins.

· · · · · · · · · · · · · · · · · ·
Autumn Wreath Making

To mark the season, I'm making an autumn wreath. For this you will need:

WIRE WREATH FRAME

FLORIST'S WIRE

SEASONAL GREENERY AND HARD BERRIES
SUCH AS HAWTHORN AND ROSEHIP

Wreaths are really easy to make. Simply start adding your leaves to the wire frame, secured by twisted florist's wire, gradually working your way around the frame until you are back where you started. Put plenty of leaves on; you don't want your wreath to look sparse. Now wire on the sprigs of berries where you would like them. You can put this on your altar or hang it on your door. The leaves represent the season that is passing away; the berries, as they contain seeds, are the promise of what is to come.

September 2: Hop Harvesting

In Kent, Herefordshire, Shropshire, and parts of Worcestershire, England, hops were a vital crop. Picking was done by seasonal workers, generally people who worked in other industries during the rest of the year and made a kind of family holiday of it. Though the work was extremely hard, many remembered the experience fondly. As with other harvests, there were peculiar customs related to hop picking such as "cribbing," when male strangers were seized by the women and thrown into the cribs, the wooden frames that contained the picked hops. In order to be released, he would have to kiss all the women present. Unmarried female pickers were also cribbed at the end of the season. A king and queen of the pickers were chosen, with the man wearing women's clothing and the woman, male clothing. Gaily bedecked with ribbons and sprays of hops, they were led in procession by the head pole-puller in front of the last load. In 1956 the *Worcester Journal* reported:

> On some farms, the last day of picking had its age-old ceremony of hoisting the last and best pole of hops, saved specially for the occasion.

· · · · ·

The pullers' caps and hats were decorated with rosettes, dahlias, asters and sprays of hops. Then a procession was formed, making its way to the farmhouse, headed by the busheller beading his metal measure to a drum, and followed by the pole-pullers, sack-holders and the pickers. At the farmhouse a feast was prepared and the farmer and his wife were toasted.[185]

Unfortunately, the growing of hops in the UK has declined as a consequence of cheaper imports and the cost of harvesting, and the traditional customs have passed away into history. However, there are still several festivals that celebrate the hop harvest. On the first Saturday of September at Canterbury Cathedral there is a procession around and into the cathedral led by the Hop Queen in a hop bower, followed by country dancers and Morris men with two hooden horses.

BEER RECIPE

YEAST

2 PINTS HOPS

2 GALLONS WATER

1 POUND SUGAR

1 POUND MALT

Activate the yeast according to the instructions on the packet. Put the hops in a large pan and add just enough of the 2 gallons of water to cover. Boil for 15 minutes, then strain the liquid into a brewing bin. Add the sugar and malt and stir to dissolve. Add the rest of the water. When the mixture has cooled to 20°C, add the yeast, cover, and stand for 5 days. Bottle in screw-topped bottles and leave for 7 days before drinking.

---

185   https://www.britishnewspaperarchive.co.uk/home/newspapertitles, accessed 12.10.19

Mid-September

Most plants are now completing their life cycle, and this is my time for collecting seeds. Some are edible, like poppy, nigella, sunflower, and pumpkin. Others, like vegetable and annual flower seeds, I collect to sow next spring. They have to be collected on a dry day as soon as the seed heads have ripened (they usually change colour to brown or black), but before they open and drop the seeds. I put them in paper bags and hang them up in the kitchen until the seeds drop out, though some pods have to be crushed to encourage this. Afterwards, they are put in small paper envelopes, labelled, and stored in an airtight container.

CARAWAY SEED CAKE

This is a traditional seed cake that was often served at harvest festival suppers, partly because caraway was thought to be a charm to faithfulness and loyalty, and the farmer wanted to keep his workers!

- 110 GRAMS BUTTER
- 170 GRAMS CASTOR SUGAR
- 3 EGGS
- 2 TABLESPOONS COLD MILK
- 225 GRAMS PLAIN FLOUR
- 1 TEASPOON BAKING POWDER
- 50 GRAMS GROUND ALMONDS
- 1 TEASPOON CARAWAY SEEDS

Cream the butter and sugar together. In a separate bowl, whisk the eggs with the milk, and gradually add this to the creamed butter and sugar. Fold in the flour and baking powder, then add the ground almonds and caraway seeds. Bake in a loaf tin lined with baking parchment for an hour at 160°C/325°F/gas mark 3.

September 14: ROOD DAY

Rood Day is said to commemorate the rescue of the True Cross by Emperor Heraclius of Constantinople in 614. There were several proverbs referring to the fact this is the time of deer mating: "If the hart and the hind meet dry and part dry on Rood Day fair, for six weeks of rain there'll be no mair."[186]

On this day in 1752 Britain abandoned the Julian calendar of Julius Caesar and adopted the Gregorian calendar, meaning that some days had to be dropped to fall into alignment with the new calendar. It meant that they went to bed on September 2 and woke up on September 14, having "lost" eleven days. Some people really thought that they had been deprived of eleven days of their lives, and there were riots in the streets. It is the reason that many of the feast days and calendar customs are elevens days adrift.

Late September

As the sun nominally moves out of the harvest period of Virgo, it enters the sign of Libra, the scales, where the grain is weighed and measured. The scales of Libra are an obvious symbol of balance and harmony and, by logical extension, justice. In Greek myth they belonged to Dike Astraea ("star maiden"), the goddess who upheld natural law. Astraea was a daughter of Zeus and Themis, a personification of justice. As mankind became wicked, she was the last immortal to leave Earth, taking her place in the constellation Virgo, while the scales of justice she carried became the constellation Libra.

September 21: ST. MATTHEW'S DAY

The church took over the autumn equinox for St. Matthew, patron saint of tax collectors and bankers, and fixed this to September 21. In the English Midlands, St. Matthew's Day is viewed as the first of three windy days, also called "windy days of the barley harvest." One of the many traditional English sayings associated with the day is:

---

186 "Mair" is Scots dialect for "more."

St. Mathee, shut up the Bee;

St. Mattho, take thy hopper and sow;

St. Mathy, all the year goes by

St. Matthie sends sap into the tree.[187]

This indicates that it is time to shut up the bee hives and make the autumn sowing of seeds.

The Autumn Equinox

The scales of Libra are a perfect symbol of the autumn equinox,[188] when day and night stand at equal length, a point of balance that we acknowledge before the scales tip and the hours of darkness start to outweigh the hours of light. As we withdraw from our outdoor activities and turn towards the warmth of the hearth fire in winter, it is time for us to go deep within, to pursue our own spiritual transformation.

The autumn equinox marks the culmination of all the work of the agricultural cycle. It is a time of plenty and celebration as we give thanks to the gods for all they have given us during the year, but it is also a time of sacrifice—the bright God of the Grain has made his sacrifice so that we may eat. He departs from us to go into the underworld (the seed is returned to the earth in the autumn), where he will rule as the Lord of the Dead until Yule. This riddle of death, transformation, and rebirth is the deepest mystery of our teaching.

In the coven our equinox ritual is threefold. In the daylight we go to the wheat field to thank the agricultural land that gives us our bread. We make offerings of wine, bread, and flowers, and the Year King makes his sacrifice (a drop of blood).[189] We circle back inwards to the garden, where seeds ripen, ready to grow next year, and light the brazier and make similar offerings in thanks for what this domestic land has provided. Lastly, we withdraw to the hearth, the centre of domestic and spiritual nourishment, where we offer milk and honey to the household deities because it is by the hearth that we will spend much of the winter.

---

187   Blackburn and Holford-Strevens, *The Oxford Companion to the Year.*

188   Because of precession, Libra no longer rises on the ecliptic at the equinox.

189   The Year King is the man chosen annually to be our sacred king.

Autumn Equinox Ritual

The following is a ritual you can do alone or with friends. The altar is decorated with autumn fruits. You will need a single ear of wheat. Place this on a dish, under a cloth. The revealing of this was the central mystery of the Rites of Eleusis and speaks of the mystery of life, death, and rebirth. We like to make a corn dolly, which is placed on the altar and which will play its part in further rituals. You will also need a yellow candle, a brown candle, and some bread and wine.

Say:

> The year ebbs and lengthening shadows cloak the land
>
> Cooling the rich earth and the ripened seeds
>
> As day and night stand equal
>
> And the year falls into darkness
>
> As the wheel turns.

Light the brown candle and say:

> I honour thee, golden-haired Goddess, Queen of the Harvest
>
> In your right hand the sickle and in your left, the glorious fruits.

Light the yellow candle and say:

> I honour thee, O fallen God of the Corn, King of the Harvest
>
> Marked for sacrifice as the Goddess raises high her sickle
>
> And sends you to the land of the west, which greets you as its lord
>
> As the wheel turns.

Think about what you have harvested this year and what you have learned. Say:

> I give thanks to the Lord and Lady for my own harvest this year:
>
> The things that I have achieved—actions grown from the seeds of my thoughts.

Uncover the ear of wheat:

> This is the final mystery that we must know:
>
> For every beginning there is an end; for every end, a beginning
>
> The tomb is but the earth-womb of the Mother
>
> And the Lord of Death will return to us as the Son of Light
>
> As the wheel turns.

Reflect on the cycles of life, death, and rebirth.

Take up the wine and place your hand over it to bless it with the words:

We have gathered the grapes

And pressed the wine

We give thanks for its gift

And as we drink, we ask the gods

To bless us with joy and wisdom. Blessed be.

Drink, then take up the bread and place your hand over it in blessing. Say:

We have gathered in the harvest

And give thanks to the Goddess for bearing it

We give thanks to the God whose sacrifice means that we may eat.

Blessed be.

Reflect on this for a while, and when you are ready to finish, say:

The Lord and Lady have given us their blessings and we have given thanks.

May this ritual end with love and blessings. Blessed be.

Corn Dolly

Take five hollow straws about 8 inches (20 cm) long and tie them in the middle. Fold the bunch in half and tie again to make the head. Take four more straws about 4 inches (10 cm) long and tie them together a short distance from the ends; these will form the arms of the figure. Slot this into the straws that form the body. Tie the ends of the longer straws to make the legs. This should give you a figure about 3 inches (7.5 cm) tall.

September 29: MICHAELMAS

In Christian times Michaelmas (the Feast of Michael and All Angels) absorbed some of the traditional celebrations of the autumn equinox. It falls on September 29 and is one of the legal quarter days in England, the others being Lady Day (March 25), Midsummer (June 24), and Christmas (December 25), which approximate to the solstices and equinoxes. St. Michael was one of the archangels who fought against the devil and his minions, and he is therefore seen as a protector against the forces of darkness and has been honoured as such for centuries. This perhaps makes him a fitting guardian against the dark winter days, when the forces of negativity, cold, bane, and death are stronger. Most of his churches are built on high places—often over Pagan sites—such as Mont St. Michel in Brittany, the church on the Tor at Glastonbury, and the church on the tumulus at Carnac.

It used to be said that harvest had to be completed by Michaelmas. Consequently, it was the date on which agricultural employment contracts ended. Every year on the day after Michaelmas, farm workers would travel to the hirings at the nearest market town to find new employment for the following year, carrying the implements of their particular trade. Thus domestic workers carried a mop, carters carried a whip, shepherds a crook, and so on. It was also the time for rented farms and lands to change hands.

Traditionally a goose, fed on the stubble from the fields after the harvest, was eaten on St. Michael's Day. More than 20,000 geese from the Lincolnshire Fens would be sold to provide the traditional Michaelmas dish. An old rhyme says: "Whosoever eats goose on Michaelmas Day/Shall never lack money his debts to pay." After the meal the breastbones were examined, and if they were brown, the winter would be mild, but if they were blue or whitish, the winter would be severe. Breaking the wishbone today and making a wish derives from this custom. The goose is an important bird in European folklore. Wild geese are associated with the sun and sun gods; large flocks pass over in the spring, and the bird was therefore connected with the lengthening of the days. In autumn the birds migrate again, and their departure signifies the onset of winter.

Altar Shrine Light

In our tradition the God is not invoked between the autumn equinox and Yule, as during that time he rules the underworld as the Lord of Death, and we do not summon death. Instead, we remember him with a night light on the altar in a red jar, and this is the day I light it for the first time. It will be burned each night until the winter solstice, when the Lord of Light is reborn.

THE EMBER MONTH

October

. . . . .

October is the glowing month that stands between the end of growth and the barrenness of winter, when Mother Nature puts on a final glorious show and the trees are a fiery blaze of leaves, the last burning embers of the autumn. The year is aging, growing tired and mellow. Earth has given us all she has, and we have harvested her bounty. Now, after the autumn sowing, it is time to feed the land and let it rest.

An old Kentish proverb says "There are always nineteen fine days in October," and though there is now a crispness in the air as the days become visibly shorter, October weather is often still fine and fairly warm here. However, the longer, cooler nights mean the fields and hedgerows are shrouded in mist most mornings, making the trailing gossamer webs of spiders pearly white in the hedgerows. As children we collected them in a hoop of twigs to make "magic mirrors" in order to see the future.

The rooks circle and ride the rough autumn winds over the brown ploughed fields, while pheasants scavenge in the stubble. Smoke plumes from house chimneys and drifts from the bonfires smouldering in cleared gardens and vegetable plots, making bonfire smoke the scent of this month. The oak trees drop their acorns, and the squirrels are busy collecting nuts to bury to keep them through the winter. The natural world prepares itself for the coming season with a flurry of activity and seasonal migrations. In the parklands, the stags are belling, calling out during the rutting season as they compete for mates, fighting with a rattling clash of horns. Most of the insects have disappeared now, and the birds who relied on them for food are getting ready to fly south, gathering in flocks, rows of them perching on the telegraph wires outside my office window.

In October, as the world descends into the dark half of the year, Mother Earth draws her energy back into her womb to protect the sleeping seeds (and the dead) that lie within it, deep in the earth. It was for this reason the ancients made offerings and poured libations into caves and chasms at this time of year, to nurture the regenerative underworld. In Rome the Mundus, the passageway to the underworld—the domain of Ceres, the mother of vegetation—was opened, and fruits were placed in the pit.[190] As the Mysteries of Eleusis drew to a close in Greece, two unstable round vessels were taken into the sacred place, one in the east, one in the west, and together they were overturned to pour a libation to a cleft in the earth.[191] They also celebrated the Thesmophoria—a three-day women's festival of Demeter, goddess of agriculture, and her daughter Persephone, goddess of spring, who spends winter in the underworld—when sacrifices of pigs, dough cakes, and branches of pine trees were deposited into the sacred caverns of Demeter to be devoured by the sacred serpents there. At the next year's festival, the decayed remains were retrieved and placed on the altar before being sowed with the seed-corn to ensure an abundant harvest.[192] The name of the festival comes from *thesmoi*, meaning "laws," and *phoria*, meaning "carrying" in the sense of the Goddess as "law-bearer," the one who maintained the natural balance, which constitutes the divine law of the gods.[193]

---

190   W. Warde Fowler, "Mundus Patet," *Journal of Roman Studies* 2 (1912) online at
         http://penelope.uchicago.edu/Thayer/E/Journals/JRS/2/Mundus*.html, accessed 4.10.19.
191   Lawrence Durdin-Robertson, "Juno Covella," *Perpetual Calendar of the Fellowship of Isis*,
         www.fellowshipofisis.com, accessed 10.9.19
192   Fowler, "Mundus Patet."
193   Anne Baring, Jules Cashford, et al., *The Myth of the Goddess: Evolution of an Image* (London:
         Penguin, 1993).

The old myths show us a world in which everything is alive and connected by the great matrix of nature, and they demonstrate that the relationship between us and the gods, between us and Mother Earth, should be a reciprocal one. This was the covenant the old Pagan religions recognised—a sacred agreement to maintain the balance. This is a covenant that the modern world has broken,[194] where Mother Earth is seen as a commodity that is raped and pillaged for her gifts. We should take heed because the old myths also tell us what happens when the covenant is destroyed and balance is lost: the powers of chaos gain ascendancy. Nearly every creation myth in the world speaks of a primal chaos, a formless void that existed before the sun was set spinning on its course, bringing the light, regularised time and the seasons that allow life to exist, a chaos that always strives to return. Myths and folklore tell us that each winter, as the sun weakens and seems about to die, the powers of chaos try to creep out of the underworld until they are sent scurrying back by the increasing light of the spring sun, but there are also stories of the final triumph of chaos, of Ragnarök[195] and the Apocalypse, when the scales tip too far for the balance to be restored. With the climate crisis, the impoverishment of soil through modern farming methods, and the mass destruction and pollution of habitats causing mass extinctions, we are at that tipping point.

This touches on the core purpose of the witch: maintaining balance. In tribal and old village societies, whenever conflict, disorder, and imbalance manifested, the village wise woman, cunning man, or shaman would be consulted to discover how the covenant with the gods/Mother Nature had been damaged and what must be done to put it right. Witches are healers, not just of human bodies but of cosmic harmony. In late September the sun moved out of the harvest sign of Virgo and entered the constellation of Libra, the scales where the grain is weighed and where we spend most of October. But there is more to the scales of Libra than assessing crops. They are a symbol of cosmic balance and weigh the souls of those who transgress against that balance.

The heavenly scales belong to the goddesses of justice whose festivals fall under Libra. In Greece she was Themis, who personified *themis*, the natural law that comes from the gods, as opposed to *nomoi*, the laws created by men.[196] She was represented

---

194   Alex Evans, *The Myth Gap* (London: Penguin Random House, 2017).

195   This myth does say that two humans will repopulate the world after the destruction.

196   John Lewis, *Early Greek Lawgivers* (Bristol Classical Press, 2007).

with scales in one hand and a sword or cornucopia in the other. One of her daughters was Dike Astraea ("star maiden"). The Romans had the goddess Justitia ("justice") similarly portrayed, and also revered Fides (Christianised as St. Faith), goddess of trust and good faith, honour, contractual obligations, and the mutual duty between two parties. The scales of Justice are a familiar symbol, and statues of the goddess of justice sit outside many law courts such as the Old Bailey in London, but really the justice of these goddesses is a matter of cosmic balance.

This is an idea exemplified by Maat, the Egyptian deity of justice, divine order, and universal harmony, who is usually pictured wearing an ostrich feather and holding the ankh, or key of life. Her law governed all the worlds, and even the gods had to obey it. She was present before the dawn of creation, when Atum, the creator, wishing that his heart might live, breathed in the essence of Maat, and everything began. It was the pharaoh's duty to maintain the rule of Maat, and Egyptian social organisation was meant to be a reflection of the divine and natural order; if the pattern should be transgressed against, then chaos and its consequences would follow. The pharaoh carried an effigy of the seated Maat as a sign that he represented her, while judges wore a lapis lazuli emblem of her on their breasts. Egyptians were urged to "speak Maat, do Maat" and to live "by Maat, in Maat, and for Maat."[197] The goddess is right action embodied.

At death, the human soul was conducted by Thoth, god of wisdom, into the Hall of Double Justice and the presence of Osiris, lord of the dead, together with the forty-two assessors or judges of Maat, who passed final judgement on the soul. The heart, which represented the person's essence, was weighed in the scales of Justice against the feather of Maat. If the person had led a good life, then the scales would balance perfectly. A crime against the rule of Maat was an offence that disturbed cosmic harmony as documented in the forty-two laws, which included cruelty to animals and polluting the environment.[198] The feather of Maat was light, and the heart that was weighed against it must belong to one who has trodden lightly on the earth.

Maat represents balance in all its aspects, the expression of the natural, immutable law of the universe that is held in equilibrium.

197 E. A. Wallis Budge, *The Gods of the Egyptians: Studies in Egyptian Mythology* (New York: Dover Publications, 1969, 1904).

198 Evelyn Rossiter (commentaries), *The Book of the Dead* (Liber SA: Fribourg, 1979).

When the work of the growing year is done and we move into the reflective period of winter, it is time to take stock and examine what it is in our lives, and in the world around us, that has slipped out of balance, and strive to return it to equilibrium. This is when we make atonement, a word that has come to signify making reparation for a wrong, but which originally meant at-one-ment, the state of being at one, in harmony, with the world and other people and, moreover, with the gods. Where we have strayed, we must bring ourselves back to the path.

Early October

Tradition has it that at the beginning of October swallows begin their seasonal migration from Britain, taking all the luck and blessings of the summer with them. Like the animals and birds, it is time for me to make preparations for the winter. The frosts will be here soon. Putting the garden to bed for the year always feels slightly sad, but life is a cycle and it will be renewed in the spring, so this is not an ending, just needful preparation for next year.

I cut my withered annual plants, put them on the compost heap, and collect the last of the seeds from my flowers. It will soon be too cold for growth in the greenhouse, so I'm collecting the last of the tomatoes, bell peppers, chillies, and cucumbers. This is chutney-making time, when the last of everything goes into the jam pan.

With everything removed, I clean and tidy the greenhouse so all the pots of frost-tender flowers and herbs can go inside for winter. The tools are cleaned and put away in the shed. One of the last things is to manure the vegetable plot. A traditional English proverb states: "In October dung your field/And your land its wealth will yield." Any gardener or farmer knows that if you want to get something out, you have to put something in, which is all the gods ask of us.

However, there is plenty left to forage. Now that the leaves are dying back, it is easier to find oak moss (*Evernia prunastri*), a grey-green curly lichen that grows on oak trees. I gather it for its musky forest scent in incense making and the fact that it acts as a fixative, giving perfume a longer life. I dry it and use it in potpourris and loose incense connected with the element of earth or nature magic, and to honour the wild god of the woodlands.

The sloes are black in the hedgerows—the small, very sour fruits of the black-thorn tree (*Prunus spinosa*). They only sweeten after the first frosts, but according to folklore, they have to be picked before November 11, when the blackthorn sprites curse them, just as blackberries must be picked before Michaelmas, echoing the old idea that any food left in the earth now belongs to the spirits of the land. Sloes make the most wonderful liqueur.

I always look forward to finding horse chestnuts (*Aesculus hippocastanum*) in autumn, the shiny brown conkers once beloved by schoolchildren for their games, but they are so much more useful than that. The tree is so named because the nuts used to be made into liniments to treat muscle sprains in horses. They contain aescin, a compound that has anti-inflammatory properties equally effective for human sprains and bruises, as well as treating varicose veins, spider veins, haemorrhoids, and cellulite. NB: Horse chestnuts are slightly toxic and must not be eaten.

The dew-spangled haws are glistening like rubies in the hedgerows. These are the small oval fruits of the hawthorn tree (*Crataegus monogyna*). The same plant that gave us the frothy white May blossoms at the start of summer now gives us an autumn bounty. The taste of the raw berries is pretty disappointing, but they can be used to make delicious wines, jellies, liqueurs, tinctures, and ketchups.

Roses all bear edible fruits called hips, but I collect the crimson berries of the wild roses (*Rosa canina*). Rosehips can be made into wine, jellies, liqueurs, tinctures, and syrups, added to garlands, wreaths, and decorations, or dried and used for rosehip tea, potpourri, and natural beads for jewellery making. During World War II, hard-pressed British housewives even used them as a substitute for raisins when baking.

END-OF-SEASON CHUTNEY

1 TEASPOON PEPPERCORNS

½ TEASPOON MUSTARD SEEDS

SMALL MUSLIN BAG

3 RED PEPPERS

3 GREEN PEPPERS

450 GRAMS TOMATOES, QUARTERED

350 GRAMS ONIONS, CHOPPED

450 GRAMS APPLES, PEELED, CHOPPED, AND CORED

225 GRAMS DEMERARA SUGAR

1 TEASPOON ALLSPICE

425 MILLILITRES MALT VINEGAR

Tie the peppercorns and mustard seeds in a muslin bag. Chop the peppers finely. Combine all the ingredients in a pan, bring to boil, and simmer for around 1½ hours until soft and pulpy. The mixture should reduce considerably by the end of cooking. Remove the spice bag. Turn into clean, warm jars.

. . . . . .

SLOE GIN

8 OUNCES SLOES

4 OUNCES SUGAR

14 FLUID OUNCES GIN

I wait until the first frost before gathering the berries, but if you want to be sure of getting some, you can pick them as soon as they ripen. Remove the stalks and wash the fruit. Either prick the sloes or put them into the freezer for 24 hours. Put them into a screw-top jar (they should take up no more than half the space), layering with the sugar. Pour in the gin, put on the lid, and shake to dissolve the sugar. You can strain and bottle after 3 months, but it is much better if you leave the fruit in for at least 6 months. If you can, leave it to mature at least a year before drinking. You can substitute whiskey, vodka, or brandy for gin.

. . . . .

SLIDER

Don't throw the berries you strain from your sloe gin away—use them to make slider. Put them in a jar and cover them with still hard cider. Leave this for 6 weeks, strain, and drink.

· · · · · · · · · · · · · · · ·

HORSE CHESTNUT SALVE

Use the salve on affected areas such as varicose veins, spider veins, haemorrhoids, and cellulite once or twice a day.

HORSE CHESTNUTS

VEGETABLE OIL (OLIVE, SUNFLOWER, ETC.)

BEESWAX

HORSE CHESTNUT TINCTURE (OPTIONAL)

First peel the nuts, then put them into a coffee grinder and powder them up as much as possible. Put powdered/chopped nuts into a double boiler and just cover them in vegetable oil. Put this on the stove over a low heat for around 2 hours, making sure the water in the double boiler does not boil away. You don't want the nut/oil mixture to boil or simmer, just be gently warmed for the duration. Remove from the heat and allow the oil to cool before straining through a coffee filter. Now take the oil and gently warm it through again over a low heat and add beeswax. How much wax you add depends on how runny or set you want your salve to be. I use about 20 grams beeswax per 100 millilitres of oil, but you may like to vary this. There is no right or wrong way, and part of the fun is using your initiative. (Remember, you can always reheat and add more wax, but you can't take it away.) Take it off the heat. At this stage, you can also add some horse chestnut tincture for an extra boost to the salve's effectiveness if you wish (at about 5 percent), whisking briskly until it is incorporated. Pour into small glass jars, fit the lids, and label.

October 1: RENEWING OUR COVENANT WITH THE GODS

In ancient Rome the first day of October was held in honour of the goddess of faithfulness, Fides (Christianised as St. Faith, whose feast day falls on October 7). The goddess was represented with an outstretched right hand, and her symbols were ears of corn and fruits, joined hands, and a turtle dove. She was the goddess of trust and good faith, honour, contractual obligations, and the mutual duty between two

· · · · ·

parties.[199] For me, her message is clear: the relationship between us and other people, between us and the gods, us and the earth, should be a reciprocal one. There is a sacred agreement between us and the gods to maintain the balance. October is the time we renew our covenant with the gods.

Ritual of Covenant

Spend some time in meditation, reflecting on what you may be doing or thinking that puts you out of balance with the gods, other people, and Mother Earth. What thoughts or actions might you take to put you back in harmony? What actions might you take to restore harmony to the world? This is at-one-ment, making yourself at one with the gods.

Write a covenant between you and the gods. This should not be long, complicated, and too detailed, but it might say something like this:

> I will honour the gods and listen to their guidance. I will honour Mother Earth as sacred. I will honour and protect all life, whether human or of fur and feather, scale and fin, leaf or shoot. Where I take I will also give, and thus maintain the balance. This I vow.

Or perhaps:

> I pledge allegiance to Mother Earth, who sustains us, and tread lightly upon this sacred world, treating all the Mother's creatures with compassion, uniting us all in harmony.

Go to your altar, hearth, or sacred place. Light a purple candle and call your gods to be present. Make an offering of incense to them, and call upon them to witness your covenant. Read it out loud. Roll it up and tie it with a red ribbon, and place it on your altar or in another safe place. Take it out periodically during the year to re-read it and reflect on how well you have kept your promise and what you can do better. Renew it each October, rewriting your vows to account for changing circumstances and insights if you wish.

---

199   Peck, *Harper's Dictionary of Classical Literature and Antiquities.*

Mid-October

According to the chronicles of the monk Bede (c. 673–735 CE), there were two seasons in Anglo-Saxon England. Summer comprised the six months during which the days are longer than the nights, and winter the others, with winter beginning at the October full moon (the Anglo-Saxons followed a lunar calendar), during the month of Winterfylleth, roughly our October. We don't know how they celebrated this, but they may have had three public winter festivals in the manner of the Norse: at the start of winter, at midwinter (Yule), and at the start of spring.[200] Some modern-day heathens celebrate Winter's Night, the full moon of October, to give thanks to the gods, particularly fertility deities such as Frey and Freya, and ask for a prosperous year to come. Some also honour the *disir* (ancestral spirits of personal fate) and *alfar* (elves).[201]

Winterfylleth marked the beginning of the Norse winter, when preparations for winter began and sailing ceased. According to Nigel Pennick, "Long-distance sailing and other summer activities also stopped on this day, as preparations for the winter took priority."[202] In Rome it was the festival of Fortuna Redux, the goddess who oversaw the safe return from journeys, especially at this time when the sailing period was drawing to an end, and also the Rite of the October Horse, during which a horse was sacrificed to the god Mars, who was both the god of war and the god who protected agriculture, to denote the end of the military campaigning season as well as the end of agricultural work for the year, and thus the start of winter.

As the colder weather comes, most of my work moves indoors, and the hearth fire becomes all the more important. Our wood-burning stove powers the central heating for the whole house in winter, and getting enough fuel to keep it going is a year-long quest. However, not all wood is equal, and some is hardly worth the effort of storing and burning, as the old rhyme tells us:

200 *The Ynglinga Saga, Or the Story of the Yngling Family from Odin to Halfdan the Black,* online at Sacred Texts, https://www.sacred-texts.com/neu/heim/02ynglga.htm, accessed 27.9.19.

201 https://www.patheos.com/blogs/pantheon/2010/09/wyrd-designs-%E2%80%93-the-holy-tides-%E2%80%93-winter-nights/, accessed 24.9.19.

202 Nigel Pennick, *The Pagan Book of Days* (Rochester: Destiny Books, 1992).

Logs to burn! Logs to burn!
Logs to save the coal a turn!
Here's a word to make you wise
When you hear the woodman's cries.
Beechwood fires burn bright and clear
Hornbeam blazes too
If the logs are kept a year
To season through and through.
Oak logs will warm you well
That are old and dry
Logs of pine will sweetly smell
But the sparks will fly.
Birch logs will burn too fast
Alder scarce at all
Chestnut logs are good to last
If cut in the fall.
Holly logs will burn like wax
You may burn them green
Elm logs like to smouldering flax
No flame to be seen.
Beech logs for the winter time
Yew logs as well
Green elder logs it is a crime
For any man to sell.
Pear logs and apple logs
They will scent your room
Cherry logs across the dogs
Smell like flower of broom.
Ash logs smooth and grey
Burn them green or old
Buy up all that come your way
They're worth their weight in gold![203]

---

203   Attributed to Honor Goodhart, printed in *Punch*, 27 October 1920.

. . . .
PINE CONE FIRELIGHTERS

I collect fallen pine cones in the park and woods to make into firelighters.
Dipped in melted wax, they are excellent for starting the fire.

October 11: GODDESS OF HEALING

In ancient Rome this was the Meditrinalia (from *mederi*, "be healed"), a festival in honour of the new vintage, when libations were offered to the gods for the first time each year. The Romans drank the new wine mixed with the old at this time, which was considered health giving. The goddess Meditrina is a goddess of health, longevity, and wine.

Goddess of Healing Rite

The last of my outdoor grapes have been harvested and pressed. I will use some of this juice, mixed with some wine from last year's vintage, in this ritual. (You could also mix a little grape juice with wine.) Put the mix into a cup, light a red candle on the altar or hearth, and say:

> *I drink new and old wine*
>
> *I cure new and old disease*

Drink the wine blend. Leave a little in the cup to take outside and pour as an offering onto the earth in thanks.

October 18: ST. LUKE'S DAY/ST. LUKE'S LITTLE SUMMER

Today traditionally heralds a spell of warm weather in England. Luke is said to be one of the twelve apostles and author of one of the four gospels retained within the Christian Bible. He seems to be associated with romance. This was often the time when people set the date for their weddings and lovers exchanged tokens on St. Luke's Day.

ffffff

Late October

We enter the sign of Scorpius, which both the Greeks and Mesopotamians saw as a scorpion. In Greek myth it was the enemy of Orion the Hunter, who had boasted that he could kill anything created by Mother Earth, which so angered the goddess that she sent a giant scorpion to kill him. After his death, Orion and the scorpion were placed in the heavens but on opposite sides of the sky, Orion with his hunting dogs (Canis Major and Canis Minor) at his feet. Whenever Scorpius rises in the east, Orion flees behind the western horizon, so they seem to be pursuing each other still, but just in case, Zeus placed Sagittarius's arrow pointing directly at the star Antares, the scorpion's heart.[204] No wonder, then, that Scorpio is the sign of darkness, mystery, and death, the sign that oversees the melancholy season when nature seems to be dying around us. But this seeming darkness and death is but the precursor to the transformation, regeneration, and rebirth that is the mystery of Scorpio.

During this time, we start to look for artificial light and warmth, and many of the folk festivals reflect this idea of keeping a flame burning in the darkness with torchlight parades and bonfires. During late October, right up until the late 1980s, children would have been out in the streets of England collecting money and wood for Bonfire Night (November 5), pushing carts and wheelbarrows containing scarecrow-like figures called "guys," beseeching "Penny for the guy!" In the north of England this was called Cob-Coaling, and children went from door to door in the days and weeks leading up to Bonfire Night asking for wood for the fire, as well as money for fireworks:

> We've come a cob-coaling, cob-coaling, cob-coaling
> We've come a cob-coaling for Bonfire Night.

A Somerset tradition called Punkie Night still takes place on the last Thursday in October in Hinton St. George. According to a local legend, all the men of Hinton St. George went off to Chisleborough Fair, but to get home they had to cross a dangerous ford in the dark. The women decided to go out and meet them, and made lanterns from mangel-wurzels (large root vegetables) hollowed out and fitted with candles. This seems to be a story to explain the tradition of Punkie Night, when children beg for candles to put inside carved mangels or turnips called "punkies," though it seems to have more to do with Halloween. The children go out in groups and march through the streets, their lanterns dangling on strings, singing traditional punkie songs:

> It's Punkie Night tonight, it's Punkie Night tonight
> Give us a candle, give us a light

---

204   https://horoscopes.lovetoknow.com/Constellation_Scorpio, accessed 17.9.19.

If you don't, you'll get a fright
It's Punkie Night tonight, it's Punkie Night tonight
Adam and Eve would never believe it
It's Punkie Night tonight.

A punkie king and queen lead the proceedings, chosen for their lantern designs, which usually consist of flowers and animals rather than the more recent Halloween spooky offerings.[205]

Protective Magic

Just like the influence of a waning moon magnified many times over, the seasonal tide of natural and magical energies turns to decline and decrease as the year winds down. Any magic and spellwork I do now until the winter solstice will be concerned with banishing, shrinking, and winding down. A healing spell performed in the spring will be concerned with growing health, for example, but a healing spell as winter dawns will be targeted at shrinking the disease. It is important that we recognise the flow of energy and work with it.

As part of the preparation for winter, I take magical measures to safeguard my home and garden, using protective wards. Small mirrored ornaments are hung in the window to reflect back any negativity, along with little representations of eyes. I brought a number of ceramic eyes back from Malta, where eyes are painted on the prows of the boats, and some glass ones from Egypt. The eye reflects evil back to anyone (or anything) sending it. My outbuildings and sheds are protected with hag stones hung over the key holes. These are naturally holed stones associated with the hag goddess herself, long believed to have a protective influence. They may sometimes still be seen hanging in barns, stables, and other farm buildings throughout the UK. Sometimes a small one is added to the property's bunch of keys.

Temporary threshold step and hearth stone patterns were once traditional in Britain, made with the aim of keeping out bad luck and evil influences. The step was washed with water, left to partially dry, then the patterns were made with sand or chalk upon it. They had to be made in a continuous line, without stopping, for the magic to work: crosses, overlapping circles, or diamond shapes, sometimes with

---

205   Day, *Chronicle of Celtic Folk Customs.*

designs such as lucky horseshoes or prickly thistles to ward off ill-wishing.[206] The tangled patterns were thought to stop spirits entering since spirits always travelled in straight lines and got lost trying to follow the tangled designs.

October 31: HALLOWEEN

Today we usually call the last day of October Halloween, a name that comes from the Roman Catholic Church's Feast of All Saints' Day, celebrated on November 1 but beginning at vespers on the evening of October 31—hence "All Hallows Eve"—and then extending into All Soul's Day on November 2, making a three-day feast of All Hallows.

The Church of Rome probably instituted the festival to displace the Pagan Roman Feast of the Lemures, during which the dark and formless spirits of the angry dead not given proper burial were propitiated. St. Augustine described them as evil and restless manes that tormented and terrified the living.[207] It was a three-day festival in May. The church supplanted this with a feast of the Christian martyrs, celebrated since the mid-fourth century CE on May 13. The Christian feast was moved to its current November date by Pope Gregory III (731–741), though the Eastern Orthodox Church of the Byzantine Tradition continues to commemorate All Saints in the spring, on the first Sunday after Pentecost. In 1890 the folklorist Sir James Frazer suggested that the feast was moved to the beginning of November to replace the festival of Samhain in the public mind in Celtic countries, so Samhain must have been a feast of the dead.[208] However, the church in Germany was celebrating All Saints Day on November 1 when the church in Ireland was still celebrating it on April 20, so this is unlikely.[209] The Irish *Martyrology of Oengus the Culdee* (eighth or ninth century) contains a note stating that All Martyrs was on April 17 and All Saints of Europe on April 20.[210]

However, this was the time from which northern Europeans reckoned that autumn tipped into winter, with all that this implied. Henceforth comes a time of gloom, bleakness, and cold. It was widely believed that the powers of increase and

---

206 Nigel Pennick, *The Spiritual Arts and Crafts* (Cambridge: Spiritual Arts and Crafts Publishing, 2006).

207 St. Augustine, *The City of God*, 11.

208 Frazer, *The Golden Bough*.

209 Hutton, *The Stations of the Sun*.

210 https://celt.ucc.ie//published/G200001/index.html.

the good spirits retire from the land now, taking its goodness with them, which is why crops and wild fruit picked after a certain date were said to be cursed or unfit to eat. The powers of darkness, blight, and bane start to emerge from the underworld to wreak havoc. In Ireland Halloween is often called Pooka Night, and after this time the Pooka fairy renders all the crops not collected unfit to eat, while in Wales gryphons blight any crops left in the field after Halloween.[211] Wicked fairies such as the Scottish Unseelie Court become very active, along with the Cailleachs, hag fairies, and winter witches. This is a process that escalates throughout November and December until the rebirth of the sun/son at Yule/Christmas starts to send them back to the underworld.

Thus the season of danger, chaos, and the world turned upside down begins. John Stow wrote in 1603:

> These Lords beginning their rule on Alhollon Eve [Halloween], continued the same till the morrow after the Feast of the Purification, commonly called Candlemas day: In all which space there were fine and subtle disguising, Maskes and Mummeries...[212]

In the reign of Charles I, the young gentlemen of the Middle Temple (trainee lawyers) considered All Hallow Tide as the beginning of the Christmas season.[213] Children celebrated it as Mischief Night, playing pranks such as knocking on doors and running away, hiding objects left outside, or tying door latches. Often they wore masks or were otherwise disguised to avoid being recognised.[214]

The three-day Christian Feast of All Hallows, in combination with existing local folklore, gave rise to a variety of interesting customs, likely a curious intermingling of Christian and Pagan belief. It was widely supposed that the dead could return at Hallowmas,[215] and the three days of All Hallows were certainly regarded as a time of especial supernatural activity, when ghosts, spirits, and witches were abroad and particular precautions had to be taken against them. Candles were lit to ward them off, and if the candle continued to burn after midnight, its possessor would be

211   Anna Franklin, *The Illustrated Encyclopaedia of Fairies* (London: Paper Tiger, 2004).
212   John Stow, *Survey of London, 1603* (Adamant Media Corporation, 2001).
213   Miles, *Christmas in Ritual and Tradition*, and www.sacred-texts.com, accessed 11.9.19.
214   Day, *Chronicle of Celtic Folk Customs*. In some areas this took place on the night before Halloween or the night before Bonfire Night.
215   Nicholas Rogers, *Halloween: From Pagan Ritual to Party Night* (New York: Oxford University Press, 2002).

immune from the attentions of witches during the coming year.[216] Prayers were said to shorten the time souls might be spending in purgatory, and the church bells were rung either to comfort the dead or ward them off, depending on which source you read. Bonfires were built in churchyards to ward off spirits, according to some,[217] or to light the souls out of purgatory, according to others.[218] Visits to the tombs of dead relatives were made, sometimes laying flowers or pouring holy water or milk on the graves.[219] In many places feasts were laid out for the dead, while in others cakes and bread were baked and distributed to the poor in return for their prayers on behalf of a soul in purgatory.[220]

As an uncanny period, it was a time for divination and taking omens, and these were many and varied, some in fun and some in deadly earnest. In England, for example, Halloween was occasionally called Nut Crack Night from the custom of taking omens from the cracking of nuts in the hearth fire. For instance, you might find out whether your sweetheart would be true by naming two nuts and seeing whether they burned together or jumped apart, or by naming the nuts for two possible partners and seeing how they burned.[221] More gloomily, in Scotland a blindfolded seeker might divine what the future had in store by reaching towards three dishes—meal for prosperity, earth for death, and a net for tangled fortunes—and the first they touched would be their lot.[222] To ascertain who would live for another year, each person in the family filled a thimble with salt and emptied it out in a little mound on a plate. If any heap was found fallen over by morning, the person it represented was destined to die within a year. In Scotland and on the Isle of Man, the ashes of the hearth would be smoothed over at night and inspected for marks and prints the next morning, and fates were deduced from them.[223]

As part of the festival of All Hallows, people, mainly children, in England went out "souling," going from door to door or travelling around the local farms singing songs

---

216   T. F. Thistleton Dyer, British Popular Customs, Past and Present (London: G. Bell, 1876).

217   Rogers, Halloween.

218   http://www.wyrdwords.vispa.com/halloween/history/, accessed 4.10.19.

219   Rogers, Halloween.

220   David Cressey, Birth, Marriage, and Death: Ritual, Religion and the Life-Cycle in Tudor and Stuart England (New York: Oxford University Press, 1997).

221   Sharpe's London Magazine of Entertainment and Instruction for General Reading, volume: v.27, 1865, and Mary E. Blain, Games for Hallow-e'en (1912), http://www.gutenberg.org/ebooks/5890.

222   Kelley, The Book of Hallowe'en.

223   Ibid.

in return for apples, soul cakes, or ale. The practice started in the Middle Ages, when the cakes were offered in return for prayers for those souls suffering in purgatory, but after the Protestant Reformation, which did away with the notion of purgatory, the custom became one of just giving out the cakes as gifts.[224] Sometimes people would keep the cakes for good luck. The recipes for the cakes varied: sometimes they were made of oats, some contained currants and spices, and in some areas it was traditional to consume seed cakes during All Hallows, which coincided with the end of sowing the seed for winter wheat.[225] Parkin, a ginger cake, was popular in the north of England, while in Lancashire harcake was offered to visitors on the day.[226]

We don't celebrate the Christian festival of Halloween with a ritual, but it is a tipping point when the tide of the year starts to shift. As such we might practice divination on this night, but more often we just join in the fun, dress up, eat sweets, and have a party.

. . . . . .

HARCAKE

60 GRAMS BUTTER, SOFTENED

500 GRAMS FINE OATMEAL

15 GRAMS GROUND GINGER

350 MILLILITRES GOLDEN SYRUP (CORN SYRUP)

1 EGG, BEATEN

200 MILLILITRES GUINNESS OR BROWN ALE

Preheat the oven to 190° C/375° F/gas mark 5. Prepare a 10 × 8-inch baking tin by lining it with baking parchment. In a mixing bowl, rub the butter into the oatmeal. Add the ground ginger and syrup. Stir together, then gradually add the beaten egg and the brown ale. Pour into the tin and bake for around 90 minutes, though this will depend on your oven, so keep checking. Cover the top with foil if it is browning too much. Leave to cool and turn out before cutting into squares.

---

224 Day, *Chronicle of Celtic Folk Customs.*

225 J. Brand, *Popular Antiquities* Volume 1 (London: F. C. and J. Rivington and Others, 1813).

226 Day, *Chronicle of Celtic Folk Customs.*

THE DEAD MONTH

November

· · · · ·

In November the golden days of autumn give way to bleak winter. The hours of daylight dwindle down; night comes early and dawn comes late. The fields are devoid of life. Tired leaves fall to earth and carpet the ground, their green summer youth forgotten. In the hedgerows all that was fair and blossoming lies rotting on the sodden ground, swathed in tendrils of mist and clinging dew. We are surrounded by a rank and decaying earth. The powers of growth are winding down, while the powers of darkness and cold gain ascendancy. This month sees the first of the snows and frosts.

As the sunlight fails during this month, the hedgehogs in my garden are seeking a place to hibernate, the squirrels in the woods are spending more time sleeping, and the badgers keeping more often to their dens. In the garden pond the frogs and newts have disappeared, probably sheltering in the muddy bank or in the compost heap, away from the frost. Snails huddle together under heaps of dead plants and woodpiles; they hate the cold and glue themselves together and withdraw into their shells. Butterflies are dreaming through the winter in the leaf litter or the nooks and crannies of my sheds till spring. Even the owls will fall silent in November. I know that many small animals and birds will die over the winter of starvation and cold, whatever preparations they make.

It feels like a melancholy month when the colours have faded out of the world and all becomes grey—grey skies and grey heavy moisture in the air. Nevertheless, there are wonderful compensations in the clear, frosty mornings, vivid winter sunsets, the bare brown earth, and the beautiful naked branches of the trees. We turn to the hearth and the warmth of the crackling fire and the cheer of the singing kettle on the hob. This month sees festivals that signify keeping a light burning in the darkness with bonfires and fireworks, with Martinmas, Bonfire Night, and Diwali, the Hindu festival of lights, that we usually attend in nearby Leicester, where the biggest celebration of Diwali outside of India takes place.

This is the death time of the year, when the earth sleeps and the world falls silent, and we enter the season of the Crone, the hag of winter.

Beware, this is no gentle old lady—she is wild, fierce, and elemental, just like winter itself. She is the storm rider, the shapeshifter, the ground freezer, the plant witherer, the bringer of death, and the collector of souls. She has had many names in many places—Ceridwen, Hecate, Frau Gauden, Perchta, Nicneven, Reisarova, Frau Holda, Befana, the Hag of Beare, Babushka, Beira, Gyre-Carline, Mag Moullach, Gentle Annie, Lussi, and Saelde, amongst numerous others.

In Scotland she is the Cailleach Bheur ("the blue hag"), whose face is blue with cold, her hair as white as frost. With her holly staff in her hand and a carrion crow perched on her shoulder, she strides across the land, beating down the vegetation and hardening the earth with ice.[227] In her great cauldron, the whirlpool of Corryvreckan, she washes "the plaid of old Scotland" until it is white with snow.[228] In Germany she is Frau Holda (or Frau Holle), who makes it snow when she shakes her feather pillows out. In Leicestershire, my home county, she is Black Annis, the blue-faced hag who haunts the Dane Hills, dealing death.

Winter is a time of death—the death of plants, the death of animals, and the death of those humans for whom the season is too harsh—so it is not surprising that the hag of winter is a death goddess and a collector of souls. In this role she often leads

227 McNeill, *The Silver Bough, Vol. 3.*
228 Mackenzie, *Wonder Tales from Scottish Myth & Legend.*

the Wild Hunt, flying through the midnight skies accompanied by wild women and ghosts, gathering the recently dead. In Norse myth these are called the *túnridur*, the "hag riders," or the *gandreid*, "witch ride." In Norway the goddess Reisarova leads the *aaskereida* ("lightning and thunder"), a spectral host who rode black horses with eyes like embers, while in Germany the Furious Host is led by Frau Holle, Percht, or Berchta ("shining"). Slovenians call the goddess leading the hosts of the dead Zlata Baba, or "golden crone."

The Tyroleans said that whoever got in Wild Berchta's way as she tore through the night with the Wild Hunt would sink into trance and upon awakening be able to predict how the next harvest would be, and this leads us to something important about the hag of winter: there is a deep connection between fertility and winter death. Perchta fructified the land by ploughing it underground, while her *heimchen* (the souls of the dead babies she collected) watered the fields. While the Maiden begins it, the Mother bears it, and the Harvest Queen reaps it, the fertility of the next year's harvest is fundamentally the Crone's gift—the sleeping seeds in the underworld are in her care.

The fierce and powerful vision of the Crone Goddess found in myth is fundamentally at odds with the sanitised and patronising view of her I often come across: the Crone as the kindly, wise old woman, waiting for death, who exists solely to patiently pass on her years of accumulated wisdom—a concept reflecting our own society, with its heritage of patriarchal monotheism, where old women are seen as useless, past sex, past childbearing, past working. That characterisation doesn't fit any of the old ladies I know—most of whom are pretty formidable—and it certainly doesn't fit the stories of the Hag, who might be considered the most elementally powerful goddess of all.

At this dark time of year, we might be drawn to consider our own personal November, our own cronehood, however far away it might be. At some point in our lives we are forced to acknowledge that beauty must fade, physical strength decline, and that one day we too will die. And yet…and yet…in this dismal season, when the earth is bare and the trees skeletal, when everything showy is stripped away, we feel the underlying bones of creation and we see more clearly into its deepest secrets. We approach its elemental power, and this is the true knowledge of the Crone, the *coron* or "crowned one," the Cailleach or "the veiled one," the Hag or "the sacred one."

And this is a secret that only the wise may know.

Early November

November 1: SAMHAIN

November begins with the Christian feast day of All Saints and the modern Pagan festival of Samhain. Samhain was one of the four quarter festivals of the early Irish, though it was not mentioned in contemporary Scottish, Welsh, or Continental literature at all.[229] The Irish word *Samhain* is usually glossed as "summer's end," from *sam*, "summer," and *fuin*, "end," though others argue that it may derive from the Proto-Celtic word **samani*, meaning "assembly," as great tribal assemblies were held at Samhain.[230] We can speculate that with the agricultural work of the year completed and the warring and trading seasons over, it would have been the time when travellers returned home to their hearths with new stories to tell and experiences to share.

Sadly, we don't know how the Pagan Irish celebrated Samhain or even how they regarded it, or whether the Celts in other areas marked the occasion at all. Samhain certainly appears in many Irish stories recorded during the Christian period, and it was recorded as a Pagan festival by the Christian chroniclers, but while some describe great assemblies on that date, none of them mention any religious or druidic rites (unlike the practices attested around Beltane), though doubtless there were some.[231]

In 1890 the folklorist Sir James Frazer suggested that the feast of All Hallows was moved to the beginning of November to replace the festival of Samhain in the public mind in Celtic countries, and therefore Samhain must have been a feast of the dead.[232] However, the church in Germany was celebrating All Saints Day on November 1 when the church in Ireland was still celebrating it on April 20, so this is unlikely.[233] Where known European feasts of the dead took place, whether Christian or Pagan, they were part of a spring purification to prepare for the year ahead. When the Catholic Church introduced the doctrine of purgatory, where souls spent a time of suffering before going to heaven, the medieval church gradually instituted a three-

---

229   Hutton, *The Pagan Religions of the British Isles.*
230   J. A. MacCulloch, *The Religion of the Ancient Celts* (Createspace Independent Publishing, 2018).
231   Hutton, *The Stations of the Sun.*
232   Frazer, *The Golden Bough.*
233   Hutton, *The Stations of the Sun.*

day festival of the dead called All Hallows, as it was believed that the prayers of the living could alleviate the suffering of those in purgatory. However, this was developed in Germanic countries and only later spread to Celtic lands.[234]

The suggestion that it was the Celtic New Year dates back no earlier than 1886 and was proposed by John Rhys, who asserted that because the Celts marked their days from the evening before (as did the Saxons, Jews, and Muslims, amongst many others, though he didn't mention this), they must start their year in winter, even though no contemporary classical source mentioned it.[235] Frazer used Rhys's idea to support his own theory that Samhain had been the Pagan Celtic feast of the dead. After the introduction of the Roman calendar, Samhain was certainly associated with the Christian three-day feast of All Hallows in Ireland.

However, the one thing we know for certain is that it was considered the start of winter in Ireland. In the fifteenth- or sixteenth-century manuscript *Tochmarc Emire*, the hero Cúchulainn explains the structure of the Irish year: "For two divisions were formerly on the year, namely, summer from Beltane the first of May, and winter from Samhain to Beltane."[236] The Brythonic Celtic languages simply name the day the "first of winter," from the Latin *calend*, which denotes the first day of a month, so in Welsh it is *Nos Galen-Gaeaf* ("night of the winter calends"), in Breton as *Kala-Goañv*, and in Cornish *Kalann Gwav*.[237] It ushered in the dark and cold season when death is close and when the spirits of blight and bane are released onto the land.

Nevertheless, as Pagans, we take our cues from the natural world, which is the manifestation of the spiritual. It is time to acknowledge the role of death, seasonally and personally, and mourn what has passed and remember what has been. We think of all the lives that have touched ours and of the ancestors who have brought us to this place.

---

234 Ronald Hutton, *Halloween? It's more than trick or treat*, https://www.theguardian.com/commentisfree/2014/oct/28/halloween-more-than-trick-or-treat-origins?fbclid=IwAR13rqBx1oqclv4giBmWmYstGVhsyM9GxrOxP8Q8Jo7eo_j3zBs2xsZoo6U, accessed 5.11.19.

235 John Rhys, *Lectures on the Origin and Growth of Religion as Illustrated by Celtic Heathendom* (HardPress Publishing, 2012).

236 https://www.ancienttexts.org/library/celtic/ctexts/emer.html, accessed 20.11.18.

237 *Samhain: Season of Death and Renewal* by Alexei Kondratiev (1997), http://www.imbas.org/articles/samhain.html, accessed 20.12.19.

Samhain Ritual

Set up the altar and decorate it with three black candles and enough small tea-lights for the number of dead you want to remember. If you wish, you can add pumpkin lanterns, a skull, a cauldron, and photographs of those you want to remember. Have soul cakes and a cup of wine ready (I like to use clary sage wine) and burn a visionary incense such as mugwort.

Light the black candles and call to the Crone:

> Crone of Winter, I call to you. Lady of the midnight skies, keeper of
> the ancient wisdom, I call upon your dark aspect this night, the lady
> of the dead and the yet to be born. Hag Queen, keeper of the keys to the
> underworld realm of transformation, be with me. Lady, in this darkness
> show me your understanding and grant me your blessing.

Take up the cup of wine and say:

> Dark Queen, bless the wine in this cup in token of your cauldron
> that contained three drops of wisdom for all the world. Let the cup
> be filled in the name of the Dark Goddess, for I would speak once more
> to those who have passed from us and I would see those who are yet to be.

Drink from the cup. Say:

> Harken to the voice of my soul and hear me. Harken, for I call upon
> those who have passed from this life, back through the generations of man
> to the time of my first parents. I light the beacon that you are guided to this place,
> and I call upon you to join me in this place and eat of the food I offer you.

Call out the names of the people you wish to join you. For each one, light a tealight from the black candles and place it on the altar, along with an offering of a soul cake and some personal encouragement. Spend some time meditating, remembering, and listening. When you are ready to end the ritual, say:

> I have rejoiced this night in the knowledge that time is no barrier
> and that friendship endures. Therefore go to your appointed places
> disturbing not those who would fear you, nor harming any substance of this
> world. Remember that we will meet again some other Samhain night.

Put out all the candles and say:

It is not for me to bid the Lady to be gone. Instead, I ask that she is with me all my days, guiding my path. This rite is ended. Blessed be.

. . . .
Soul Cakes

1 POUND PLAIN FLOUR

1 TEASPOON MIXED SPICE

6 OUNCES BUTTER

6 OUNCES CASTER SUGAR

3 EGG YOLKS

3 OUNCES CURRANTS

MILK

Mix flour and spice. Cream butter and sugar in a bowl. Beat in egg yolks. Add flour and spice mixture and the currants. Add enough milk to form a soft dough. Use a big tablespoon of batter per cake. Make into flat cakes and mark with a cross. Place on a greased baking tray and bake at 180°C/350°F/gas mark 4 until golden brown, about 10–15 minutes.

November 3: ST. HUBERT'S DAY

According to the myth, Hubert loved hunting so much that he even went out on holy days. In reproach for this behaviour, the stag he chased turned back to him, and between its horns was an image of Christ on the cross, and a voice cried out to him to give up his vain pursuits and contemplate his salvation. Hubert immediately went off to join a monastery and contemplated so hard that he became a bishop. St. Hubert is the patron saint of hunters as the deer he encountered is said to have reminded him that animals are God's creatures too and should be regarded with compassion, that only clean shots should be taken, that only old or sick stags should be shot, and females with young should never be killed. In Flemish Belgium special little cakes are made that are adorned with the horn of the saint and are eaten not only by human beings but also by dogs, cats, and other domestic animals.

The same story is told of St. Eustace, and it appears to be a Christian rewriting of an earlier tale in which a human meets an animal (usually a white stag or doe) from the otherworld, and many such tales appear in Celtic literature.[238] It may even be a memory of the Horned God himself, who at this time of year becomes the Lord of Death and winter hunting. Though he is the protector of all that lives upon the earth, he is also the dark hunter that culls them in season.

Rite of the Cairn

We do not invoke the God between the autumn equinox and Yule, for now he is the Lord of Death, but we do mark the deaths of the animals and plants that have died to feed us at this time.

Each person prepares a pebble, painted with symbols or figures that represent the plants and animals that have been killed so that we might live. These are laid on a cairn (a commemorative pile of stones), with each person speaking of the lives of those beings and their deaths with gratitude for their sacrifice. If you work alone, you can begin your own cairn, which you can add to year after year. It brings the message home that our lives affect other creatures that are sacrificed so we might live.

November 9: THE DREAMING BEAR

This is the feast day of Saint Ursinus, whose name means "bear," a name borne by a number of dubious saints celebrated around the calendar, and it is tempting to think that they relate to earlier Pagan customs and beliefs since the bear cult features in the lore of all the countries of the north.[239] The bear is one of the most revered animals in the world, often thought to be a god incarnate or a visitor from the realm of spirits. The Celts certainly venerated the bear and had several bear gods and goddesses, while the legendary King Arthur has a name that means "great bear" (Welsh *Arth Vawr*).[240] The constellation of Ursa Major, the Great Bear, is known in Wales as "Arthur's Wain" (wagon). It travels closely around the North Star and, unlike other constellations, never sinks below the horizon, but it is highest in the sky in the spring and lowest in the autumn, when, according to American Indian legends, the bear is seeking a place for its winter hibernation.[241]

---

238   Walter, *Christianity*.
239   Joseph Campbell, *The Way of Animal Powers* (New York: Harper and Row, 1988).
240   Marion Davies, *Sacred Celtic Animals* (Chieveley: Capall Bann, 1998).
241   Krupp, *Beyond the Blue Horizon*.

The bear hibernates in the winter, entering a cave or some quiet, secluded place. It emerges in the spring, with the female often having given birth in the meantime, appearing with cubs in tow. This led to the bear being associated with regeneration and rebirth and adopted as a solar symbol; many sun gods are said to have been born in a cave at Yule. The mythology of the bear is thus inextricably linked with its winter retreat into hibernation and its apparent renewal in the dreaming darkness.

Rite of Winter Dreaming

At this season activities outdoors come to an end and it is time for winter dreaming, for deep inner work. In the darkness the path of inner knowing is illuminated. Only in silent retirement from the world can the voice of your soul be heard, and only when you listen to it will you discover your spiritual power. Your rational, conscious mind is continually analysing and questioning, weaving its own view of reality stitched together by beliefs and ideas, but spiritual insight springs from your subconscious, and its quiet voice speaks a different language, communicating in symbols and metaphors. This can only happen when the chatter of the thinking mind is stilled. This is a time to rest and be passively open to the unconscious influence of the otherworld and growth that is slow and unforced. All birth takes place in darkness, from ideas in the mind to the seeds in the ground. Seeds of ideas planted now can burst forth next spring, transformed and strengthened by their time in the unconscious.

Prepare a dark, quiet place where you can sit comfortably. You can lie down if you wish, but take care that you do not fall asleep. Have a single candle only, well shaded. Burn a visionary incense such as mugwort.

Invoke the spirit of the bear:

> I call upon you, spirit of the bear.
>
> You walk between the worlds
>
> Earth bear, sky bear.
>
> You are the keeper of darkness
>
> The place of wisdom.
>
> You are the keeper of silence
>
> Where the voice of the soul is heard.
>
> You are the keeper of stories

The knowledge of the ancestors.
You are the keeper of dreams
Where all realms entwine.
Let me wake to the dream.

Sit or lie in meditation, but put the candle out first. In this case, it doesn't matter whether you fall asleep, as your dreams will be teaching dreams.

Dream Pillow
During the long nights of November, you can also take advantage of the power of your sleeping dreams by creating a vision sleep pillow stuffed with herbs such as mugwort, hops, passionflower, or clary sage. Stuff a muslin bag with your herbs, and place it beneath your own pillow as you sleep. Have a pen and notebook beside your bed so that you can write your dream down when you awake.

Mid-November

In November all the festivals of the ancient world in the northern hemisphere concerned the transition to winter, heralded by the appearance of the winter stars. By November the summer constellations are fading from the sky and the winter constellations are rising. As the days shorten, Orion the Hunter appears earlier and earlier and by midwinter dominates the southern sky. Orion not only sets in the same area as the winter sun, but it rises in the same area too—in effect, it might be seen as following the sun. In Homer's time the first visible setting on the western horizon at sunrise of Orion, the Pleiades, and the Hyades marked the beginning of the winter.

The ancients used the heavens as their visible calendar, and we often underestimate the power and importance of star cycles and star myths in the ancient world. Many calendar systems, whether sacred or pastoral, utilised the positions of the Pleiades, a bright star cluster that lies on the shoulder of Taurus the Bull. In Lithuania the Pleiades are known as *Sietynas* or *Sietas*, and it was noted that the cluster travelled through the sky during the long nights of November along a similar trajectory as the Sun in summer, hence the saying "The Sietynas goes along the same road as the sun in summer" and "(The Pleiades) go around the earth at the same time as the sun; only the sun goes in the daytime and it moves at night."[242] The Greeks thought that the Pleiades led the eternal dance of the stars around the heavens, marking the coming of summer in May and the coming of winter in November. During November the stars of the Pleiades rise in the east as the sun sets, reach their highest place in the sky— almost directly overhead—at midnight, and then set at sunrise. They can be seen in the sky for nearly the entire night.

November 11: MARTINMAS/SAMHAIN OLD STYLE

Pope Martin I (649–654 CE) established Martinmas as an important church festival, and it is probable that it was an attempt to absorb and Christianise earlier Pagan end of harvest/coming of winter traditions. If we want to find the folk customs of the start of winter, we have to look at Martinmas on November 11 rather than Samhain on November 1, as most of the old coming-of-winter customs were celebrated on this date. The confusion comes from the adoption of the Gregorian calendar in Britain and Ireland in 1752, when eleven days were "dropped" from the calendar to make it astronomically correct, so this is the real natural point of year Samhain would have fallen, and some witches (such as my coven) celebrate Samhain Old Style on this date.

Martinmas was considered the first day of winter for all practical purposes, for, as the Germans said, "St. Martin comes riding on a white horse," alluding to the coming winter snows. (Certainly, after we celebrated Samhain Old Style last year, St. Martin came riding in on his white horse, as it snowed as soon as we had finished.) After the holiday, women moved their work indoors for the season, and men turned from agricultural work to other crafts.

The feast day celebrated the end of the harvest and its bounty, the time when the autumn seeding was completed, when fattened animals were slaughtered before winter grazing became scarce, and when the newly produced wine was ready for drinking. Indulging in large quantities of food and drink played a central role in the festival, and in France an upset stomach caused by too much food and drink is still known as *mal de Saint Martin*, or "Saint Martin's sickness." People who got drunk on Martinmas were often called "Martinmen," as were those who squandered their resources in riotous living.

---

242 http://www.lnkc.lt/eknygos/eka/eastr/stars4.html.

In his eighth-century chronicles, St. Bede (c. 672–735) noted that the Anglo-Saxon term for November was *Blot Monath*, or "Blood Month," in reference to the customary slaughtering of animals that took place during that month. Doubtless some were given in offering to the gods, the rest used as foodstuff for the cold months ahead. In more recent centuries, German farmer's almanacs called November *Slachtmaand*, or "slaughter month." In Western Europe Martinmas was the traditional day for slaughtering livestock before grazing became scarce in the winter, making it an unusual opportunity for most people to eat fresh meat, as well as the time to cure meat for the coming season and make sausages and puddings from the offal. These were then cured for the winter by being smoked and dried in the chimney. Families often clubbed together at Martinmas to form a "mart" to buy a cow or other animal that was butchered, from which black puddings and sausages were made.[243] An old English saying was "His Martinmas will come, as it does to every hog," meaning "he will get his comeuppance" or "everyone must die."

Throughout Eastern and Western Europe, it was traditional to invite friends and acquaintances to "eat the goose" on St. Martin's Eve or on St. Martin's Day, and in many places it still is. In Hungary, for example, this was the day to slaughter and eat the goose a family had been fattening up, and the more a person ate and drank at Martinmas, the stronger and healthier they would be. According to one Hungarian saying, "If you don't eat goose on Martin's Day, you'll starve all year," which is a sentiment shared in many other places.

In the past, great bonfires roared on Martinmas in Germany and the Netherlands, so much so that in the fifteenth century, the festival acquired the nickname *Funkentag*, or "spark day." Young people leaped through the bonfire flames and danced about them, and the ashes were strewn on the fields to make them fertile. In some places little candles were placed in floating nutshells on rivers. In later days in northern Germany people continued to jump over lit candles set on the parlour floor.

Martinmas also absorbed some of the winter bear customs. The Martin Bear or Straw Bear is a well-known figure in folk tradition and still appears in places such as Germany, Austria, England, Ireland, Poland, and even in North America in areas with strong Germanic traditions. Straw Bears are generally seen as good-luck bringers who appear from the beginning of November to the beginning of February—

---

243 *Hone's Everyday Book*, https://archive.org/details/everydaybookorguo1hone/page/n10, accessed 20.11.19.

the period of the solar winter. Pagan antecedents or shamanic traditions are often claimed for such performances. Even today, in many parts of Europe, on St. Martin's Day, a man appears dressed as St. Martin, accompanied by a bear-like guiser. In Germany the figure is called *Pelzmärte*, which might mean "furry Martin" or "Martin with a fur coat" or "skin Martin."[244]

While Martinmas customs continue in some parts of Europe, in Britain most of them have died out, subsumed in the Remembrance Day observances and parades that commemorate the members of the armed forces who have died in war. It was begun in 1919, and the date was chosen because the hostilities of the First World War ceased on the eleventh hour of the eleventh day of the eleventh month in 1918—a serendipitously suitable date on which to remember the dead.

My coven celebrates Samhain on the Old Style date, generally renting a cottage for a week-long retreat where we can devote ourselves to meditations, discussions, spellwork, and ritual, as well as visiting local sacred sites and shrines. One thing we always do is to visit a cave, the dark and damp underworld womb of the Goddess, where it is impossible not to reflect on cycles of creation far vaster and slower in evolution than our own short lives. Fossils of extinct species remind us that nothing is permanent and that expressions of life evolve and pass away to emerge in another form.

Rite of the Winter Crone
Have ready a cauldron (or large dish); offerings of salt, water, and earth; 2 green candles; and 1 black candle.

Say:

> The wheel turns. The Crone brings an end to growth as she
> hardens the earth with frost. Hers are the darkest months of the year.
> Everything dissolves in her cauldron as all things return to the source.

Light the black candle and say:

> Crone Goddess, I call
> Grandmother, teacher
> Storyteller and lore keeper
> Mistress of the cauldron

---

244 Walter, *Christianity*.

Of inspiration
Of manifestation
Of transformation
Of initiation
Crone, I call.

Go to the cauldron and say:

All life springs from the sea.
All life springs from the Goddess.
Salt and water are within me.

Add salt and water to the cauldron:

All things young and fair must fade, all that is vital eventually grows weary,
all that is strong becomes weak, and all that is full of promise and hope must
pass away. All things that live must die and return to the womb of the Goddess.
But as the mound is raised above the seed, the seed prepares itself for rebirth,
and all things shall be transformed by death. Earth is within me.

Add earth to the cauldron:

The year itself returns to the otherworld womb from which it came,
but know this: the secret wisdom of the Crone is that the wheel shall
turn once more. Rebirth follows on the heels of death, just as spring
follows on the heels of winter. Let the candles be lit in token of our hope.

Light the green candles and reflect for a time on the meaning of the cauldron and
the wisdom of the Crone. Then say:

The cauldron of creation is the essence of life in motion.
I carry the hope of the Goddess in my heart, safe in the knowledge
that the wheel shall turn. This rite is ended. Blessed be.

⟨⟨⟨⟨⟨⟨⟨

Late November

We enter the sign of Sagittarius the Archer, represented as a centaur with a drawn bow and an arrow that points at Antares, the star at the heart of Scorpius the Scorpion. In Greek mythology Sagittarius is usually identified with the wise centaur Chiron, who tutored Herakles, Achilles, and Jason.[245] Accidentally shot by Herakles and bearing a wound that would never heal, Chiron offered to take the place of Prometheus, the Titan eternally punished by the gods for giving fire to humankind. In recognition of this sacrifice, Zeus placed him in the stars as the constellation Sagittarius.[246]

For the Babylonians, Sagittarius was Nergal, god of the underworld, who was either depicted as a winged figure with a scorpion tail, firing an arrow from a bow, or associated with *Pabilsag* ("chief ancestor").[247] Pabilsag rules the time of year when the sun descends to its lowest ebb and the gates to the netherworld are opened, symbolising the transition between death and new life. The centre of the Milky Way lies within Sagittarius, and the Milky Way was the ancient pathway of souls to the afterlife in many mythologies.[248] Sagittarius is the gateway to Capricorn, the sign in which the winter solstice fell in in ancient times, which was considered the cosmic gate to the spiritual kingdom, while the gate of Cancer (at the summer solstice) was the gate to incarnation.[249]

Stir Up Sunday

In late November winter has taken hold and we struggle for light and warmth. Our thoughts begin to turn towards preparations for Yule and the rebirth of the sun, which will rekindle the spark of the year and set us on the path to warmth and light once again.

---

245 Others say that the creature represented is the satyr Crotus, son of Pan, who invented archery, placed in the stars at the behest of the Muses to demonstrate the art.

246 Ian Ridpath, *Star Tales* (Lutterworth Press, 2018).

247 White, *Babylonian Star-Lore.*

248 Krupp, *Beyond the Blue Horizon*, and Gavin White, www.babylonian-astrology.com.

249 In antiquity Capricorn was the location of the sun at the winter solstice, but due to the procession of the equinoxes, this has actually shifted to Sagittarius. In 600 years it will be in Scorpius.

In Britain Stir Up Sunday, the last Sunday before Advent, is the day to make the Christmas or Yule pudding, a dessert that remains a mystery to our American cousins.[250] The Christmas pudding began its career as the plum pudding, a concoction of plums, spices, wines, meat broth, and breadcrumbs. The plums and meat have disappeared from the modern version and have been replaced by dried fruits and nuts. Traditionally, it should be made with thirteen ingredients. Lucky charms and silver coins were incorporated in the mix to bring good fortune, such as a silver coin meaning wealth, a ring meaning a marriage, and so on. Every member of the family should have a stir. In Suffolk it was thought that each person should stir sunwise three times, making three wishes, only one of which would come true. The round pudding is covered with brandy and flamed, and we can use it to symbolise the fires of the sun and associate the thirteen ingredients with the twelve signs of the zodiac plus the sun itself.

November 25: ST. CATHERINE'S DAY

St. Catherine was supposed to be yet another Christian virgin who refused to marry a Pagan—in this case, an emperor. He ordered her broken on a wheel, making her the patron saint of all who use wheels—spinners, carters, wheelwrights, and so on. Fire came down from heaven and the wheel broke, so she was beheaded, which led to her becoming the protector of unmarried women and the accidental inventor of the spinning Catherine Wheel firework. She was deleted from the official list of saints in 1969 as there was no evidence of her ever having really existed. It is probable that she was a Christianised version of an earlier goddess, represented as she is with a wheel, as were so many deities of the sun, fate, time, and the seasons. As such, I honour her today.

In folk custom her festival was celebrated mainly by unmarried girls making merry together, which they called "Cathar'ning," usually a simple procession with a girl representing Catherine, dressed in white and collecting money, apples, and beer. A favourite game involved jumping over a two-foot-tall "cattern candle" without putting out the flame, which meant bad luck, chanting:

> *Kit be nimble, Kit be quick*
> *Kit jump over the candlestick.*

---

250   See page 65 of *The Hearth Witch's Compendium* for a Yule pudding recipe.

In England it was a day for eating sweet cattern cakes flavoured with caraway, and in Somerset farmers had special cattern pie shaped like a wheel and filled with mince, honey, and spices, and washed down with "hot pot," made from warm beer, rum, and eggs.

Cattern Day Ritual

I take this as an opportunity to celebrate the Goddess of the wheel, keeping the light burning in the darkness. Place a symbol of a wheel on the altar (you can draw one if you don't have anything suitable). Have ready some cattern cakes and a large white candle—I use a 50-hour one—and light it each night from now till Yule.

Light the candle on your altar or hearth, and offer one of the cakes beside it with the words:

Goddess of the wheel
Keep this light burning in the darkness
As a symbol of our hope
For we know the wheel will turn
And all things shall pass
And be remade anew.

. . . .

CATTERN CAKES

½ CUP (4 OUNCES/125 GRAMS) BUTTER

½ CUP (4 OUNCES/125 GRAMS) SUPERFINE (CASTOR) SUGAR

1 LARGE EGG

1½ CUPS (8 OUNCES/250 GRAMS) SELF-RAISING FLOUR

½ LEVEL TEASPOON GROUND MIXED SPICE

4 LEVEL TABLESPOONS GROUND ALMONDS

⅓ CUP (2 OUNCES/60 GRAMS) SULTANAS

Cream the butter and sugar together. Gradually beat in the egg with a spoonful of the flour to prevent curdling. Sift in the rest of the flour and spice, then add the almonds and sultanas. Mix well until the dough binds together. Knead lightly and roll out on a floured board to ¼ inch (½ cm) thick by 8 inches (20 cm) wide. Cut into ½ inch (1 cm) strips and twist round to make about 30 flattened spiral shapes, or Catherine Wheels.

. . . . .

November 30: REMEMBRANCE DAY FOR LOST SPECIES

I came across this idea recently, and it struck a deep chord within me. At this time of year we explore the themes of death and remembrance—In Britain, we celebrate Remembrance Sunday with parades for fallen service men and women, and at Samhain we have rites for the ancestors who have gone before us. But why don't we grieve for extinct species? Where are our rituals for coping with extinction, ecological destruction, or environmental loss?[251]

Remembrance Day for Lost Species was begun by artist Persephone Pearl after she saw an exhibit in the Bristol Museum of a thylacine, an animal that went extinct in 1936. Legend says the world's last thylacine died cold and alone, mistakenly locked out of its night-time quarters at the zoo in Hobart, Tasmania, during an unusually cold night in 1936. The animal, which was never even identified as a male or female, perished from exposure. Pearl realised that we barely remember it, let alone weep for it, and began the first Remembrance Day for Lost Species in 2011, with artists, activists, and the general public finding ways to mark and mourn with performance, ceremony, poetry, and art installations, each in their own way.[252]

Remembrance for Lost Species Ritual

We formulated this ritual and celebrate it with our Outer Circle. You can do this alone or you can gather a group of fellow mourners. Research an extinct species or lost environment. Think how you feel about it, what you want to say about it, and how you would like to express your grief about its passing. Prepare a card "tombstone" on which you can write this. If you are doing this with a group, each person should choose their own subject.

The altar is set up in the centre of the sacred space, with a large cauldron and lit tealights, one for each species you wish to honour, grieve, and remember.

> **Leader:** *In this place that is not a place, in this time that is not a time, we gather together to mark the death time of the year. All things young and fair must fade, all that is vital eventually grows weary, all that is strong becomes weak, and all that is full of promise and hope must pass away. We remember our ancestors, we*

---

251   https://www.theguardian.com/environment/radical-conservation/2016/nov/19
       /extinction-remembrance-day-theatre-ritual-thylacine-grief, accessed 20.10.19.
252   https://www.lostspeciesday.org/?page_id=14, accessed 20.10.19.

remember loved ones who have passed away. But who stands for the species that have become extinct, that die unmarked and unmourned?

All: *We stand. We stand for them. We mourn them.*

Each person comes forward in turn to speak about their chosen animal or environment and express what they want to say. They put out one tealight and place their tombstone against the cauldron until all the lights are extinguished.

Drummer: *The Goddess is always with us, the steady heartbeat that supports us always as we remember and honour those that have gone before.* (Begins a quiet, slow drum beat like a heartbeat and chants:) *Honour, remember, honour, remember, honour, remember…*

All join in. This continues as long as seems appropriate.

Leader: *All things return to the womb of the Goddess, the great cauldron of creation, there to dissolve and be remade and await another dawn. Here is the cauldron of Ceridwen, which transforms all things, which can regenerate all things in her underworld womb. In her lies our hope.* (Places the extinguished lights in the cauldron.)

Leader: *The ocean of time is wide, and as your spirits sail upon its winds and tides, know this: nothing passes from the records of the keepers. Each leaf, each feather, each child, each joy, each life is noted, is recorded, is held. All beings across time are potent within the record. All are held in the womb of the Goddess, ready so that when the time is right, they can and will return. Remember that what is lost to the mundane lives on within the Universal Spirit. You have the power within you to elicit change, and change elicits the returning of life. And all things, when the time is right, may return.*[253]

Go forth and make change. You are the life bringers.

This rite is ended. Blessed be.

---

253   This passage was written by Dave Manley (or Dave the Flute, as we like to call him), our bard.

THE MONTH OF REBIRTH

December

• • • • •

Sheltered in our warm houses and able to buy food from the supermarket all year round, we find it hard to conceive what winter meant for our ancestors. Just imagine for a moment. During the summer and autumn, the long hours of light and warmth provide a bountiful harvest of greenery, grain, and fruit. Animals have plenty of grazing and have reproduced, supplying meat, milk, and cheese. But then winter comes. Darkness and cold increase daily, causing plants to shrivel and die and animals to perish while struggling to find fodder. Humans die from cold and hunger. The great source of life, the sun, is weakening daily. Each day it is lower and lower on the horizon, and each day the hours of daylight grow fewer. Darkness is spreading; everything is winding down, threatening to come to a standstill. The year has declined and languishes in the season of its old age, standing on the edge of its grave.

If the sun does not regenerate, then time itself will come to an end—life will be extinguished, and the world will return to the dark womb of chaos from which it emerged. And when the sun decays towards its death at Yule, that primal chaos threatens to return.

In the myths of many cultures, before the sun was set spinning on its course—creating the hours, days, and seasons—there was only chaos; it was the beginning of regularised time that brought the cosmos into being. In Greek, *chaos* did not mean "disorder," as it does today, but primordial emptiness, space, and darkness, a confused mixture of the four elements, a formless mass without order but containing everything in potential. The world began when Cronos, the god of time, set the world in motion and confined the forces of chaos to the underworld. But although chaos was locked away, it continued to exert an influence. They believed there is a gateway to the underworld that cracks open as the sun declines. As darkness increases, the immortal spirits of chaos creep from the underworld.

In many parts of the world, it is thought that the dead return at Christmas. In Scandinavia the dead revisited their old homes and had to be made welcome. Before people went to bed, they made sure the house was left tidy, with a fire burning in the hearth. Food and ale were left out on the table. In Poland the dead were invited inside to warm themselves and funeral foods were eaten. In Portugal the souls of the dead are welcomed at Christmas with crumbs that are scattered for them on the hearth. In ancient times seeds were left out for the dead so they could return with fruits and grains from the otherworld at harvest time. In Lithuania food would be left on the table, as it was believed that once the family was asleep, the dead would come in and feast.

Only the sun's rebirth can send the spirits of chaos back and restore time and order to their proper courses. Until then, the world is turned upside down and the Kingdom of Misrule is established.

The great source of life is failing. The Sun God is dying. Will he be overcome by the powers of darkness and chaos or will he fight and overcome? The fate of the whole world rests with him. Eventually everything comes to a standstill. For three days the sun does not move on the horizon. The great Wheel of the Year has stopped turning. Then, on the shortest day, in the time of greatest darkness, the sun is reborn.

Each sunrise the sun demonstrates the victory of life over the forces of death and darkness; it is a metaphor for human spiritual and physical life, reflecting our own experiences of birth, growth, decay, and death, as well as our hope of rebirth, our struggles against negativity, and the triumph of spirit. For our ancestors, the eternal cycle of the sun was the central paradigm of their spiritual beliefs.

The ancient Egyptians, Mesopotamians, and Teutons (among others) all had a twelve-day festival around the winter solstice. The twelve days represent the twelve signs of the zodiac or the twelve months the sun must past through in the coming year. The idea was adopted by Christianity in the fourth century.

Modern Christians celebrate December 25 as the birthday of Jesus Christ, but this is a date that was not fixed until the fourth century and is still not accepted by some Eastern churches. Various sects have celebrated Christmas on 136 separate dates, and every month of the year as been mentioned as the possible one in which Christ was born. The first evidence of the birth of Jesus being celebrated was in Egypt around 200 CE, when it was celebrated on May 25. The Nativity of Christ was not considered an important festival by early Christians, unlike Easter, which celebrates the resurrection. The celebration of a birthday was rejected as a Pagan tradition by most Christians during the first three hundred years of Christianity. However, partly in reaction to the claims by Gnostics that Jesus had not been mortal, Christians began to emphasise the Nativity, though a date could not be agreed upon.

The celebration of Christmas arrived in Britain around the early fifth century. By 1100 Christmas was celebrated all over Europe. The Protestant Reformation in sixteenth-century Europe saw a rejection of the Roman Catholic Church. Turning to the Bible, they found no evidence of a date for Christ's birthday and no commandment to celebrate it. Puritans called Christmas by such pejorative names as Old Heathen Feasting Day and abolished the Christmas celebration by an act of Parliament in 1647, a ban not lifted until the Restoration. Parish officers were subject to penalties for allowing the decking of churches and allowing services to be conducted on Christmas Day. However, the much-loved feast was not so easily suppressed, and many people protested; there were riots in several places. In 1647 evergreen decorations were defiantly hung up in London, and the Lord Mayor and City Marshal had to ride about setting fire to them.

The Puritans had a point: every element of the Christmas story and every Christmas custom is Pagan in origin. But while Christians see time as linear and believe that the birth of the divine child came but once, two thousand years ago, Pagans view time as cyclical and know that the Child of Light—and with him the world—is reborn and renewed every year.

· · · · ·

Early December

December 1: THE THREE FATES

During the longest nights of the year, families would have spent their time huddled around their hearths, pursuing what crafts they had sufficient light for, telling stories, and listening to the cold winds outside, imagining the spirits of misery and chaos getting closer. Ancestral spirits were propitiated with libations poured onto the hearth. St. Jerome, in the fifth century, reported the laying of tables with an abundance of food on the first day of December, condemning it as a Pagan charm to ensure abundance during the coming year. In the early eleventh century, Burchardus of Worms said that people still laid tables with food and drink and three knives for "those three Sisters whom the ancients in their folly called Parcae."[254] The Parcae were the three Roman goddesses of birth and midwifery, later associated with the Greek Fates, the Moirai; like them and other fate goddesses, including the northern Wyrd Sisters, they spin, weave, and cut the metaphorical thread of human life. It is fitting to associate their midwifery with the imminent birth of a new cycle, the rebirth of the sun and thus all life on earth. Possibly the name *Modranicht* ("night of the mothers"), which Bede says the Pagan Angles gave to Christmas Eve, may be connected with this practice.[255]

Offering to the Three Fates

It is fitting to begin December with an offering to the Three Fates, the weavers of destiny. Put out three small cups of red wine, fruit, and bread, along with three knives. This is a way of honouring the powers that will bring more provisions during the coming year. Have three candles ready: white, red, and black.

Light the white candle and say:

> *Goddess who upholds the primal law of the universe, to which even the gods are*
> *subject, allow me to know and release what cannot be changed, the things that*
> *have already been: the deeds of myself and others.*

---

254   Miles, *Christmas in Ritual and Tradition.*
255   Ibid.

Light the red candle and say:

> *Goddess of becoming, drawing together the threads of the past and the layers of*
> *my thoughts and deeds to make the present, allow me to understand how my*
> *actions now are weaving my future.*

Light the black candle and say:

> *Goddess of that which may become, allow me to understand the web of possible*
> *futures, for my destiny and my soul are one and the same. Goddesses of Fate,*
> *look kindly upon my offerings and keep me in your care. Blessed be.*

Allow the candles to burn out.

December 4: ST. BARBARA'S DAY

In Christian tradition, this is St. Barbara's Day. Barbara is said to have been imprisoned in a high tower by her father to discourage her many suitors, but when he found out she had converted to Christianity, he handed her over to his henchmen for torture and eventually beheaded her himself, whereupon he was immediately struck dead by lightning. Therefore she is invoked against lightning, tempests, and explosions. Finding no evidence for her existence, the Roman Catholic Church removed her from the list of saints in 1969. Her real origins lie in earlier Pagan goddesses. In Dutch Pagan tradition there were three chief goddesses, Anbet the Earth, Wilbert the Moon, and Barbet the Sun. In Germanic lore there were three sister goddesses, Einbet, Barbet, and Wilbet, and in some areas these were the names given to the Norns, three fate goddesses.[256] Slavonic art portrays both St. Barbara and St. Catherine with the solar haloes, which are usually reserved for important male saints. St. Catherine is associated with the fiery wheel and Barbara with lightning, and both originally may have been solar maidens.

In many places the Christmas season begins with the feast day of Saint Barbara, and it is especially associated with wheat and omens for the next harvest. In Lebanon a special dish of grain called *kahmie* is served. In southern France, especially in Provence, wheat grains are soaked in water, placed in dishes, and set to germinate in the warm chimney corner or a sunny window. If it grows fast, crops will do well in the coming year.

---

256 Pennick, *The Goddess Year.*

There is an old custom of cutting cherry branches on December 4 and putting them in water to encourage them to blossom. They are commonly called St. Barbara's boughs. If they bloom in time for Christmas, it indicates a good harvest for the coming year; if not, it portends bad luck.

Barbet Ritual
To honour the Goddess today, bring in a fruit tree branch and encourage it to blossom by putting it in water in a warm place. If it flowers, it is a blessing for the coming year.

December 5: EVE OF ST. NICHOLAS
St. Nicholas was said to be the bishop of Lycia, who died on December 6, 346 CE, though there is no historical evidence of his existence. He had a great reputation for giving gifts and took over the legends and functions of the gift-giving spirits of the season (such as Woden and the Winter Hag), even being identified with the modern Santa Claus. In the Netherlands children put their wooden clogs (or sometimes baskets) by the hearth on the Eve of St. Nicholas, hoping that St. Nicholas, riding through the air on his white horse, will pause, come down the chimney, and fill them with sweets. Carrots and hay are left out for his white horse. This could be a Christianisation of the legend of Woden flying through the air on his eight-legged horse around the winter solstice to deal out reward or punishment.

St. Nicholas has a variety of helpers, sinister winter spirits—sometimes horned, often hairy with blackened or hideous faces—that carry rods to punish naughty children and evildoers, even dragging some away to hell. They go by a variety of names in various regions and include Knecht Rupprecht, Pelznickle, Zwarte Piets, Furry Nicholas, Rough Nicholas, and Klapperbock.

Modern gift-giving spirits, such as Santa Claus, have their origin in much older Pagan legends. The Hag Goddess comes into her power in this season and flies through the midnight skies, accompanied by wild women, ghosts, and other spirits, collecting the souls of the dead, especially those unbaptised at the time of their death. She is usually described as a spinner or a crone who has a long nose or perhaps a nose made of iron, or she has iron teeth.[257] She sometimes carried a pitcher of live coals or

---

257 The Russian witch goddess Baba Yaga had iron teeth and flew with witches at the summer solstice.

a cauldron to burn the distaffs of lazy spinners.[258] However, though she was severe in her punishments, she rewarded those who pleased her, and her passing blessed the land with fertility. It was she who gave newborns their destiny.

Mid-December

Up until recent decades, "bringing in the green" was one of the most widespread features of the season. Evergreen plants were collected from gardens, woods, and hedgerows and used to decorate hearths, make wreaths, and bedeck houses and churches. Stow, in his *Survey of London* (1603), recorded that not only were houses and churches decorated with evergreens, but also the conduits, standards, and crosses in the streets.[259] These decorations were either taken down on Twelfth Night or as late as Candlemas. The custom is ancient. The Romans decorated their houses with evergreens during the Saturnalia and January Kalends, and in spite of church condemnations they survived. In the sixth century, the bishop Martin of Braga forbade the adorning of houses with laurels and green trees.

For the old Pagans, the evergreen was a symbol of immortality as it had the power to survive the winter death that struck down all other forms of vegetation. Evergreens represent the continuation of life during the death time of winter. Particularly precious were plants like the holly, ivy, and mistletoe, which actually bear fruit in wintertime. Decorating your home with evergreens is an act of magic far more significant than tacking up shiny plastic decorations.

The Romans used holly as a decoration during the Saturnalia winter festival and would send fresh holly boughs as a greeting to friends. In Germanic myth the holly was associated with Frau Holle (Holde or Holda), the winter hag. The early Christians forbade the practice as a Pagan custom, but the association of holly and the winter solstice continued unabated, so the church was forced to reinterpret it, identifying the holly with Christ, the white flower emblematic of his purity, the prickles his crown of thorns, and the red berries the drops of his shed blood. In the Middle Ages, Christian mythographers decided that St. John the Baptist was born at the summer

---

258 Max Dashu, http://www.suppressedhistories.net/secrethistory/witchtregenda.html.
259 Thomas K. Hervey, *The Book of Christmas* (The Folklore Society, 1888).

solstice, at the time of the weakening sun, announcing his own power would wane with the birth of Christ at the winter solstice, the time of the strengthening sun,[260] associating Christ with the waxing year and John with the waning, represented by the holly and oak respectively.[261] Many popular superstitions still linger round the use of holly at Christmas. Tradition says that no branch should be cut from a holly tree, but rather that it should be pulled free. Sterile holly (holly without berries) was unlucky in decorations. In some western counties of England, the boughs removed from churches were treasured for luck throughout the year.

Mistletoe is an evergreen, woody parasite growing on the branches of trees, mainly apple and pear but occasionally on ash, hawthorn, and oak. It was considered a potent magical plant because it did not grow on the earth but on the branches of a tree, in a "place between places." It grows into a ball, imitating the sun, and the leaves are fresh and green all year long, making it a plant symbolising immortality and life in the dead time. Because the evergreen mistletoe bears its fruit in winter, it is an emblem of fertility. The Roman historian Pliny wrote that the mistletoe was one of the most important magical plants of the Celts. He recorded that the druids called it "all healing" and it served as a symbol for the winter solstice. In Norse mythology the mistletoe was used to slay the sun god Balder and afterwards given into the keeping of Frigga, the goddess of love, and it was ordained that anyone who passed beneath the mistletoe should receive a kiss to show that it had become a symbol of peace and love.[262] A berry had to be plucked off with each kiss for luck.[263] Though other evergreens were included in the decorations of churches, mistletoe was the one omission, being considered too Pagan. The exception was at York, where on Christmas Eve mistletoe was carried to the high altar of the cathedral and a general pardon and season of peace was proclaimed. In the coven we each keep a single piece of Yuletide mistletoe throughout the year as a symbol of hospitality and to burn as part of next year's Yule ritual to signify the ending of another cycle.

---

260 Walter, *Christianity*.

261 In a reversal of the usual borrowings from Pagan to Christian, many modern Pagans have adopted this as the oak and holly king theme but switch the roles around so that the holly king gives up his power to the oak king at Yule and regains it at the summer solstice; Williamson, *The Oak King, the Holly King, and the Unicorn*.

262 Thomas K. Hervey, *The Book of Christmas* (The Folklore Society, 1888).

263 Miles, *Christmas in Ritual and Tradition*.

Ivy is an evergreen plant that begins to grow on the ground but which then climbs the nearest tree in a spiral fashion. This associates the plant with the sun, since the path of the sun during the year is a spiral one, depicted as such on Neolithic monuments such as Newgrange. Any plant with a spiral growth pattern was thus considered a plant of immortality and sacred to death and resurrection gods such as Dionysus and Osiris. As a symbol of rebirth, ivy was carried in a basket representing Bacchus. In Christian allegory it represented the eternal life and the resurrection of Christ. Church ivy saved from Christmas was fed to ewes to induce the conception of spring lambs. An ivy leaf placed in water on New Year's Eve that was still fresh on Twelfth Night meant that the year ahead would be favourable.

The Christmas evergreens had a sacred nature, as evidenced by their careful hanging and disposal. In Shropshire people never threw them away for fear of misfortune, but either burnt them or gave them to the cows; it was very unlucky to let a piece fall to the ground. The Shropshire custom was to leave the holly and ivy up until Candlemas, while the mistletoe bough was carefully preserved until the time came for a new one next Yule.

December 12: ST. LUCY'S EVE

Saint Lucy, Lussi, or Lucia ("light") was said to be a Christian virgin who refused to marry a Pagan and was martyred for it. In one version of her tale, her eyes were pricked out prior to execution; in another version, her suitor praised her beautiful eyes, and she plucked them out and sent them to him. She is often pictured with her eyes on a plate beside her and thus became the patron saint of the blind. Whether an actual person called Lucia ever existed or not, the saint seems to have taken her mythology and characteristics from local Pagan deities and so is seen differently in different regions. In Italy it is likely that she acquired attributes of the Roman goddess Juno Lucina or Lucetia, the Mother of Light, who also carried a tray and a lamp, bestowing the gifts of light, enlightenment, and sight, and who was also known as the opener of newborn children's eyes.[264] In Scandinavia she seems to have taken on characteristics of the goddess Freya, who was known as the Vanadis, or the shining bride of the gods. The *lussekatter* (Lucy cats)—the golden saffron rolls that are served at this time in Scandinavian countries—are said to be the devil's cats that Lucia subdued, and the cats were pictured at her feet; cats were also associated with Freya and

264   Susan Granquist, 1995, http://www.irminsul.org/arc/001sg.html, accessed 12.12.18.

pulled her chariot. Freya's special season was Yule, when she dispensed wealth and plenty. The traditional shape of the rolls is a crossed shape, where the arms are rolled inward and in the curve are bright pieces of fruit or small candles in the form of a solar wheel.[265] Lucia may also have some aspects of the Norse sun goddess Sunna, whose emblem is the fiery wheel.

St. Lucy's Eve was a mysterious and dangerous time in many parts of Europe, a time when witches were thought to be especially powerful. In Britain witches and fairies would kidnap anyone who went to bed without any supper. In Lower Austria witchcraft had to be averted by prayer and incense; a procession was made through each house to cense every room. On this evening, too, girls were afraid to spin lest in the morning they should find their distaffs twisted, the threads broken, and the yarn in confusion. Between Lussi Night and Christmas, trolls, ghosts, and evil spirits were thought to be active. It was particularly dangerous to be out during Lussi Night. On St. Lucy's Eve in Scandinavia, candles are lit and all electrical lights are turned off, and the *Lussevaka* ("Lucy wake") vigil is held, staying awake through the *Lussinatt* to guard the household against evil. It was also a time when the future could be divined. In Austria a mysterious light called *Luzieschein* ("the Lucy shining") was observed by boys outdoors at midnight, and the future could be foretold from its appearance.

December 13: LITTLE YULE

Though the winter solstice is the shortest day of the year, it is not the date of either the earliest sunset or the latest sunrise. The earliest sunset occurs around Little Yule and the latest sunrise around New Year, at the beginning of January.

In Sweden the Christmas season begins with St. Lucy's Day and as such is sometimes referred to as "Little Yule." It is thought that to celebrate the day with vigour will help a person live through the winter days with enough light. In the home, the oldest daughter rises first and wakes the rest of the family. She is dressed in white with a red sash and wears a nine-candle wreath, while her younger sisters will just dress in white and carry a single candle as they take breakfast to their parents, with hot coffee and *lussekatter* ("Lucy cats," i.e., yeast rolls). For the day, the elder girl is called Lussi (Lucy) or Lussibruden (Lucy bride). The family then eats breakfast in a room lit with candles.

---

265   Susan Granquist, 1995, http://www.irminsul.org/arc/001sg.html, accessed 12.12.18.

On Little Yule we hold the first of our three Yule rites with the lighting of the Yule log (the others being the Yule rite proper and the last the wassailing of the orchards). The Yule log is an old custom once widespread in Europe, the winter counterpart of the midsummer bonfire. Traditionally it was a huge block of wood, often chosen and set aside earlier in the year, lit with great ceremony and burned throughout the festive season. It was very unlucky if it went out, and a piece would be kept throughout the year to guard the house from fire and lightning, or steeped in water to cure many ills amongst humans and cattle, while the ashes were thrown on the wheat fields to protect the crops from mildew. The Yule log must never be bought but should be received as a gift, found, or taken from your own property. In some parts of the Scottish Highlands, the head of the household would find a withered stump and carve it into the likeness of an old woman, the *Cailleach Nollaich* ("Christmas old wife"), a sinister being representing the evils of winter and death. Burning her drove away the winter and protected the occupants of the household from death.

The First Rite of Yule

We usually celebrate this ritual with the coven's outer circle. None of us has a big enough fireplace to burn a massive log throughout the season, so we light a symbolic small fire, putting a fire pit in the courtyard laid with fuel, and everyone is given a sparkler. We have a large cup and some warm wassail drink waiting. Everyone wears ivy and mistletoe. We keep a partially burned piece of the old Yule log to start the fire. (If you don't have one, take a small log and put on it some symbols—runes, pictures, or glyphs—of the old year.)

Light the fire and say:

> We open the season of Yule with this, the first of our three ceremonies of Yule, when we light the Yule log and usher in the time of peace and love on earth.

> This is the old Yule log, representing the old year. (Put the old log on the fire.)

> This is the new Yule log, representing what is to come. (Place the new log on the fire.)

Consider this for a moment. We then give out the sparklers and everyone lights them on the fire. Then it is time for the wassail toast. Pour the drink into the cup and say:

> I wish you peace, joy, and health. Wassail!

The cup is passed around the circle, and as each person drinks they shout *wassail* ("be of good health"), which everyone shouts back in good cheer and blessing.

Then there may follow the singing of songs and carols. At the end, say:

We await the rebirth of the sun. May this be a time of peace, joy, and love.

Blessed be.

Don't forget to rescue a bit of the new Yule log to save for next year.

December 16: OFFICIAL START OF THE MINCE PIE SEASON

In the past, little fresh food was available at this time. However, Yule was a time of great feasting and merrymaking. It was a time when special carefully hoarded and stored foods—sweets, costly spices, dried fruit, liqueurs, and spirits—were brought out to celebrate the rebirth of the sun and impart a little cheer in the depths of winter. It was also an act of trust in the harvest yet to come next autumn. Seasonal treats included mince pies. For those who don't know, mince pies are small, individual shortcrust pastry pies or tartlets filled with sweet mincemeat, i.e., dried fruit and spices. There is a superstition that you should eat a mince pie every day of the twelve days, and each one eaten will give you a month of good health in the coming year. I certainly shall!

· · · · · · · ·

MINCEMEAT

1 POUND CURRANTS

1 POUND RAISINS

1 POUND SULTANAS

1 POUND COOKING APPLES, PEELED, CORED AND FINELY CHOPPED OR COARSELY GRATED

1 POUND CHOPPED VEGETARIAN SUET

3½ OUNCES BLANCHED ALMONDS, ROUGHLY CHOPPED

1 POUND LIGHT MUSCOVADO SUGAR

1 TEASPOON CINNAMON

1 PINCH GRATED NUTMEG

1½ TEASPOONS MIXED SPICE

1 LEMON, GRATED RIND AND JUICE

· · · · ·

1 ORANGE, GRATED RIND AND JUICE

7 OUNCES MIXED CANDIED PEEL, CHOPPED

7 FLUID OUNCES DARK RUM

9 FLUID OUNCES DRY SHERRY

Mix everything together in a really large bowl. It's a good idea to get stuck in and use your hands for this. Cover the bowl and set aside for a day so that the flavours can develop. Give it a good stir now and again. Pack the mincemeat into sterilised jars and seal with greaseproof paper jam pot covers and tight-fitting lids. Store in a cool place—if you have the time, let the mincemeat mature for 2–3 weeks before using it for mince pies.

December 17: SATURNALIA

Many of our customs of Christmas stem from the Roman Saturnalia, a winter festival spanning several days beginning on December 17. The equivalent of the Greek Cronus, Saturn was a major Roman god of the seasons, the calendar, agriculture, and the harvest, depicted holding a sickle in his left hand and a bundle of wheat in his right. In Roman mythology, after Jupiter defeated him, Saturn fled to Rome and established a golden age there as an earthly king, a time of perfect peace and harmony. When the era was over, Saturn departed to sleep on a magical island but will one day return and bring back another golden age, just like King Arthur. The feast of Saturnalia was meant to recapture something of this perfect time—no taxes could be collected, no wars declared, and no prisoners executed. Presents were given, and feasts and merrymaking were the order of the day.

It was an annual period of license, when the customary restraints of law and morality were thrown aside and everyone gave themselves up to excessive mirth and jollity.[266] Catullus called it "the best of days." Masters changed places with their servants, and the slave might dine with his master or even be waited on by him. Every house had its *Saturnalicius Princeps* ("master of the Saturnalia"), the Lord of Misrule, chosen by lot, who had to act as foolishly as possible and was free to order others to do his bidding. His command was law, whether it was to dance naked, to sing, suffer a dunking in icy water, or carry a flute girl round the house. Trees were decorated and houses hung with holly and other greenery. Slaves wore the badge of freedom

266   Frazer, *The Golden Bough.*

known as the *pillius* and were exempt from punishment; there was a school holiday and a special market. Senators left aside their togas for more informal clothes, and people greeted each other with "Io *Saturnalia*" ("hail/praise Saturn") rather in the manner we say "Merry Christmas."

Midwinter's Eve

We have reached the nadir of the year. Ancient man would have realised that we depend on the sun for life—in the summer the long hours of daylight and warmth make the crops grow, but in the winter darkness and cold, they shrivel and die. Each day, up to the winter solstice, the sun grows weaker and weaker. Each day it is lower and lower on the horizon, and each day the hours of daylight grow fewer. Darkness is spreading; everything is winding down, threatening to come to a standstill. As the Roman writer Lucan (39–65 CE) described it:

> Nature's rhythm stops. The night becomes longer and the day keeps waiting. The ether does not obey its law; and the whirling firmament becomes motionless, as soon as it hears the magic spell. Jupiter—who drives the celestial vault that turns on its fast axis—is surprised by the fact that it does not want to turn.[267]

If the sun does not regenerate, then time will come to an end, life will be extinguished, and the world will return to the dark womb of night from which it emerged.

❦❦❦❦❦❦

Late December

We enter the sign of Capricorn. The constellation of Capricorn was called "the House of Death," as in winter all life in the northern hemisphere is at its lowest ebb. Capricorn is the second faintest constellation after Cancer. It is generally represented as a mythical creature, half goat, half fish, an association that goes back to the Bronze Age and was recorded in the Babylonian star catalogues. In Greek myth, the constellation is sometimes identified as Amalthea, the goat-nymph that suckled the infant god Zeus. The goat's broken horn was transformed into the cornucopia, or horn of plenty. Some ancient sources claim that this derives from the sun "taking nourish-

---

267   Quoted in Christian Rätsch and Claudia Müller-Ebeling, *Pagan Christmas: The Plants, Spirits, and Rituals at the Origins of Yuletide* (VT: Inner Traditions, 2006).

ment" while in the constellation in preparation for its climb back northward. The Roman astrologer Manilius associated Capricorn with that which needs a "renewal of flame" because its season brought back a renewal of the sun's light following the winter solstice.[268] Macrobius wrote that souls descended to earth through the gate of Cancer, the Gate of Men, but Capricorn was called the Gate of the Gods because through it, men ascended to their seats of immortality and became gods.[269]

It was a common belief that the sun spent each night or each winter in a cave. Most solar deities are said to have been born from a cave: Zeus was born in the Dictean Caves on Crete; the god Krishna was born in a dark dungeon; Apollo was born under Delos, where no rays of sunlight could penetrate; the Phoenician god Melkarth woke from his winter sleep in his sacred cave at the winter solstice; and the Japanese sun goddess Amaterasu lived in a cave for a time. In early Christian stories, Jesus was born in a cave (the Greek text of the Gospel of St. Luke uses the word *katalemna*, meaning "cave," not "stable"), and in Bethlehem the Church of the Nativity is built over a cave. The Sun God was reborn from the chthonic realm, bringing order out of chaos and light out of darkness.

Winter Solstice

At the solstice the sun is still for three days, as though time itself is frozen. The word *solstice* is derived from Latin and literally means "sun stands still." The sun usually rises at a different point on the horizon each day and travels northeast to its farthest position at the summer solstice, and it appears to stand still for three days before heading southeast, reaching its southernmost position at the winter solstice, where it seems to rest again for three days before heading north once more.

And then, in the very moment of greatest gloom, the sun is reborn. Life and hope are rekindled—the light will grow, warmth will increase, and spring, summer, and harvest will come. The Wheel of the Year, which has been briefly stilled, will spin on. The old year, the old cycle of existence and time, dissolves back into the primordial chaos. The sun reborn and the New Year represent the world rejuvenated and reality renewed. Even today we have the familiar image of Father Time (Saturn or Cronus),

268 Manilius, *Astronomica* (c. AD 10), trans. G. P. Goold (London: Harvard Heinemann, 1997).

269 In the same way, the sun is responsible for the birth of each New Age every 2,000 years. Because of precession, the Gate of the Gods moves to Sagittarius.

depicted as an elderly bearded man carrying a scythe, the personification of the old year who passes the duty of time on to the New Year's baby.

Modern Pagans usually call the festival Yule, the modern English version of the Old English words *ġeól* or *ġeóhol*. The meaning is uncertain. According to *The Barnhart Concise Dictionary of Etymology*, Yule comes into modern English from Jól, deriving from Old Norse *hjól*, meaning "wheel."

In the Northern Tradition, Yule was the time that marked the death of Balder, the sun god, the result of the jealousy of the trickster Loki. Loki knew that everything in nature had promised not to injure Balder except the mistletoe, which was considered to be too insignificant to worry about. He searched for the mistletoe until he found it growing on an oak tree on the eastern slope of Valhalla. He cut it off and fashioned a dart from it, returning to find the gods engaged in the amusement of tossing spears, axes, and stones at Balder and watching them bounce off of him harmlessly. Then Loki handed the twig of mistletoe to the blind god of darkness, Höder, directing his hand and encouraging him to throw it. When the mistletoe struck Balder, he fell lifeless to the ground, his spirit sinking into Hel, the underworld.

Rite for Yule

I've written this ritual so that it can be performed alone or easily adapted for group work, with the parts shared out. Make a representation of the old year. This should be a dark, bent, misshapen thing that holds everything outworn and spent that you want to pass away with the year. It can be made of crumpled paper if you like, or you can come up with something much more inventive if you wish. We generally make a boat that is holed, with bent masts and crooked decks.

In the centre of the circle is a lit brazier (you can substitute a cauldron or metal dish with a candle in it), representing the cauldron-womb of the Goddess at the core of creation. Around it is a spiral of unlit lamps or candles.

Say:

> The year has reached its lowest ebb; all is darkness and death.
> The forces of chaos threaten to overwhelm the world.
> The Sun has ceased in his course, lingering three days in his grave.
> Time itself stands still.

Carry the symbol of the old year along the spiral on an inward course to the centre, saying:

> *Go back to the source*
>
> *Your time is over.*

At the centre, say:

> *Goddess, great mother,*
>
> *Your womb is the dark void of space*
>
> *Which holds the seed of all potentials*
>
> *You are the beginning and the end and the beginning once again*
>
> *Take back the spent year and all its forces of chaos.*

The symbol of the old year is burned on the brazier.

Say:

> *In this darkness we must find hope.*
>
> *In this darkness we must find light.*
>
> *The Wheel of the Year must spin on.*
>
> *The Sun must be reborn!*
>
> *Goddess, great cosmic mother,*
>
> *Your celestial womb is the source of all things*
>
> *It births the elements*
>
> *Goddess, great cosmic mother,*
>
> *Give us the spark of life*
>
> *The reborn sun*
>
> *Renew creation so that the wheel of life spins on.*

Take a light from the brazier and gradually light the lamps (or candles) of the spiral so that the light begins at the brazier, which represents the womb of the Goddess at the centre of the cosmos, and travels outwards until it reaches the edge. As you light each lamp, say:

> *Death moves to life and dark turns to light*
>
> *The light is reborn!*
>
> *The wheel spins on*
>
> *Life is renewed.*
>
> *With the Sun we are each reborn.*
>
> *Blessed be!*

In the coven, after we have performed this ritual, we go indoors to the hearth fire and the sparkling Yule tree and exchange presents. These are always handmade, and we have an injunction that they should not cost more than a pound (just over a dollar) per person. It's amazing what people come up with under these strictures, and we've had far more meaningful and personal gifts than we would have done if they had been bought. Coveners have knitted hats, made sets of runes, incense, candles, bath salts, engraved glasses, pyrographed placemats, baked cakes and sweets, and produced homemade liqueurs.

December 24: CHRISTMAS EVE

In folk belief there is a sense of the nearness of the supernatural on Christmas Eve. Throughout Northern Europe there were traditions that the family ghosts returned at Christmas time to share the festival with their living relatives, along with other less welcome spirits.[270] In Sweden the trolls were believed to celebrate Christmas Eve with dancing and revelry. Anne Boleyn is alleged to have been seen haunting her old homes, her headless ghost reported at Rochford Hall in Essex and Hever Castle in Kent. For this reason, it was a tradition to tell ghost stories at Christmas time. Charles Dickens penned several such tales for his readers, and until recently, the BBC televised a dramatised supernatural tale every Christmas Eve.

Christmas Eve divination was also a common practice. In England a dumb cake was made by single girls from salt, wheat, and barley, and baked in complete silence. (*Dumb* may just mean "silence" or be from Middle English *doom*, meaning "fate" or "destiny.") It was placed in the oven and the front door opened at midnight. The spectre of the girl's future husband was supposed to enter the house and stride into the kitchen to turn the cake. Otherwise, children might cut an apple and count the pips. The one whose apple had the most pips could look forward to the most happiness in the twelve months ahead. In Scotland the ashes of the fire were checked on Christmas morning. A foot shape facing the door foretold a death in the family, while a foot facing into the room meant a new arrival.

---

270   In Brittany there was the custom of leaving food for the ghosts while the family attended church.

December 25: Sol Invictus and Happy Mithrasmas

December 25 was the fixed day of the winter solstice in the calendar established by Julius Caesar in Rome in 46 BCE. Actually, the solstice usually falls around December 21 (though it varies), and the difference is due to an error in the Julian calendar that calculated the year on 365¼ days, which meant a discrepancy of one day in the Julian calendar in 128 years.

By 274 CE the emperor Aurelian had established the sun cult as the Roman state religion, with the traditional birthday of Sol (Sun) as December 25, though by then the actual solstice had happened two and a half days earlier.[271] It blended a number of Pagan celebrations of the birth of the Sun God into a single festival called *Dies Natalis Invicti Solis*, the "birthday of the unconquered sun." Roman women would parade in the streets, crying "Unto us a child is born!"

There are thousands of sun gods and goddesses around the world with remarkably similar characteristics: they battle the forces of darkness and dispel evil; they illuminate the sky; they see everything on their path and uncover those secrets hidden by darkness; they represent truth, justice, and enlightenment; and they bring healing. These gods have several things in common: they are usually counted as the saviours of mankind (because the sun saves the world from darkness and brings life); many were thought to have incarnated upon the earth in order to help humankind; they are born of a virgin mother; they are born in a cave or underground chamber; there is a star in the east; there is a flight into a distant country (while the sun is still too weak to finally triumph over darkness); they are sacrificed to benefit humankind; and finally they descend into the underworld and rise again on the third day. Mithras, for example, was born of a human virgin on December 25, his birth attended by shepherds. When he reached adulthood, Mithras healed the sick, made the lame walk, gave sight to the blind, and raised the dead. Before returning to heaven at the spring equinox, Mithras had a last supper with twelve disciples (representing the twelve signs of the zodiac).

When Constantine replaced the Pagan Diocletian as emperor of the Western Roman Empire in 305 CE, he sought to unify sun worship and Christianity into a single monotheistic state religion and summoned the Council of Nicea in 325 CE to settle disputed points of doctrine and orthodoxy. The council opted to mark

---

271   Krupp, *Beyond the Blue Horizon.*

Christmas on December 25 to coincide with the Roman festival celebrating the birth of the unconquered sun.[272] This identification of Jesus with the Pagan Sun God was a doubled-edged sword for the Christians, however, and Tertullian had to assert that Sol was not the Christians' god, while Augustine denounced the heretical identification of Christ with Sol. In 386 CE St. Chrysostom, archbishop of Constantinople, preached:

> But Our Lord, too, is born in the month of December…the eight before the calends of January…, But they call it the "Birthday of the Unconquered." Who indeed is so unconquered as Our Lord…? Or, if they say that it is the birthday of the Sun, He is the Sun of Justice.[273]

Pagan customs and observances persisted. Tertullian condemned Saturnalia customs such as exchanging gifts and decorating homes with evergreens. The biographer of St. Eligius recorded that the bishop would caution his flock:

> (Do not) make *vetulas* (little figures of the Winter Hag), little deer or *iotticos* or set tables at night or exchange New Year gifts or supply superfluous drinks.

The early church flourished in Egypt, with the result that many elements of ancient Egyptian mythology were incorporated into the Jesus story. The most prominent Egyptian deities of the time were Osiris and his consort Isis, who had been worshipped for thousands of years and who had gradually assumed the powers of various other gods.

Osiris was a god who chose to become a man to guide his people; as such, he was called "the Good Shepherd" and depicted with a shepherd's crook. As a corn god he died, was buried, and was brought back to life. As grain he fed his people and was called the "Resurrection and the Life." His flesh was eaten in the form of wheaten cakes. Like Mary, Isis was called "the Star of the Sea" and "Queen of Heaven," a virgin who brought forth a son titled "the Saviour of the World," the hero who brings order back into the universe. Isis and her son Horus were forced to hide from an evil king until Horus became a man. According to Plutarch, Osiris was betrayed by Typhon (Set), the power of darkness, killed and dismembered when the sun enters the sign of

---

272 The Eastern Church refused to accept December 25 for another three hundred years.

273 Quoted in Allan J. Macdonald, *A Jolly Folly? The Propriety of the Christian Endorsement of Christmas* (Wipf, 2017).

the Scorpion and reborn as Horus at the winter solstice. The Temple of Luxor shows images of the god Thoth announcing to Isis that she will conceive Horus and then of the virgin birth and the adoration. The pictures and statues of Isis suckling her son Horus are the prototypes of the Virgin Mary and her child.

Horus's birth was heralded by the evening rising of the three stars of Orion's (Osiris's) belt just before the rising of the birth star Sirius (Isis) shortly afterwards in the east, marking the place where the newborn sun would rise. The Egyptians represented the newborn sun Horus by the image of an infant, which they brought forth and exhibited to his worshippers.[274] The celebrants retired into certain inner shrines, from which at midnight they issued with a loud cry, "The Virgin has brought forth! The light is waxing!" Macrobius (395–423 CE) reported that a figure of the baby Horus was laid in a manger and a statue of Isis was placed beside it. The festival lasted twelve days to reflect the twelve months (or twelve zodiac signs) of the year.

Twelve Days Out of Time

The twelve days of Christmas officially begin on December 26, called Boxing Day in the UK. According to some, they are the last six days of the old year and first six days of the new year. The ancient Egyptians, Mesopotamians, and Teutons (among others) all had a twelve-day festival around the winter solstice. The idea was adopted by Christianity in the fourth century because, the apologists said, it took the Wise Men twelve days to find Jesus. They start on Boxing Day because "Christmas Day was a holy day," or maybe because the old way of counting days was that they began at sunset, so Boxing Day starts on the eve of December 25. If, as Pagans, we celebrate the solstice on December 21, that neatly and conveniently takes the twelve days of Yule to New Year's Day.

The sun reborn at Yule is a weakling babe, and for twelve days all is still uncertain. Only at their conclusion does the sun gain enough power to turn the tide and send the winter spirits back to the underworld. These first twelve days are the most dangerous and uncanny days of the year. They exist outside of normal time and do not belong to the year proper; time is in suspension. Finnish shamans call this period "the Dreaming" or "God's Trance Hour."[275] The strangeness of these days is reflected in many of their other names: the Balkan "unbaptised days," the Slovenian "wolf

---

274   Frazer, *The Golden Bough*.
275   Nigel Jackson, *Compleat Vampire* (Chieveley: Capall Bann).

nights," the Germanic "raw nights," and the Bulgarian "heathen days" or "dirty days" when demons attack the World Tree.[276] In Scotland no court had power during the twelve days. In Finland and Sweden the twelve days of Christmas were declared by law to be a time of civil peace, and anyone committing a crime during them could expect a stiffer sentence than normal.

Many of the ancient beliefs and customs surrounding the twelve days remain to this day. They are a time of danger, the eerie, and the supernatural, haunted by spirits that might punish or reward.

As the twelve days represent the twelve months of the coming year, many omens were taken from them. In England it was said that the weather on the first day would reflect the weather in January, the weather on the second day the weather in February, and so on.

The threat of the precarious twelve days that follow before the sun gains enough power to combat it is reflected in the folk tales of ghosts and fairies temporarily freed from the underworld. In Guernsey the powers of darkness are supposed to be especially active between St. Thomas's Day (December 21) and New Year's Eve, and it is dangerous to be out after nightfall. In the Orkneys precautions had to be taken against supernatural visitors, especially from the influence of the trows, the ugly and malicious fairies of the Northern Isles who leave the underworld at Yule.[277] In the Scandinavian countries on Christmas Eve people stayed indoors so as not to meet the spirits. In Sweden the trolls were abroad. In Iceland the thirteen Yule lads, or *Jolasveinar*, appear. Though today they have become cuddly gift bringers, leaving presents for good children and potatoes for naughty ones, originally they were terrifying characters, the sons of two undead trolls, Gryla and Leppaludi, who stole and ate naughty children. The Yule lads start arriving during the days before Christmas to cause mischief.

The Hag Goddess comes into her supremacy during the twelve nights and flies through the midnight skies accompanied by wild women, ghosts, and other spirits, collecting the souls of the dead, especially those unbaptised at the time of their death. Frau Gauden and her twenty-four daughters were often seen during the twelve nights, and where she passed by with her dogs, the harvest would be good. In northern Germany the hag was Frau Holle or Frau Holt. To placate the Crone and her host,

276   The "Pagan Days" by Max Dashu, http://www.matrifocus.com/IMB07/scholar.htm.
277   Anna Franklin, *The Illustrated Encyclopaedia of Fairies* (London: Vega, 2002).

people would leave out offerings. In Germany the *Hollenzopf* ("Hölle's braid") plaited loaf was left out. Holda, whose name means "the kindly one," brought rewards for diligent spinners, and on every New Year's Eve between nine and ten o'clock she drove a carriage full of presents through villages where respect had been shown to her. At the crack of her whip the people would come out to receive her gifts. In Hesse and Thuringia she was imagined as a beautiful woman clad in white with long golden hair, and, when it snows hard, people said that "Frau Holle is shaking her feather-bed." She is derived from the Germanic sky goddess Holda or Hulda, who was also a goddess of fertility, the hearth, and spinning.[278]

More frightening are the Greek Kallikantzaroi who appear during the twelve days. They are half-animal, half-human monsters, black and hairy, with huge heads, red eyes, goats' or asses' ears, lolling red tongues, ferocious tusks, long curved claws, and animals' feet. Though they normally live in the underworld, at this time they attempt to climb up the world tree to emerge on earth. In the Macedonian plain of Saraghiol, the Kallikantzaroi emerge from a stone named Kiatra Schuligan, beneath which an abyss opens, black and deep, and the sound of laughter, sobs, and screams can be heard issuing from it, along with the sounds of pipes and beating drums.[279] The signal for their final departure does not come until Twelfth Night with the Kalanda festival, when the "Blessing of the Waters" ceremony takes place. Like other such creatures elsewhere, they are often said to be spirits of the dead. Children born at Christmas are susceptible to becoming Kallikantzaroi, as are people with inept guardian angels. In some places they are thought to be transformed humans placed under a spell after being born with a caul during the twelve nights.

This is a characteristic they share with the werewolf, a man who is supposed to change into a ravening wolf—"man-wolves" is the name given to the Kallikantzaroi in southern Greece. The connection between Christmas and werewolves is not confined to Greece. According to a belief in the north and east of Germany, children born during the twelve nights become werewolves, while in Livonia and Poland that period is the special season for the werewolf's rapacity.[280] The wolf is associated both

---

278 Ibid.
279 This Macedonian lore of the Kallikantzaroi connects high rock formations with the dead, especially infants who died without baptism. Similar associations were made by the Scots, who used to have a custom of burying unbaptised babies among inaccessible rocks. The child's spirit entered into the rocks and became the echo (called "child of the rock" in Gaelic).
280 Nigel Jackson, *Compleat Vampyre* (Chieveley: Cappall Bann, 1995).

with the wild side of nature and the time of chaos and boundaries. In Norse myth the Fenris wolf embodies the forces of night and chaos and will bring about Ragnarok, when those forces will overwhelm the world.

December 31: NEW YEAR'S EVE

New Year's Eve is a day of omens and taboos when people believed that it was important to banish the old year completely and ensure good luck and prosperity for the new one. Creditors had to be paid off to avoid starting the new year in debt and thus setting a pattern for the future. Lending as much as a light for a candle was considered very unlucky.

As the liminal point when one year shifts into the next, New Year's Eve was often considered a dangerous and magically charged night of the year, making it necessary to protect the home and its inhabitants from the supernatural. In Iceland, for example, cows gain human speech, seals take on human form, the dead rise from their graves, and the elves move house. In the Scottish Highlands houses were decorated with holly to keep out the fairies. It was the tradition to keep the fire, which was usually damped down at night, burning away merrily all through New Year's night, fuelled along with a special incantation. If the fire went out that night, it was a very bad omen for the coming year. In Silesia it was the custom to fire shots into bushes and trees to drive out evil spirits and witches. Fireworks were traditional in Germany for the same reason. In Denmark the same thing is done, with the aim of chasing away trolls and evil spirits. This seems to be an end-of-year custom designed to make enough noise to chase away the spirits of darkness.[281] In Switzerland the people parade through the streets dressed in costumes and hats representative of good and evil spirits.

Ritual purification was common. On the last night of the year, Strathdown Highlanders would bring home great loads of juniper, which was kindled in the different rooms with all the windows and doors closed to fumigate all the household members and farm animals.[282] In Germany juniper twigs collected during the year were brought in and burned to protect the house. Austrians considered this a *rauchnacht*, or "smoke night," when all rooms and animals must be purified with the smoke of burning wormwood and holy water.

---

281   Walter, *Christianity.*
282   W. Grant, *Popular Superstitions of the Highlands of Scotland* (London: Archibald Constable, 1823).

In several places it was customary to "burn out the old year" with bonfires. In Herefordshire and surrounding counties, one tradition was the weaving of a globe of hawthorn twigs that was then set alight and carried around the fields. The custom was widespread on farms and in villages in Herefordshire and Radnorshire during the nineteenth century. In parts of Worcestershire on New Year's morning, a crown was made of blackthorn that was then baked in the oven before being burned to ashes in a cornfield, the ashes then being scattered over the ground.

This is also St. Sylvester's Day. *Sylvester* means "forest" or "wood." An Austrian custom involved a masked figure called the Sylvester (a sort of wildman) who hid in the corner at inns and leapt out when a young man or woman passed to give them a kiss. The Sylvester wore a wreath of mistletoe, perhaps an emblem of the fertility that he bestows with the kisses. When midnight came, he was driven out of the room as a representative of the old year.[283]

It was important to "let the New Year in" in the proper manner. First footing customs are found throughout Britain. It was considered most important that the first-foot (i.e., the first person over the threshold after midnight) should not come empty-handed but must offer a gift of spiced ale, whiskey, shortbread, oak cakes, sweets, or fuel for the fire. An offering of food or drink must be accepted by sharing it with everyone present, including the visitor. Fuel must be placed onto the fire by the visitor with the words "A good New Year to one and all, and many may you see." The first foot had to be a man or a boy, preferably dark haired, as it was very unlucky for a red-headed man—or, in some places, a fair-haired man—to "let in" the New Year.[284]

Divinations were also practiced. One involved placing a ring in a water-filled bowl, with young unmarried people dunking for the ring; the one who succeeded in retrieving it without the use of his or her hands was guaranteed to be married within the year.

The coming weather was also considered. According to one rhyme:

If New Year's Eve night wind blows South,

It betokeneth warmth and growth;

If West, much milk and fish in the sea,

If North, much cold and storms there will be;

---

283   Walter, *Christianity.*

284   Owen, *Welsh Folk Customs.*

If East, the trees will bear much fruit;
If North-east, flee it, man and brute.

New Year's Eve Ritual

To set the tone of prosperity for the coming year, we practice the custom of first-footing. We choose a dark-haired man to be the first person across the threshold after the stroke of midnight, and he must bring in and present to the householders the following:

- a piece of coal to represent warmth

- a silver coin to represent prosperity

- a glass of whiskey to represent good cheer

- a branch of evergreen to represent long life

- a loaf of bread to represent enough to eat during the year

- a pinch of salt to represent hospitality

CONCLUSION

• • • • •

In this book I've shared with you some of how I celebrate the cycle of my year. The festivals and customs of the year reveal deeper themes and greater truths than are revealed by solely concentrating on the eight sabbats, and I hope that I've inspired you to celebrate the whole year. Always listen to what Mother Nature is telling you, and create your own seasonal celebrations and rituals based on where you are.

APPENDIX

Weights
and Measures

Volume
(Liquid Measures)

IMPERIAL	METRIC	US CUPS
½ FLUID OUNCE	15 MILLILITRES	1 TABLESPOON
1 FLUID OUNCE	30 MILLILITRES	2 TABLESPOONS
2 FLUID OUNCES	60 MILLILITRES	¼ CUP
2½ FLUID OUNCES	75 MILLILITRES	⅓ CUP
4 FLUID OUNCES	120 MILLILITRES	½ CUP
5 FLUID OUNCES	150 MILLILITRES	⅔ CUP
6 FLUID OUNCES	180 MILLILITRES	¾ CUP
8 FLUID OUNCES	250 MILLILITRES	1 CUP
10 FLUID OUNCES (½ PINT)	310 MILLILITRES	1¼ CUPS
20 FLUID OUNCES (1 PINT)	620 MILLILITRES	2½ CUPS

Weights
(Rough Equivalents)

IMPERIAL	METRIC
½ OUNCE	15 GRAMS
1 OUNCES	30 GRAMS
2 OUNCES	60 GRAMS
3 OUNCES	90 GRAMS
4 OUNCES	110 GRAMS
5 OUNCES	140 GRAMS
6 OUNCES	170 GRAMS
7 OUNCES	200 GRAMS
8 OUNCES	225 GRAMS
9 OUNCES	255 GRAMS
10 OUNCES	280 GRAMS
11 OUNCES	310 GRAMS
12 OUNCES	340 GRAMS
13 OUNCES	370 GRAMS
14 OUNCES	400 GRAMS
15 OUNCES	425 GRAMS
16 OUNCES (1 POUND)	450 GRAMS

Ingredient Weights
(Rough Equivalents)

ITEM	US CUPS	IMPERIAL	METRIC
BUTTER	1	8 OUNCES	225 GRAMS
OATMEAL	1	3 OUNCES	85 GRAMS
SUGAR, GRANULATED	1	7 OUNCES	200 GRAMS
SUGAR, SOFT BROWN	1	8 OUNCES	220 GRAMS
SUGAR, POWDERED	1	4 OUNCES	110 GRAMS
FLOUR	1	4½ OUNCES	125 GRAMS
APPLES, SLICED	1	4 OUNCES	223 GRAMS
CHEESE, GRATED	1	4 OUNCES	110 GRAMS
CORNFLOUR (CORNSTARCH)	1	4 OUNCES	110 GRAMS
MAYONNAISE	1	8 OUNCES	225 GRAMS

Temperatures

FAHRENHEIT	CELSIUS
32°F	0°C (FREEZING POINT)
70°F	21°C (AVERAGE ROOM TEMPERATURE/ LUKEWARM)
212°F	100°C (BOILING POINT OF WATER

Oven Temperatures

CELSIUS	FAHRENHEIT	GAS MARK	DESCRIPTION
110	225	¼	VERY COOL/SLOW
130	250	½	
140	275	1	COOL
150	300	2	
170	325	3	
180	350	4	MODERATE
190	375	5	
200	400	6	
220	425	7	HOT
230	450	8	
245	475	9	VERY HOT

BIBLIOGRAPHY

Blackburn, Bonnie, and Leofranc Holford-Strevens. *The Oxford Companion to the Year*. Oxford: Oxford University Press, 1999.

Bogle, Joanna. *A Book of Feasts and Seasons*. Gloucester: Action Publishing, 1992.

Bouyer, Louis. *The Christian Mystery: From Pagan Myth to Christian Mysticism*. Translated by Illtyd Trethowan. Edinburgh: T & T Clark, 1990.

Briggs, K. M. *The Fairies in English Tradition and Literature*. Chicago: University of Chicago Press, 1967.

Carmichael, Alexander. *Carmina Gadelica*. Vol. 1. Edinburgh: T. and A. Constable, 1900.

Cormac's Glossary. Translated and annotated by John O'Donovan. Edited by Whitley Stokes. Calcutta: O. T. Cutter, 1868.

Danaher, Kevin. *The Year in Ireland*. Cork: Mercier Press, 1972.

Day, Brian. *Chronicle of Celtic Folk Customs: A Day-to-Day Guide to Folk Traditions*. London: Hamlyn, 1998.

The Encyclopaedia of Islam. Edited by C. E. Bosworth, E. van Donzel, W. P. Heinrichs, and C. Pellat. New York: Leiden, 1993.

Fowler, William Warde. *The Religious Experience of the Roman People, from the Earliest Times to the Age of Augustus; the Gifford Lectures for 1909–10, Delivered in Edinburgh University by W. Warde Fowler*. London: Macmillan and Co., 1922.

Fox, William Sherwood. *The Mythology of All Races*. Forgotten Books, 2018.

Frazer, James George. *The Golden Bough: A Study in Magic and Religion*. Hertfordshire: Wordsworth Editions, 1993.

Funk & Wagnalls Standard Dictionary of Folklore, Mythology, and Legend. Edited by Maria Leach and Jerome Fried. San Francisco: Harper & Row, 1984.

Green, Marian. *A Harvest of Festivals*. London: Longman, 1980.

Green, Miranda. *Gods of the Celts*. Gloucestershire: A. Sutton, 1986.

Grimm, Jacob. *Teutonic Mythology*. J. S. Stalleybrass edition. London: George Bell & Sons, 1883.

Hines, Derrek. *Gilgamesh*. Knopf Doubleday, 2009.

Hutton, Ronald. *The Pagan Religions of the British Isles: Their Nature and Legacy*. Oxford: Blackwell, 1991.

———. *The Stations of the Sun: A History of the Ritual Year in Britain*. Oxford: Oxford University Press, 1996.

Jones, Julia, and Barbara Deer. *Cattern Cakes and Lace: A Calendar of Feasts*. London: Dorling Kindersley, 1987.

Jones, Prudence, and Nigel Pennick. *A History of Pagan Europe*. Barnes and Noble, 1995.

Kelley, Ruth Edna. *The Book of Hallowe'en*. Boston: Lothrop, Lee & Shepard, 1919.

Kightly, Charles. *The Customs and Ceremonies of Britain: An Encyclopaedia of Living Traditions*. New York: Thames and Hudson, 1986.

———. *The Perpetual Almanack of Folklore*. New York: Thames and Hudson, 1987.

Krupp, E. C. *Beyond the Blue Horizon: Myths and Legends of the Sun, Moon, Stars, and Planets*. New York: HarperCollins, 1991.

Long, George. *The Folklore Calendar*. London: P. Allan, 1930.

Mackenzie, Donald Alexander. *Wonder Tales from Scottish Myth & Legend*. London: Blackie and Son, 1917.

Matthews, John. *The Winter Solstice: The Sacred Traditions of Christmas*. Arelsford: Godsfield Press, 2003.

McNeill, F. Marian. *The Silver Bough, Vol. 2: A Calendar of Scottish National Festivals, Candlemas to Harvest Home*. Glasgow: William MacLellan, 1959.

———. *The Silver Bough, Vol. 3*. Stuart Titles, 1961.

Miles, Clement A. *Christmas in Ritual and Tradition, Christian and Pagan*. London: T. Fisher Unwin, 1912.

Miller, Dean. *Animals and Animal Symbols in World Culture*. New York: Cavendish Square, 2014.

Nilsson, Martin P. *Primitive Time-Reckoning: A Study in the Origins and First Development of the Art of Counting Time Among the Primitive and Early Culture Peoples*. Gleerup, 1920

Ó hÓgáin, Dáithí. *Myth, Legend and Romance: An Encyclopaedia of Irish Folk Tradition*. New York: Prentice Hall Press, 1991.

Olcott, William Tyler. *Star Lore: Myths, Legends, and Facts*. Mineola, NY: Dover, 2004.

Owen, Trefor M. *Welsh Folk Customs*. Llandysul: Gomer Press, 1994.

Peck, Harry Thurston, ed. *Harper's Dictionary of Classical Literature and Antiquities*. New York: Harper and Brothers, 1898.

Pennick, Nigel. *Folk-lore of East Anglia and Adjoining Counties*. Cambridge: Spiritual Arts and Crafts Publishing, 2006.

Pennick, Nigel, and Helen Field. *The Goddess Year*. Chieveley: Capall Bann, 1996.

Raven, Jon. *Black Country & Staffordshire: Stories, Customs, Superstitions, Tales, Legends, and Folklore*. Tettenhall: Broadside, 1986.

Roud, Steve. *The English Year*. Penguin, 2006.

Rufus, Anneli. *The World Holiday Book*. HarperSanFrancisco, 1994.

Shaw, Philip A. *Pagan Goddesses in the Early Germanic World*. London: Bristol Classical Press (Bloomsbury Academic), 2011.

Simpson, Jacqueline, and Steve Roud. *A Dictionary of English Folklore*. Oxford: Oxford University Press, 2000.

Staal, Julius D. W. *The New Patterns in the Sky: Myths and Legends of the Stars*. Blacksburg, VA: McDonald and Woodward, 1988.

Tongue, Ruth L. *Somerset Folklore*. Edited by K. M. Briggs. London: Folk-Lore Society, 1965.

Walter, Philippe. *Christianity: The Origins of a Pagan Religion*. Rochester, VT: Inner Traditions, 2006.

White, Gavin. *Babylonian Star-Lore: An Illustrated Guide to the Star-Lore and Constellations of Ancient Babylonia*. Solaria, 2008.

Williamson, John. *The Oak King, the Holly King, and the Unicorn: The Myths and Symbolism of the Unicorn Tapestries*. New York: Harper & Row, 1986.

• • • • •

INDEX

RECIPE INDEX

RECIPE INDEX